Daddy
Needs
a Drink

Robert Wilder

Daddy
Needs
a Drink

An Irreverent Look at Parenting
from a Dad Who Truly Loves His Kids—
Even When They're Driving Him Nuts

delacorte press

DADDY NEEDS A DRINK
A Delacorte Press Book / May 2006

Published by Bantam Dell
A Division of Random House, Inc.
New York, New York

Book design by Lynn Newmark

Delacorte Press is a registered trademark of Random House, Inc.,
and the colophon is a trademark of Random House, Inc.

Library of Congress Cataloging-in-Publication Data
Wilder, Robert.
Daddy needs a drink : an irreverent look at parenting from a dad who
truly loves his kids—even when they're driving him nuts / Robert Wilder.
p.   cm.
ISBN-13: 978-0-385-33925-4
ISBN-10: 0-385-33925-9
1. Parenting—Humor.   2. Child rearing—Humor.
3. Fatherhood—Humor.
PN6231.P2 W55 2006
818/.602 22   2005054764

Printed in the United States of America
Published simultaneously in Canada

www.bantamdell.com

BVG   10   9   8   7   6   5   4   3   2   1

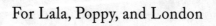

For Lala, Poppy, and London

Contents

Daddy
Needs
a Drink

Hoarding Names

In terms of upbringing, my wife, Lala, and I led mirror lives as children. I grew up with three brothers in New York and Connecticut with my dad, while Lala was raised in Colorado and Wyoming with a trio of sisters and her mother. Even though we've known each other for fifteen years, there are still many things I do not understand about Lala or the female species in general. I believe some simple concepts can be taught to men, such as the length of the menstruation cycle or the appreciation of a closetful of narrow footwear; we can even learn to spot and compliment a recent haircut if given the proper training. However, some of the abstract and less forensic female notions still remain puzzling to me.

My wife has been nesting her whole life, even before she thought about having children. A folk artist by trade and by obsession, she's the kind of person who believes if a week goes by without rearranging furniture, you're halfway to the grave. When she was pregnant with our first child, the change-it-up home show occurred even more frequently than usual. I'd come home from waiting tables at 2 A.M. to find Lala covered in paint and standing by a half-finished wall, a color swatch in each hand.

"Do you like the Daredevil or the Blaze of Glory?" she'd ask, shoving the cards in my face.

"They both look red to me," I'd say.

"Come on, really," she'd plead, desperate for a way out of the latex corner she'd painted herself into.

"Truly, I can't tell the difference." I'm not color-blind, yet shades of the same hue just don't move me in a decision-making direction the way a dinner menu does. My indifference toward interior decorating goes deeper even: I simply don't care. It's hard for Lala to believe, but for this caveman, if I don't trip on anything in my house and I have a place to sit that's not wet, I feel pretty good. I'd rather have things put away and no dishes in the sink than Tiffany lampshades and a red velvet couch. Except for their lack of underwear that supports, I often envy those silly little Tibetan monks with their polished floors and black pillows. If they had cable and beer on tap, I'd be hard-pressed not to pony up and join.

Lala is a determined creature, and now that a baby was on the way, the choices she offered me were no longer just about tinge and tincture. She stood on the second rung of our ladder, her brush moving across the ceiling in long strokes while her large belly kept her from getting to those hard-to-reach places. She knew better than to ask me for help, however, just as I knew better than to ask her to shout the football score to me while I was on the toilet.

"What do you think of the name Hemingway?" she called down.

"Are you kidding?" I asked.

"No, why?" She paused and faced me, resting her brush on the top rung.

"I'm an English teacher and a writer."

"So?"

"What would you think of a math teacher with a kid named Hypotenuse or Pythagoras?"

"You overthink things. I like the sound of it." She craned her neck and eyed her handiwork above our heads. "Hemingway Wilder." She sighed, hoping to gain my sympathy.

"Where'd you get that name anyway?" I asked, slightly changing the subject.

She shrugged. "From my list."

I then became enlightened on one of the strange behaviors of the Carroll sisters and, as I found out later, other women I have met. Starting at the age of pretend weddings with younger siblings or household pets, some women keep lists of names for their future children. Even though I grew up in a household where eating in your boxers was acceptable dinner dress, I knew that women had a distinct vision of their perfect wedding, complete with seating diagrams, fabric swatches, and guesses as to which bridesmaid would most likely go down on smelly Uncle Louie.

I had no idea that ever since she was running barefoot in her grandfather's silo Lala had been hoarding names. She had dozens for girls, fewer for boys (everyone knows boys' names are harder, she informed me), and a handful that could fit either team or a very special sheepdog. When I was a kid, what people called me held virtually no importance, since all the Wilder boys had almost interchangeable names. The four of us have each other's first names as middle names and vice versa. My parents had been unable to produce offspring for ten years and had almost given up until my older brother Rich was born. Since they thought he'd be their last, my mom and dad named him after my mother's grandfather and father: Richard Edward. I popped out two years later, and I got my father's part of the bargain: Robert (his father) Thomas (his grandfather). Out of exhaustion or distinct lack of imagination, my two younger brothers got stuck with a rearranging of what had already come before: Thomas Edward and Edward Robert Wilder. Sometimes I feel that such an inbred naming process makes us southern somehow by proxy.

Lala would ask me for my opinion on what we should call our child, and most of the time I felt neutral about the choices, not unlike when she showed me swatches labeled Weeping Sky and Dodger Blue. Even I grew bored with my own dull responses, so I took on a more proactive male role by trying to predict the nicknames or associations that might plague our offspring during their undoubtedly misspent youths-to-be.

"I think Bea is cute," Lala said one day while she rolled Coca-Cola Red onto our antique refrigerator.

"No way," I said. "I'd look at our daughter and think of Bea Arthur. That woman gave me nightmares."

"How about Macaulay?"

"Besides being too Irish, it would remind me of Macaulay Culkin."

"So?"

"I don't want my kid associated with that creepy child actor. He's a bit too close to Michael Jackson. I read that M.J. has a photo of Macaulay in his bathroom. Gives a whole new meaning to *Home Alone*."

"Jesus, nobody but you would think like that." She shook her hand disapprovingly at her academic egghead of a husband.

"You never know."

Our daughter's name wasn't even on Lala's list. Her mother, Beverly, had a dream that our first child would be a girl named Poppy. We thought Beverly had been working at Grier's furniture store, a former mortuary, for far too long, and treated her whole idea as silly. When we did find a time and way to get pregnant, however, we jokingly referred to the embryo as Poppy, and it stuck. Every other name—Addison, Grayson, Kirkum—all sounded too formal next to a fun floral forename. I even held back from sharing with Lala all the possible scenarios on the middle-school playground—Pop Goes the Weasel, Popcorn, Soda Pop, and far less pleasant things that pop for a girl during adolescence.

After Poppy was born, the name game did not go away as I'd hoped. A year later, my brother Rich called to tell me that his wife just had a baby girl, and they had named her Madeleine with the middle name Joan after my late mother.

"Well, that's rude," Lala said, slamming a wooden paint stirrer against the kitchen counter she had sanded only moments before.

"Why? Did you want to use Joan on our next kid?"

"Are you kidding? I hate that name." She took her fingernail and picked at a rough spot of Formica. "Now Poppy will have two cousins named Maddie. That's just great." Lala's older sister Kate had registered the Madeleine trademark in Seattle years before. "Just think how confused Poppy will be and how exhausting for us to use last names when talking about first cousins. I wish they'd called to check with me."

This botched title search happened again not so long after

the Maddie business when Lala's younger sister Emily took Poppy's middle name, Olivia, as the first for her new daughter.

"I cannot believe this," Lala said when her sister broke the news over the phone. Emily admitted that the name had been on Lala's list, but she tried to convince her it had been on Emily's as well. The case is still pending in appellative court. "From now on," Lala told me, "we are not sharing our list with anyone. When people at work ask you which ones you like or what other names we had for Poppy, you absolutely cannot say." She paused, and her eyes lit up like the square of Goldenrod taped to the wall over our bed. "Better yet, let's think of some phony names to throw those name snatchers off the scent!"

"Like what?"

"I don't know." She shrugged, then looked around the house for inspiration. Rectangles of colored paper lay scattered on tables like a shrunken game of fifty-two pickup. "I got it," she said, weeding through the cards and choosing a few. "Rose, Coral, Scarlet, Indigo."

"Indigo? Who the hell do you think I am, Lenny Kravitz? No one will buy that."

"I don't care. Those are the ones you'll tell all those name stealers."

"You are out of your skull." I waved my hand at her.

"Oh am I?" she asked, wagging one spackled finger. "Tell that to your daughter when she comes to you in tears because all her cousins have the same goddamn names. We might as well move to Russia."

"Russia?"

"You know what I mean. Vladimir this, Boris that. I wonder if they have a problem with name theft over there. I bet you they do."

Lala treated this name theft business like national security secrets stolen from Los Alamos Laboratory, only a *Home Improvement* episode from where we live. She wasn't the only one mucking about with this moniker malfeasance. A college friend's wife, Margaret, belongs to a mommies' group. When Margaret found out she was pregnant, she joined a birthing class that ended up forming into a social support club for women expecting their first child. The eight *mamacitas* completed the birthing class together, survived prenatal yoga, and cheered each other on during the series of births. Now two hundred pounds thinner, the group still met to discuss postpartum depression and sex after a cesarean, staying together even as some members became pregnant with kid number two. They shared everything from husband frustrations to lactation issues and, also unfortunately for Margaret, names.

The mommies' group had gathered at a new restaurant in town to celebrate Margaret and another mom, Laura, who were both due within a few weeks of each other. While the non-nursing, non-expecting moms made up for all the lost drinking time chugging glasses of Chardonnay, Margaret, high on hormones, chatted freely about possible names for her second coming. She was due before Laura, so she believed her list was safe. She hadn't visited my multicolored house or sought the advice of Lala the Namekeeper and her stealth strategies of keeping secrets. Margaret told the assembled group her first, second, and third choices. Everyone discussed the merits of each and quickly launched into her own naming story. Laura, the other swollen one, smiled but remained silent.

Laura gave birth first and used Margaret's name for her bundle of joy. It's close to a year later now, and Margaret is still not over it. If you ask her the name of her child, she'll say, "Well, her name is Jade. We originally wanted to use Amber, but we couldn't." Then she'll drop her head, mourning those five stolen letters.

I wonder if as Jade grows up the unrealized first choice will follow her like a rap sheet. I can see her first-grade teacher calling roll: "Jade-should-have-been-Amber, please raise your hand." Then the obvious follow-up, "By any chance, are you related to the artist formerly known as Prince?"

Lala and I are finished with that whole child-having business. Our second, a boy we named London, proved also to be a difficult birth and narrowly escaped other, more unpleasant monikers. Given our finances, overscheduled lives, and dumb luck in creating one child of each gender, I figured it was time to pull the mucous plug. Why go to zone defense when you survive just fine with man-to-man? A lot of teachers at my school are having babies lately, and the naming process is a frequent topic of conversation around the faculty lunch trough. Not so long ago, I came home and told Lala that I thought Bea would fit the global studies teacher's last name quite well.

"Did you tell her that?" she asked me coldly.

"Yes?" I knew from her gaze that I was in deep shit.

"I thought we agreed not to share our names. What happened to Indigo?"

"What does it matter?" I asked. "We're done with that messy birth stuff."

"I'm saving our names for Poppy," she said, turning her attention back to priming the trim on the living room windows.

"Poppy is happy with her name," I said. "She won't want to change it."

"For later," she replied, still avoiding my now-befuddled mug. "For Poppy's children."

"Poppy is only eight years old. Are you kidding me?"

"Nope." She pulled two swatches off the wall, held by pieces of blue painter's tape, the kind that is not very sticky. "Now," she said calmly, "which do you like for the windowsill: Jamaica Bay or Wild Blue Yonder?"

Baby Oh Baby Monitor

A few weeks before our daughter was born, Lala and I were busily preparing for the arrival of the seven pounds of flesh that would forever change our lives. We had already made the obligatory trip to the strip malldom of Albuquerque, home of places with redundant and embarrassing names like Baby Depot, Babies R Us, and Steven's Everything but the Baby. Like every other wet-behind-the-ears parents-to-be, we loaded up on bedding, clothes, diapers, and other gadgets and gizmos that fool you into believing you'll actually be ready to take that alien thing home. It's pretty simple: when Americans get scared, we just buy more crap.

My sister-in-law Becky was staying with us then, to help us with the baby. Our rental house offered only about 500 square feet of living space, but it was spring, so if one of us needed room, we could walk out the door to the four-by-ten-foot strip of backyard and nervously pace like a rhino in a Mexican zoo.

The bulk of the baby gear was in our bedroom. Lala and I had set up a changing station in the far corner with a bassinet against the opposite wall, our bed jammed in the middle. The room was so cramped that you had to shuffle sideways to move from the closet to the door. The guidebooks Lala and I were reading told us to unwrap, wash, and try out the baby's stuff well before Lala's water broke, signaling a trip to the hospital and a new rug. I opened the baby monitor package, removing the two white boxes from their Styrofoam beds and placing the transmitter onto the windowsill near the bassinet. Lala and Becky ran out to the living room and plugged in the receiver, eagerly waiting like a pair of Thomas Watsons, Alexander Graham Bell's famous lackey. I flipped on the miniature radio transmitter and gave the sisters a full dose of my family's cornball sense of humor.

"Testes. Testes. One two three," I called.

"We can hear you!" they yelled as if they had been just cured of lifelong deafness.

"Help me," I cried like a baby. "I'm urinating in my own mouth."

"OK. Sounds fine. That's enough," Lala said.

"What is Aunt Becky doing with the postman? Is he hurting her?"

My act grew stale, so we all went on a walk. During the past winter, Lala had become a full-fledged mall walker, padding along with the other fatties and geezers who strapped on overpriced running shoes and did laps around picturesque landmark stores like Hot Topic, Foot Locker, and Furr's Cafeteria all-you-can-eat slopfest. Now that it was almost summer and I'd finished my graduate work, the three of us often strolled downtown so that Becky could smoke, I could drink, and Lala could scare people into thinking she was going to give birth right there on the barstool.

By the time we returned to our little *casita*, it was dark. Upon entering, we heard noise coming from the baby monitor. The little Battlestar Galactica eye raced back and forth, warning that our baby needed us. I had heard that the electronic eavesdropper could pick up transmissions from mobile and cordless telephones, police scanners, and passing truckers cruising whores on their CB radios. Like the Three Stooges, we all looked dumbly at each other and shuffled closer.

"Oh baby," the monitor moaned. "Baby, fuck me right there, yes there. Harder, harder, you fuck, won't you fuck me harder?"

We all scanned the area, thinking we were on some sort of hidden-camera show, but everything seemed in place. All the shades were drawn, our evening ritual ever since Lala had stumbled onto a peeping Tom six months before. The local police offered her two high-tech New Mexican solutions to the nighttime prowler: draw your curtains and plant cactus under your windows.

"Don't come yet, baby," the disembodied female continued. "I want it harder than that. Be a man, be a man and fuck me like it's the end of the world!"

Our discomfort and curiosity led us into the bedroom toward the point of origin. Baby monitors not only capture sounds but amplify them as well. The sexcapades came from our neighbors, whose open bedroom window was only ten feet from our spy ear. Even though we lived close enough to spit on each other, we'd never spoken to the young couple behind us. Lala and I are not rude people, yet at the time we had an oppressive landlord who, in exchange for low rent, felt completely justified in keeping track of our daily lives, where we went, and what types of visitors we allowed into our, well, his, home. Becky was not on the lease and her stay far outlasted a visit, so we spoke to no one who lived within a two-mile radius.

We'd seen this couple before, however. He was a skinny, pale hipster with a failed attempt at a goatee. She was a Rubenesque Hispanic woman who favored large Tammy Faye sunglasses and lipsticks in the extended orange family. Since they left around four in the afternoon and were so devoted to pleasing each other, we guessed that they worked somewhere in the service industry.

That first night of the broadcast, Lala, Becky, and I huddled by the window and listened to the sounds of copulation in stereo, since we could hear the live action and the immediate backyard feed. Picture me, the befuddled husband, sandwiched between my very pregnant wife and my very single sister-in-law. I could feel their hormones washing over my body, far too confusing for a repressed white guy like me. As the couple started to climax, the heat of our adjacent bodies steamed us all up. Like a drip irrigation system, our three faces began to spritz.

"Let's listen in the other room," Becky suggested, and we all retreated to the speaker to finish our program a safe distance from the live stage show.

Developed as a reaction to the kidnapping of the Lindbergh baby, the first child monitor was introduced by Zenith in 1937. It was called the Radio Nurse, and the designer, Isamu Noguchi, crafted the receiver to look like a stylized human head, if our heads had brown Bakelite grates instead of two eyes, a nose, and a mouth. The product logo depicts a baby oddly yelling "SOS" to the "guardian that never sleeps." Maybe my dad was right about kids being smarter back in the day, since an infant would have to be pretty damn sophisticated to master Morse code before he learned to crawl. The tradition of smashing baby monitors started then too, though originally people destroyed the Radio Nurse because it was designed by a Japanese person, while now we smash them because it's no longer cool to hit your kids.

Just like my father's generation gathering around the Philco to listen to *The Shadow* or Jack Benny, Lala, Becky, and I found our way to the little white box of lovin' somewhere between 10 and 11 P.M. Mountain Time. This couple was not only sexually active, they were punctual too. Our first few evenings we were silenced by what we were hearing, yet amazed at the fact that it came to us without unsightly installation or a monthly cable bill. None of us had ever given much time to porn, but the fact that this smut virtually fell in our laps made us feel titillated and morally superior at the same time. We dubbed the woman "Big Momma" since she did most of the talking as she commanded "Skinny McDick" to screw her forcefully, with laser-like precision and to delay his emission until she was damn ready. Once in a while we heard a whimper from him, something between a cry for help and a cry of pain. A few times I thought we'd have to call 911 since she outclassed him in weight, force, and profane vocabulary.

I was never sure what the sisters were thinking as we listened, but once in a while I saw Becky gazing longingly in the general direction of the bars downtown, her face red and her palms rubbing the tops of her jeans. If she left us for such pursuits, it would have been far too desperate and obvious, and she would have missed the second or third coming. As the newness wore off, our interest deepened from passive voyeurs to parties engaged in a more involved relationship. Becky psychoanalyzed the couple, trying to spot times Skinny might have faked it or estimating how long a hump-based union like this could last. Lala just rubbed her belly, happy that something so obviously rude and taboo was conveniently located in her home yet did not implicate her or the baby one bit. I wanted to bet on the duration of the sex drama or start a drinking game based on the number of times the F-bomb was dropped, but I had no takers. I did start a dialogue with the receiver, however, acting out different parts as I returned Big Momma's volleys.

"Fuck me? No, fuck you!" I'd shout like Robert De Niro in *Taxi Driver*. I played a proper English butler, nebbish Woody Allen, and Marlon Brando's Godfather, asking how I could come in her face when they'd just shot Sonny on the causeway. Most of these references and impressions pleased only me, and self-pleasure was something I was desperately trying not to think about.

The nuns at Sacred Heart would have asked why we didn't just turn that hellbox off. Because, Sisters, we had a ten-inch cableless television with poor reception and nothing to talk about but Pampers, mucous plugs, and blood-enriched placentas. Besides, I could get away with enjoying professional-grade radio porn with unpaid women sitting next to me. I'd be lying if I said that such detailed and dirty talk didn't spark my imagination. I'd never had sex like that in my life, nor did I know anyone who had and lived to tell me the tale.

Just like any fan of a celebrity whose work you admire, the three of us became engrossed in our performers' comings and goings. The couple usually didn't emerge until three or four in the afternoon, and our view lasted only a few minutes as they strolled from their porch to the car.

"Laid Man Walking," Becky would yell, and we'd race to the window to try to spot any new detail that revealed character or relationship, or would provide the backstory to last night's coitus operetta.

"They're holding hands!" I would shriek, clapping my palms like a little girl at a puppet show. Such PDA was a virtual trailer to another night's blockbuster.

"I think that's a new sweater." Becky had never seen the lime green fabric showcasing Big Momma's mountainous breasts. "I wonder if Skinny bought it for his love avalanche."

"No way he could pull that off," Lala'd tell her while enjoying a bowl of ice cream. "That sweater is fitted and she's an odd size."

We were just short of convincing ourselves to upgrade to a 2.4-gigahertz full-color baby videocam with night vision and optional handheld monitors. Not only could we evolve from radio to TV, but we'd never again miss a moment of our favorite show when performing inconvenient tasks such as sweeping, washing dishes, preparing meals, or going to the bathroom. Even though we were close to becoming true stalkers, we also realized as Lala got bigger and the due date grew nearer that we would not want that smut in the house when our little angel arrived.

As Lala's upcoming explosion of baby and liquid became more real, I stood out to a greater extent as the token male in the house. I had done my vital duty nine months earlier, and now I was more valuable as an errand boy, running to get espresso, rent chick flicks, or make purchases that were intended to embarrass me. My favorite was the breast pad, tampon, and nipple salve combo. I didn't mind the outings so much since our house felt cramped and the weather in Santa Fe in May is quite lovely. It was the last time in my life I really had nothing to do but wait. One day, I ended up going to a local café for sandwiches and coffee. The long line sloped down to the raised counter and the cement floor was slick, having just been mopped after a soy chai latte spill. The dozen of us in line studied the menu and shuffled our feet, not wanting to slip on the wet surface. Lala is a picky eater by nature, and when she was pregnant her tastes became even more particular. Deep in a burrito-versus-panini dilemma, I was surprised when it was my turn to order. I looked up, and there was Big Momma manhandling the register with long manicured nails. Her hair had been whipped up into a bouquet of curls, her shirt opened to reveal a highway of cleavage.

"May I help you?" Her lips, moistened with a shade of burnt sienna, beckoned. All the raunchy dominatrix language flooded my ears, the many and varied positions my imagination had created, providing a film for my saucy soundtrack. I saw her looming over me naked, big lips and breasts telling this stupid white fucker not to come or she'd slit my throat with a dull bread knife. I was struck dumb by my own self-imposed pressure.

"It's been so long," I said mistakenly. The plastic menu trembled in my hands.

"Excuse me?" she asked, her tone changing from friendly to angry. Like my favorite song, I recognized the chord progression from her many nightly performances. She always started off sweetly employing whispers and baby talk, but by the end of their session, she was threatening to fuck the spleen right out of poor Skinny.

"I've waited so long in line," I said, trying to cover my panic. I thought of the safe distance the clean white speaker provided in our living room, curtains drawn, Becky and Lala, my legit-imizing bodyguards, nicely by my side.

"I'm having a hard time deciding," I said, shuffling back-ward toward the exit. "Do you take orders over the phone? That might work better for me."

Papa Pia

Our daughter Poppy was barely a month old and our lives seemed relatively easy after a difficult birth. We lived in a cheap four-room adobe on Galisteo Street in Santa Fe, about five blocks south of the plaza. It was summertime, and Poppy (and parenthood, for that matter) meshed into our lives without much fuss. Although she wasn't a great sleeper, she wasn't much of a crier, so we considered that, as they say in Vegas, a push. After a month of staying close to home, Poppy either in the bassinet near our bed or in her Moses basket in the living room, we thought we would drive the hour south to Albuquerque for the weekend to shop for needed baby items and to celebrate Lala's thirty-third birthday. This parenthood thing, we decided with no apparent objection from the baby, was not as hard as people warned us it would be.

We dropped our bags off at the Hampton Inn and went to the Macaroni Grill for dinner, based on another couple-with-child's recommendation. The Macaroni Grill is a chain restaurant and, like many franchises of the sort, tries desperately not to look like a chain. Under high ceilings, side tables host clusters of wine bottles, sheets of butcher paper cover white tablecloths, fancy lights twinkle over the bar, and some retired man dressed in a cravat sings the CliffsNotes of arias at your table. It's a big restaurant—and loud, with clinking glasses and the voices of tourists, locals, and the occasional soccer team mixing together in the steamy air above your penne rustica. After an obligatory wait and a little black box vibrating us back to the hostess stand, we were seated in a room off the main hall where both the lights and noise were dimmer. I dropped Poppy, still restrained in her car seat, on a spare chair while Lala and I scanned the menu. My brother-in-law takes this kind of place public, so I know that in order to calculate potential profitability, every aspect of the business needs to be uniform—food, ambience, and service. Our waitress greeted us the way she greeted all her tables, the same way a waitress at the Macaroni Grill in Omaha greeted hers—a canned smile and a multimedia introduction. Our server was named Violet and she wrote her name on our butcher paper, upside down for her, right side up for us, a trick she embellished with a line underneath her name and a star over the i, all in crimson Crayola. I allowed this pat intro to enter as funny and cute because my brain was still freshly drunk on fatherhood. I ordered a badly missed beer and the pasta special, which had something vaguely to do with food from the sea. I don't recall what Lala ordered. I do know that she's smart enough not to order seafood at a chain restaurant in a high desert climate.

After Violet scurried away, a noise bubbled from the car seat, followed by a deeper tone, matching the belting baritone of the opera singer in the main room. I nobly offered to change my daughter because I desperately wanted to be a father who did such things in public places, and besides, it was my wife's birthday and she had been breast-feeding this kid for twenty-eight days straight. I grabbed Poppy and the diaper bag and wound my way through the tray stands and ferns made from shiny green plastic to the men's room, a black-and-white affair. Anyone who has children knows that changing tables are reserved for women's lavatories and the male bathrooms in only the most enlightened of airports in faraway places like Seattle and Vancouver. I considered my options—the floor was too unseemly and slick with a mystery liquid, the toilets small and potentially risky. The only place that seemed remotely possible was the sink—two basins side by side sunk in faux marble. Sometimes, when teaching writing, I ask my students to look at the negative space—the area in the middle of two people, say, or the gap between who we are and who we think we are. I saw a space that snaked between those two sinks, so I positioned Poppy in a slight curve so that her head was on the edge of the left-hand basin and her legs almost dropped into the one on the right. Man of men, I was proud of myself.

Over the loudspeaker in the bathrooms, an unnamed narrator with a smoky voice whispered a language lesson—the Italian word, then the English: *ciao*, hello . . . *bene*, well . . . *grazie*, thank you . . . *la cucina*, kitchen. This audio instruction is designed to add to the authenticity of the place, since the closest any of the Albuquerque employees has come to Italy is watching the movie *Gladiator*. On this most promising night, I viewed the lessons as multicultural, adding a bit of flavor to my own heroic journey. When I opened Poppy's diaper, I saw that indeed business had been transacted on the trading floor. As I reached down for an unscented wipe from the diaper bag, she exploded. It was as if a lunchbag full of mustard had been shot from a speargun. The shit sprayed the mirror, the wall, her legs, and up and down my left arm. This was how bad it was: I could not see the face of my watch. I started to sweat. Grabbing an inch of wipes, I scrubbed and dabbed and scraped her body and clothes. Just as I thought my little Mount St. Helens lay dormant, she erupted again, and this time I was a witness to this most unnatural phenomenon. The gunk discharged from her like a Super Soaker full of pureed yams. The loop of Italian lessons finished its first cycle and then repeated, taunting me: *la casa*, house . . . *la stanza*, room . . . *la finestra*, window.

Now here is where we put the men into the men's room. Two salesmen entered, their vocation obvious from their attire: oddly patterned polo shirts and pressed khakis with cell phones clipped neatly to their belts. One had sandy hair and a thick mustache. The other's flattop was as black as a crow's wing. They chatted nicely, obviously at dinner with their wives. I am dripping with sweat, tap water, and unscented-wipe juice and I pray these are Real Men, the kind that watch eight hours of football on Sunday in their La-Z-Boys, the kind that use their teeth to open almost anything, the kind that don't wash their hands. I pray for this stereotype-made-flesh even though I'm a dedicated hand washer. In fact, in graduate school, I told my classmates about a faculty member who didn't wash his hands after using the urinal, and they never looked at the piss-poor poet the same way again. At the Macaroni, I was frantically wiping, but the mess seemed to be getting worse. Poppy's temperament darkened as her head lolled back into the sink. I don't need to tell you that the two men behind me were some sort of hand-hygiene freaks.

"Hey, buddy," they called.

I ignored them.

"Hey, buddy." (Why do guys call each other buddy? Is it like when my female students call each other "bro"?) They both nodded toward me. "We need to wash our hands," they said.

I glared at them, not in their faces but in the mirror image, as if they were tellers in a drive-up window and I was closing my checking account. They waited and I scrubbed, a sanitary stand-off. Above us, the speakers rattled off Italian words and phrases, including the obscenely ironic "Where is the bathroom?" Exasperated, they turned to each other, one muttered a profanity, and they left. I breathed heavily, though not happily, and Poppy crapped again—not as much mass but equal force, a raspy Bronx cheer that sprayed the inside of her legs and the edge of the mirror. Men and boys pulsed into the room in clumps. Some saw my crime scene—a sweaty father buffing a wet baby—and left. One older man with spectacles waited patiently against the wall as if what I was doing would only be a minute and he would be pleasant and polite. Using my full store of wipes, I finally removed any visual traces of excrement. My lovely daughter shivered like a shaved rat. She was cranky from all my chiropractic movements keeping her from falling into either the basin or onto the floor. I figured I would strip her, maybe dangle her under the hand dryer for a minute to warm her up, and then change her into the extra set of clothes we so diligently kept in the side pocket of her quilted diaper bag. The end was near. I was sure of it.

The wallflower smiled at me, the kind of tentative smile you give your mechanic as he fixes your car. I reached into the diaper bag and took quick inventory: bottle, wipe box, diapers, teether. No clothes. Nothing. In a flash, I remembered unpacking everything back at the hotel and saw the onesie, booties, and cute little sweater knitted for her by a student's mother—all on the bed in a neat little pile. That's when I lost it. "Give me a fucking break," I, the doomed dad, yelled to the disembodied voice of the Italian teacher who was still instructing me on goodbye, *ciao*, and hello, *ciao*. When I screamed, the wallflower jumped out of his Rockports and shot me a look that I'm sure most violent criminals have seen at least once before they are sent up the river. Then I thought, *Why didn't he offer to help? Why didn't any of these men?* If this were the women's room, Poppy would have been fed, comforted, and swaddled in the extra clothes that someone would have had in her oversized purse for such an occasion. Probably would have bought us dinner as well. All I got from my brethren was profanity, impatience, and denial. No wonder wives get sick of their husbands. We just don't care.

At Macaroni Grill there were no Italian words for "Help me, God and baby Jesus" or "Why did we ever leave home?" There was no Roman equivalent for "give up," which is what I did. I left Poppy in her wetsuit and I wiped myself down with soap, water, and scratchy paper towels. We looked like two drowned cats. Defeated, I left my Italian gulag and limped back to our table, a no-longer-unscented wipe stuck to the bottom of my shoe. By the gape of her jaw, I could tell Lala saw us coming. This was not her vision of the perfect husband and daughter. On the table, Violet had drawn a childish picture of a gondola. My pasta looked like something you had to eat on *Fear Factor*, and my beer was flat; we had been gone for over twenty minutes. I held out my whining child, and Lala looked at me in a way that has lasted through

Poppy's eight years and my son London's first four: *Oh, Rob, what have you done this time?*

Then Violet scampered up and chirped, "How is everything?" with a smile that would sink a thousand ships.

I replied, "Are you fucking kidding me?" Grabbing a crayon with my free hand, I scribbled back and forth on that tablecloth like an autistic kid after ten candy bars and a case of Red Bull.

Violet wilted and said what she had been trained to say: "Let me give you a minute." Lala took Poppy in her arms. I did something I was good at: I chugged my beer as the retiree in a cravat came over and began *O mio bambino caro*, the new soundtrack for my life.

One-Handed

After Poppy was born, I learned to do almost everything one-handed. She loved to be held and carried around, as most babies do, and it became apparent to me that if I wanted a happy child and a fairly productive life, I needed to use my left hand as a nest for Poppy and my right as an all-in-one tool, the kind favored by really clever serial killers and the more outdoorsy of us. It's not as hard as you'd think, living a short period of your life mono-dextrously. I could cook a steak dinner and do the dishes afterward, Poppy calmly at my side. Scrubbing pots and pans proved difficult at first until I jammed them against the walls of our porcelain sink (the place was a rental) and created the proper amount of friction for optimum gunk removal. I could make the bed, do the laundry, and iron shirts, flicking Poppy's drool to check the heat of the portable mangle. Talking on the phone required only one hand, and I still typed with just my index finger, the product of a misspent youth. Opening twist-off caps and lids frustrated me until I saw all the gaps in our hundred-year-old adobe. A liter of seltzer fit neatly between our couch and the wall, the pickle jar wedged nicely under the refrigerator, and baby food could be released by a snug oval between the toilet seat and the basin of the commode. I was like my old hero MacGyver, only with one hand. I could change from my pajamas with buttons into jeans, T-shirt, and sandals, then back again at night. My greatest feat was showering (soap, shampoo, rinse, repeat) while my daughter was held melon-like outside the rain ring of the bathtub.

Poppy enjoyed escorting me on my rounds in her little five-fingered sidecar. She had the best of both worlds: the comfort of my soft grip (I'm not handy enough for calluses) and the constant stimulation of new environments and activities. She monitored my scrubbing technique as I washed my '67 Ford Galaxie in the driveway and acted as sobering backup when I approached our neighbors about their loud sex at night. She was my extra appendage, a nine-pound growth at the end of my left arm, the one I never wanted removed.

With just one child, born at the gateway to summer, Lala and I ate out often. We'd walk down Galisteo Street, past the Oasis Café and narrow shops between Alameda and Water, to the Blue Corn Café, upstairs at the Plaza Mercado. Early into our meal, I needed to use the men's room and wanted to give Lala some time to eat in peace. Poppy didn't yet fit into a booster or high chair, and she wasn't content to lie horizontally. She wanted to see the green and yellow of the peppers in my fajitas, the orange and blue paint on the walls, and the crimson faces of the drunks slamming shots of cheap tequila. Latching her into my left hand,

I carried Poppy past the hostess stand with its rack of dormant pagers to the restroom. The Blue Corn's bathroom was a simple affair: urinal in the middle, flanked by a stall on the left and sink on the right. I lifted Poppy outside the splash zone and began my transaction. I'm a pretty verbal guy and my daughter seemed consoled by my incessant banter. Here are some of the things I said to her at the urinal:

> Hey, honey.
> Hey, honey bunny.
> Sweet baby.
> Sweetness.
> Pop pop.
> Pop goes the weasel.
> The popster.
> (I'm a big water drinker.)
> Sugar.
> Sugar britches.
> Scooby.
> Scooby dooby doo.
> Darling.
> I love you, baby.

As I was about to begin my impressions of television celebrities as farm animals, a gruff voice bellowed from the shadows of the stall. *"Excuse me?"* the occupant asked in such deep tones that I thought his next sentence would be about grinding our bones to make his bread.

"Oh, shit," I squeaked. Poppy was deathly silent. I desperately needed for her to make her presence known to the gathered trousers and hiking boots next to us. "Say something," I pleaded. She smiled devilishly, then farted.

"Who the hell?" the voice started again.

"I've got a baby here," I weakly explained, making me sound even more twisted given what the guy in the stall must have thought I was really holding in my hand. I may even have pointed at Poppy, which was totally stupid given his vantage point and sitting position.

I zipped up and washed my right hand with amazing efficiency and speed: pump soap, rub fingertips across thumb meat, down to wristline and up to roots of fingers, repeat, rinse, dry. I molded Poppy into a ball and tucked her into my chest. We bobbed, weaved, reversed direction, and hurdled oncoming chairs and busboys to the end zone of our brightly colored booth. My wife, always the referee, looked at me quizzically.

"What took you so long?" she asked.

Poppy's eyes were as wide as saucers from our rapid return. A stream of servers whizzed by, their shoulders loaded with trays overcrowded with margaritas, enchiladas, and tacos.

"We were going potty," I said, scanning the footwear of passersby for a now-familiar pair of hiking boots.

"How'd you manage that?"

"Almost single-handedly," I said, and raised my right arm victoriously for the entire world to see. Poppy looked up from her cradle on my left side, wondering if there was something at the end of my arm that was worth noting—a balloon, perhaps, or maybe a bird.

"Sit down. If you don't stop acting like a dork, I'm gonna break that arm," Lala said, taking our daughter from my grip. "And you're gonna need it."

Bite Me

In terms of child labeling, no epithet carries more weight than *biter*. Your toddler can break Vatican windows, defecate in all the wrong places, and utter profanity that would make Chris Rock blush, but if he bites one kid, you might as well ship him off to Sing Sing. One of Poppy's first friends was a little girl named Angelica who looked a lot like my daughter—hydrocephalus-sized head, tiny body, and very little hair. These kids were straight out of a Diane Arbus photo. Both our families had been in the hospital at the same time, overlapping labor pains and screaming, two exhausted fathers pacing the halls like zombies in search of ESPN and a decent cup of coffee. Our kids spent much of their first year together strolling to grassy parks and spitting up on the same burp cloths. About the time when the two girls took their first steps, Angelica's parents began what would become a lengthy and painful breakup. One afternoon, her mother, Carmela, sat at our kitchen table and was telling my wife and me about her marriage troubles, when we heard the scream. Poppy ran in and showed us the chew marks on her arm. Carmela darted quickly into the playroom and scolded Angelica in rapid-fire Spanish (she is from Spain). My wife and I thought nothing of the incident; the girls had never hurt each other before. Like a newborn tiger cub, Angelica was just experimenting with her teeth.

A week later Angelica and her mother came over again. Carmela looked like dogshit—washed out, bags so heavy above her cheeks it looked as if her eyes were about to go on a long trip. The split with her husband was obviously not going well. Lala is one of those great natural listeners; total strangers in line at the grocery store feel compelled to explain to my wife the details of their affairs with TV anchormen, abuse from past priests, or botched hysterectomies. As Carmela relayed stories of difficult domestic relations, I hovered outside the playroom, not wanting to hear more complaints about the male species and still a bit nervous about last week's child bite. Much to my dismay, I was becoming a bitist.

Poppy and Angelica were playing café. My daughter sat demurely at a small-scale table, a large purple dress swallowing her body. Angelica wore a fake nose with glasses and held a book of green guest checks we had purchased at a restaurant supply store. I couldn't make out the words exchanged, but the roles were clear. Poppy acted the part of the snobby customer and Angelica was the sarcastic server, personas both girls had witnessed frequently in the many haughty Santa Fe restaurants that pretended they were in New York or L.A. Poppy ordered something that sounded like "fishy boots." Angelica dutifully wrote down the order and then caught me standing in the doorway. I swear I saw her raise her eyebrows in a Groucho Marx kind of manner, but I cannot be sure given the phony nose and glasses covering her face. Either way, she leaned in closer, pad in one hand, *Blue's Clues* crayon in the other, and bit Poppy just below her eye. Angelica's teeth formed a crescent-shaped bruise along the curve of my daughter's cheekbone. I rushed in and tried to piece together a decent sentence from Spanish learned from a drunken high school teacher and from working in restaurants staffed by people from Mexico.

"Why? Why?" I yelled. "Why to eat the head of my daughter?"

Angelica stared me down and then bit Poppy again, this time on the sad little patch of hair on top of her scalp. My wife arrived on the scene and whisked Poppy out of harm's way toward the kitchen, where they'd retrieve the "ouch mouse" from our freezer. Besides the time when my wife dropped Poppy on her head, this was the most action the misery mole had seen in a while. I stammered on like a stoned game show contestant, trying to discipline this kid, but the Romance languages were failing me. Giving up any hope of syntax, I sounded the way a dog might think: "Mouth. Bad. Head. Danger. Friend. Mean."

Carmela slumped in and said a few harsh words in her Castillian lisp, but her heart wasn't in it. Her life must have felt too overwhelming to now include constant and extreme parenting centered on her daughter's chewing habits. Angelica was no longer just an experimental biter, we realized. She had now progressed into the threatened or stressed stage. And since counseling or guidance seemed unlikely, my wife and I cut them off. We stopped phoning for playdates, and returned their calls when we knew they weren't home. This may sound awful, but we purposely went stroller shopping in Albuquerque the day of

Angelica's birthday party and blamed their lost invitation to Poppy's party on the thankfully lax Santa Fe postal workers. When Poppy and Angelica were both invited to high tea hosted by a mutual friend, I shadowed my daughter like a Secret Service agent, throwing myself in the path of Angelica's teeth if the canines or incisors came within snapping distance. All this occurred over six years ago. The two girls haven't been friends since.

The stigma attached to the term *biter* seems to have grown to mythic proportions, especially around preschools. *Kicker*, *puncher*, or even *licker* doesn't hold the same juice. My friend Marla's son Calvin went through a nipping stage at his first institutional house of play. Because of a staffing shortage, the school mixed the older and younger children at recess, and Calvin, a little brighter and more active than the two-year-old blobs stewing around him, tried to hang out with the much older and cooler three- and four-year-old crowd. He chased the upperclassmen around the play structure, sat on their big-boy chairs, and grabbed their balls when they bounced them. The older kids didn't want a lackey from the diaper set, so they snubbed him. Calvin smartly found a way to get their attention by sinking his teeth into their flesh. It makes sense. I don't know anything short of a bee sting in the eye that will wake your ass up more than another human giving you a decent chew.

Marla came in to work the next day and sighed, "I've got a *biter*," as if she'd just discovered a tumor. The preschool had sent her home with a pamphlet titled "Fighting the Biting" that discussed causes, creative cures, and categories that ranged from frustration to power struggle to "your little Hannibal Lecter." The director filled Marla in on their three-bites-and-you're-out policy and issued her a yellow teething ring on a string that Calvin would be forced to wear like a scarlet letter until he was out of the dark woods of mastication. "When a man is hurt, he makes himself an expert," the poet Tony Hoagland writes. I'd say when a day care boss is confused, she creates more policies (and punishments).

Marla said the word was out on Calvin by the time she picked him up. Outside the low building, the mob of mothers barraged her with their curbside diagnoses:

"How much sugar do you allow in his diet?"

"Is he a big TV watcher?"

"Is everything OK at home—you know, with your husband?"

"Have you checked him for any neurological abnormalities?"

"Have you tried Tiny Tot Yoga or Wee Ones Aromatherapy?"

After bite number two near the water table was documented in triplicate, Marla started carrying her cell phone with her to staff meetings, when she gave tours of our school to prospective parents, and even to the bathroom, just waiting for Calvin's final snap. She was such a nervous wreck that she finally withdrew him, because as an admissions director, she knows that leaving voluntarily is far better than getting expelled for such a foul crime. And, as she confessed to my wife in line at Whole Foods, "the suspense was fucking killing me."

I have a friend from high school named Walter Crow who lives in our hometown with his wife, Pam, and their two boys, Samuel and Nate. After Samuel was born, Pam wanted to stay home with him but needed some income, so she started a small day care. Pam is a delightful woman, the kind of wife who can drag her husband home from the bar without holding a grudge and get up early the next day eager to create some elaborate and goopy art project with the kids. A few years ago, I went back East to become godfather to another high school friend's daughter, and Walter and Pam kindly let me sleep in the "Crow's Nest," their basement decorated to look like a British pub smack dab in suburban Connecticut (Walter is proudly from England). Pam had changed professions from day care provider to caterer when her second son was born, and she had landed the post-christening gig of preparing food that was both tasty and denounced Satan. As she scooped melons into tiny balls, she told me of her days of day care.

"Everything was super. I could stay home with Sam, and some of the neighbor kids came over in the mornings and we'd play in the yard, read—you know." She paused to rinse her hands and consult her neighbor Martha Stewart's cookbook. "It was a great deal until one day Samuel bit the kid from next door. I don't know if he was jealous that I was dividing my attention in his house or what," she said, letting a bit of her Long Island Italian accent leak into her otherwise New Englandy kitchen. "But he left a mark on the kid. You see this?" She waved a piece of prosciutto ham as big as a silver dollar. "This big and the same color."

"Was the mom OK with it?" I asked, thinking about our excommunication of Poppy's only bilingual friend.

"Yeah, at first she was, but then I got worried. Sam kept biting and the kid started to look pretty bad."

"Like?" I couldn't help myself.

"Like this." She grabbed a fistful of ham scraps and flung them onto a whole cantaloupe. The meeting of two foodstuffs reminded me of a hastily assembled decapitated head at a neighborhood haunted house. Pam continued, "I tried all the methods they say—I told him no, gave him toys to play with, offered other things to bite like dirty rags and wooden spoons."

"Dirty rags?"

"I read it somewhere, I swear." Pam scraped the meat off the melon, then sliced it in half with a carving knife. "I put him in time-out. Jesus, that kid lived in time-out. He never got any time in." She formed her fingers into a claw, scraped the seeds from the fruit's cavity, and whipped them into the trash. This woman knew how to discipline produce. "I was getting so frustrated with him. I knew all the moms were about to pull their kids out. The whole neighborhood was talking. I had a biter on my hands."

Maybe it was watching Pam manhandle food or the story she was telling, but I couldn't stop from uttering aloud that most profane and biased word. "Biter," I growled through clenched teeth. There was something primal about this action that was never portrayed on Saturday morning TV. *Yu-Gi-Oh!* and *Pokémon* offer plenty of kicks and punches for young kids to emulate and enjoy, but even these tiny Asian heroes never bite their way through a cartoon-colored challenge. Yet our kids happily chew cereal as they watch. "So what did you do?" I asked, perplexed by the overt irony.

"Well," she said, rinsing the seeds and juice from her hands, "the next time he gnawed the neighbor kid, I took Sam into his bedroom and bit him, hard, on the back."

"What happened?" I was breathless. The biter now becomes the bitee.

"He freaked out! He looked at me in a way he'd never done before. Then he started wailing." Pam deftly strangled a melon ball with a noose of cured pork. "I don't think he ever realized how much it hurt until I took a chunk outta him."

"So it worked?"

"Like a charm," she answered, turning to face me. In her palm lay a perfect sphere of orange muskmelon donning a meat toga, hand-tailored in Parma. "Wanna bite?" she asked.

Driving and Rubbing

I don't know if sleep, when it comes to kids, is a more valuable commodity today than when I was a child. My memories of bedtime rituals seem rather dull and uninspired when I hear of the lengths today's parents will go to just so their son or daughter gets some shut-eye. I recall my mom and dad checking my teeth like I was a horse to see if I'd actually brushed, then sending me off to the room I shared with my older brother, Richard. If, in the confined area of my upper bunk, I didn't fall right to sleep, "tough darts," as my dad would say. I had no high-tech machines playing white noise or the soothing sounds of Maui waterfalls, no glowing night-lights or rotating colored mobiles emitting actual recordings of the human heart. If I wasn't sleepy, a few hours of staring at the ceiling six inches from my face while my brother snored below would shut down my deadened brain.

Even if, during the night, I rolled off my bed and dropped the five feet to the orange-carpeted floor, it never occurred to me to go into my parents' room for some cuddly comforting back into slumberland. I just climbed up the faux wood ladder and tried to bore myself to sleep again.

Neither of my kids is a good sleeper. Poppy has only just realized, at the age of eight, that rest might be good for her tetherball game, but London is often awake until late at night, yelling at the TV and spooning cereal into his mouth like some old retiree in a convalescent home. When Poppy was an infant and toddler, Lala and I had been sleep-deprived for so long that we were willing to try anything to get our daughter to go down. The one method we found that actually worked was driving her around in the car. Although Poppy hated getting strapped into her car seat, the bad suspension of our Daihatsu Charade over poorly maintained streets soothed her tortured soul. Later, when Lala's art business picked up and she needed time to work, I became Poppy's chauffeur. Driving around town without destination or cell phone is not the most thrilling of activities for the modern parent. I decided that I should try to get something accomplished during our jaunts, so I drew up a list of all the drive-through places in the city. At the time there weren't many locations that invited automobiles alongside their buildings, but Santa Fe had more than I had noticed before my car became my second home. I could drop off dry-cleaning, get my car washed and lubed, order fast food, and pick up prescriptions, and for a brief period New Mexico still allowed you to buy booze while buckled in your Chevy pickup truck. At Owl Liquors, I truly felt like a local, pulling up to order the hopeful lowbrow combo of a six-pack and a lottery ticket. While I never drank and drove, that chilled 72 ounces of liquid Prozac on the seat next to me was tempting given the high-pitched wailing coming from the backseat.

After becoming the drive-through dad, I learned that Poppy shared my enthusiasm for establishments that did commerce through sliding windows, so I needed something to dull her to my series of moving transactions. When Lala and I decided to go on road trips to Utah to see her grandmother or Wyoming to see her mom, Poppy would cry for hours. I hate to admit it, but in order to stop the insanity, Lala would often unbuckle herself and crawl into the backseat to breast-feed Poppy while I piloted us north on the highway. She'd lean over, unleash a breast, and let Poppy gulp-'n'-go. The other discovery we made was due to the glaring lack of a CD player in the car. Lala and I were forced to sing in order to soothe our savage spawn. Between us, we maybe know the words to six tunes, but we found one ditty that Poppy really liked: "This Is the Way We Wash Our Clothes." We sang that song more often than Céline Dion sings the *Titanic* theme in her Vegas show. Lala and I altered the lyrics to avoid crashing or killing each other, changing "wash our clothes" to "comb our hair" to "brush our teeth." Our kid would have damn good hygiene if nothing else, we figured. I wonder now what we looked like tooling down I-25, Lala pulling a Janet Jackson in the backseat while we serenaded our child with the Puritan work ethic set to music.

The catch with the whole singing bit was that once you started, you couldn't stop. The same went for the car. Singing and engine idling together made for one happy Poppy. So I'd pull up to One-Hour Martinizing with a load of shirts and sing my order to the ex-con in the window, who either threw me mad-dog stares or frantically looked around for the hidden camera. It went something like this:

"This is the way I say no starch,
say no starch,
say no starch,
this is the way I say no starch,
I need them by this Thursday."

At Owl Liquors, they didn't find it unusual that I melodized my request, since most people ordering at drive-through windows were so loaded they could drive and sing but couldn't walk the six feet to the register. Ultimately, I had to abandon my drive-through addictions since this whole song-and-dance routine on wheels became too stimulating for Poppy. What worked the best was the singing while driving in circles along the same *avenidas* in my *barrio*. Piloting the Charade, I'd repeatedly pass my landlord's brother, a guy we called the Monkey Man due to his simian features and abundance of ear hair. He was the type of man who bullied the neighborhood to buy parking stickers and installed signs so no "troublemakers" could park on his public streets. Monkey Man would be outside his house hanging another orange Trespassers Will Be Shot placard on his garage door, and I'd pass him singing at the top of my lungs, "This is the way I shave my ass so early in the morn-ing!" With each lyrical drive-by, his face transformed from vaguely friendly to curious to downright angry. Even if I waved or winked, he looked pissed. I don't know if he thought I was on smack or crazy or if he was concerned that a singing village idiot would lower his property values, but he eventually called his brother, who scowled at us long enough to make us want to find another shack to live in.

I know many parents who struggle with this relentless sleep issue. My friend Marla's son Calvin's nighttime ritual of books and stories has grown to over an hour. And forget naptime at the

Eurocentric preschool he attends. The boy just can't fall asleep on a mat even if it's made from organic and hypoallergenic natural fibers culled from a fetal lamb. His lack of narcolepsy has been labeled as "difficult" and "noncompliant" by the caregivers, who no longer have time to go outside to smoke, chug espresso, and practice their Romance-language profanity.

Another mom I know named Denise has a daughter who will not go down without a good hour of back rubbing. We were having coffee the other day in a strip mall café, and I was complaining about London's erratic sleep behaviors.

"Oh, that's nothing," she said, sipping her half-caf latte. "With my girl, it started when she was still in her crib. I rubbed her back for a good forty minutes until she finally gave in. If I stopped for even a second to deal with my muscle spasms, she'd lose it and we'd have to start all over."

"Forty minutes steady?" I was amazed. I start snoring a third of the way into *Runaway Bunny*.

"Yeah, it was hard. I had so much to do, and my arms and back were killing me. Try leaning over and rubbing—it ain't easy."

Even though a good leaning over and rubbing sounded perfect to me, I had to hear the rest. "Did you have to sing to her?" I asked, thinking of the "wash our clothes" ear worm that still hasn't left my skull after six years.

"No," Denise said, "she needed complete silence. I tried everything to keep from going nuts—meditation, recalling pages of books I just read. I even tried to remember everyone I've ever met."

"In your life?"

"In my entire life. I felt like Steve McQueen in *Papillon*. I was so tired I even started to look like him." She rubbed her eyes in remembrance of reaching over those wooden bars.

"Do you still do it?"

"No, thank God," she said, brushing her blond hair out of her eyes. "Now she just rubs my face."

"What?" I thought I'd misheard her, since the coffee shop was filled with people Wi-Fi-ing on laptops with screens the size of my car's windshield.

"She started rubbing my face at naptime and it just stuck. I lie next to her at night in her bed and she strokes my cheek." She ran the pads of her fingers across the triangle of pale skin adjacent to her eyes, nose, and mouth. It looked kind of nice, actually, so I did the same on mine. Then I realized I was a man acting out the lyrics to *Killing Me Softly*, so I sat on my guilty hand. "Forty minutes?" I asked, getting it together.

"Over and over until she falls asleep. I think I may have gotten her down to almost thirty," she said, rapping her knuckles on the wooden table.

"What happens if you're not home?" I felt a surge of panic now, like I was watching some bad suspense film starring Jamie Lee Curtis or her modern-day re-creation, Jennifer Love Hewitt. In my movie, our heroine would have to speed through traffic, blowing through red lights, just to get home for a good stroking before it got dark. And they say Hollywood doesn't offer box-office roles to women.

"We've tried other faces—my husband's, the babysitter's, Mr. Potato Head—but I guess there is no substitute."

"You do have nice skin," I admitted.

"Thanks very much. It's not like I do anything else anyway. I sort of gave up on that whole going-out thing." She turned her head wistfully toward the window.

"Tell me about it," I said. The last time Lala and I went on a date Ben was still with J. Lo. "How long will this stage last, you think?"

"I'm not sure." She finished the dregs of her overpriced coffee drink. "She's been eyeing the back of my knees lately. I'm trying to push her toward that general vicinity."

"How come?"

"That way I could put my legs up on her bed and do crunches," she said. "I need to get back into shape."

Maybe it was the caffeine or not sleeping through the night in close to a decade, but I accepted this freakish scenario far too easily: a woman doing sit-ups while her daughter caresses the flesh behind her mother's kneecaps. As the daughter grows sleepy, the mother grows strong. A happy ending if ever I've heard one.

The Baby Whisperer

My friend Todd calls me from San Francisco a few months after his daughter Anna is born. His voice is gravelly, his speech is slurred, and even his inherited midwestern pauses stretch longer than usual. I have known Todd since junior high school, and he is eternally optimistic without being bubbly, even in the direst of circumstances. When he flipped his parents' Audi on the day he received his driver's license, Todd turned to me, both of us upside down, and said, "At least it's not on fire." Twenty years later, I can tell something's up since, as my students would say, he sounds like a softcock.

"Dude, we're dying," he tells me. "The kid won't sleep. I swear we didn't get more than twenty minutes every three hours last night." According to Todd, the only time he rests is when he's traveling on business. "I'm signing up for two days in India

just so I can catch some Z's," he says. I let my old friend vent
about how it is affecting his job at a major securities firm and
with his wife at home. Most new parents need an outlet, a shoulder to die on, and I feel like a great friend to him until he asks
me, "What did you and Lala do with Poppy?"

"You don't want to know," I say.

Neither of my kids is a very good sleeper. Before my daughter
turned two, she never slept through the night. Not once.
Nothing about her slumbering patterns was regular. One evening she'd be up until midnight, giggling on the bed, and the
next day she'd be asleep by dinnertime, then awake at 2 A.M.,
wanting us to read all 432 pages of *The Complete Adventures of
Curious George*. During the summer months, Poppy's infant in-
somnia wasn't a big deal since Lala and I had flexible job hours.
She was an artist who worked at home, and like many other people with newly earned graduate degrees, I was waiting tables. In
the fall, I added teaching to my career in the service industry,
and Lala's business had picked up, so our little insomnolent was
beginning to cramp our style.

After months of very little repose, Lala and I grew irritable,
barking at each other about everything from whose turn it was to
sing "I See the Moon" at 3 A.M. to who, in our sleepwalking
states, had placed the baby monitor in the fridge next to the
long-forgotten bottle of white wine. We bought a crib from a
couple we knew and tried to relocate Poppy from our bed into
the new digs, but as soon as she saw her new gated community of
one, she wailed like a banshee. Since Lala and I were both sleepy
and cowardly, we moved her back in with us.

One morning after I'd been teaching a few weeks, I was waiting for my group of seventh graders to arrive. I stood in the circle drive in front of our school clutching a triple-shot latte. I

could barely keep my eyes open. One of my students' mothers, a tall, striking woman with silver hair, clip-clopped up to me in her Prada shoes and said, "You look like shit."

"Thank you very little," I replied. We had joked in the same way before, mostly about her son's habit of losing his sneakers. He was on his third pair in as many weeks. She was the kind of mom who, because of her lifelong beauty and money, never felt the need to hold her tongue. She liked me because although I didn't possess either of those princely assets, I had grown up with three brothers and was fluent in the language of the smart-mouth. I told her of my life without sleep and what a drag it had become.

"You should Ferberize her ass," she said.

"What's that?"

"Dr. Ferber. Look him up. He'll save your life," she said, then ran to her Range Rover to smoke a French cigarette behind tinted glass.

I learned that Richard Ferber is a famous doctor whose book *Solve Your Child's Sleep Problems* had sold cribfuls of copies to snooze-deprived parents all over the globe. His philosophy is based on a strict schedule and routine, something that didn't exactly fit our bohemian lifestyle, but at that point we were willing to trade in our paintbrushes for a pair of bullwhips.

Lala and I bought the book and spent a few nights reading aloud to each other while Poppy crawled around on the floor chasing dust bunnies we were too exhausted to sweep up. According to Herr Doktor, we needed to put our daughter in her crib at the same time each night and, while holding a stopwatch, let Poppy cry as long as we could bear it. Each night we would let her cry a bit longer until she finally wept herself into the Land of Nod.

I set up a little command station in our bedroom and stocked the corner with bottled water, earplugs, aspirin, a digital stop-watch, and a bottle of Jägermeister left over from a period in our lives when we still had fun. Lala and I told Poppy it was time for bed, and we wrapped her burrito-style in a thin blanket, leaving one arm out so she could suck her thumb or flip us off after we deserted her. We carried our darling across the narrow strip of hallway to her crib, placed her gently inside, and, as suggested, rubbed her back in a circular motion. Poppy eyed us with great curiosity since her parents were acting and speaking in the hushed tones usually reserved for funeral directors and guid-ance counselors. After we professed our love to her ten times, we scurried back to our bunker across the corridor and hid like two frightened soldiers ready for the mortar to hit. We didn't have to wait long.

"*Mama*? Dada?" Poppy called.

Nobody moved. Lala held the bright yellow sport-edition stopwatch in her hand, while I eyed the Jäger in all its emerald-colored goodness.

"Mamaaaaaaaaaaaa!" Poppy yelled. We crouched down even lower, as if she had one of those thermal-imaging machines the cops use to see through the walls of homes rented by violent felons. Poppy abandoned what little speech she possessed and regressed to primal screams and cries, the kind we hadn't heard for months. Below the wails, we listened to her rattle the bars of her wooden cage. Lala, eyes closed, whispered softly to herself. Even though she was raised Catholic among Mormons in Utah, my wife is usually not someone who speaks freely to the Lord.

"Should I pray too?" I asked her in what I believed was a spousal bonding moment.

She opened her eyes. "Pray? I'm swearing, you idiot," she

said, and I could recognize the mother tongue clearly now, the *shitshitfuckfuckdamndamnshitshit* whooshing just under Poppy's cries, which had by now evolved into full convulsions. According to Ferber, this mania was as normal as the vomit that was scheduled to erupt at any moment. Lala and I held on to each other for dear life. I spent most of my adolescence doing things that felt good but everyone said were wrong and here I was, a parent, doing something that felt wrong that everyone said was good.

Only three minutes had gone by. A hundred and eighty seconds. Lala swore once more and then joined Poppy in the crying game. I teared up too. It sounded as if our daughter was on *Fear Factor* being nibbled to death by rats riding tarantulas. Her screams grew so deep that we thought she'd choke on them.

"That's it," Lala said, rising to her feet. "I'm going in."

"Don't," I replied. "Ferber says we should stick it out longer than this. It says here in his book that crying never hurt a child."

"I don't know," Lala said. "This doesn't seem right." Though I hated quitting, even in a contest as strange as this one, I could see her point. It sounded as if Poppy's throat was clogging with mucus, and the bars rattled louder than a Gatling gun. "Fuck Ferber," Lala shouted. "I'm going."

"Don't," I said, and blocked her way. Suddenly, everything was silent. No crying child, no bubbling snottage, no shaking slats. "See there?" I said glibly. "She's exhausted herself just like the book said she would." I thumped the paperback in self-righteous glory.

Then we heard a loud thump as Poppy's head hit the floor. Even though she couldn't walk, our little Steve McQueen made her great escape by climbing onto the top rung of her cell and throwing herself off. Luckily, she fell onto the only square of carpet in the house. We both ran in, and while I checked Poppy's vital signs, Lala apologized in as many ways and languages as she knew how. She pledged to Poppy that she'd never sleep in that playpenitentiary again. Lala promised our daughter a future full of shiny candy, homemade ice cream, rides on Italian merry-go-rounds, and a fleet of Welsh ponies with elaborately braided manes. And, Lala added in a fit of biblical guilt, if we ever bought an ox, we'd slaughter it in her name.

Poppy yawned, brushed the carpet fibers from her swollen forehead, and pointed to our communal bed across the hall.

"OK, honey," Lala cooed. "It's all right now." We all marched back into the bedroom, where the stopwatch still ticked on the table with all the other Ferberware. "Get that shit out of my sight," Lala barked. "And call the Thrifty Nickel. We're selling that goddamn crib."

Todd calls me back a few weeks later and he sounds like a million bucks. He laughs easily and heartily, and the verve in his voice reminds me of a party I held in high school. Just before I passed out on my father's bed, Todd laughed that very same way. And then, once I was fully comatose, he drew penises all over my face in permanent ink. On the phone, I ask him what caused such a dramatic change in his demeanor.

"We hired the Baby Whisperer, dude," he says.

"The baby what?" The only whisperer I'd heard of starred Robert Redford as a man who loved his horsies a bit too much.

"A guy at the office recommended her to us, and luckily she had a week free." Todd goes on to tell me that this petite blond woman from England showed up at their door with a suitcase and portable cot and told them to leave and "reconnect with their spouse."

"I asked her if we could just go to bed, but she said no dice."
Todd and his wife, Sylvie, went out to dinner to a place with cloth
napkins and nary a high chair or booster seat in sight. When they
returned a few hours later, everything had changed.

"Anna was asleep between two rolled towels and the B.W.—"

"B.W.?"

" 'Baby Whisperer' is too long to say. Anyway, she'd installed
a dimmer switch so the nursery lights could be adjusted. She had
on one of those Sound Screen machines playing white noise, and
the place smelled like rose petals."

"Rose petals?"

"Yeah, she said that Anna liked that scent best of all, better
than vanilla or potpourri. She told us to go to bed, that she'd
wake Sylvie up to breast-feed once during the night, but we'd all
powwow in the morning."

Todd tells me the Baby Whisperer stayed up all night with
Anna, studying her every breath, cry, and fart. Then she spent
the next four days teaching Todd and Sylvie about their own
daughter.

"What was that like?" I ask, recalling the prenatal classes
Lala and I took that focused far more on mucous plugs and
meconium than on how to get any sleep after the placenta was
disposed of.

"She was very direct." Todd describes to me the "wind-
down" program that the Queen of Siesta created and which the
couple needed to follow or she couldn't guarantee they'd ever
rest again. "B.W. informed us that Anna liked to sleep on her
side, wanted us to squeeze her bottle until she drank the last
drop, and preferred Vivaldi to Debussy. By the time B.W. left,
Anna was sleeping twelve hours a night—7 A.M. to 7 P.M.—like
freaking clockwork."

"What did the whole deal cost you guys?" I wondered aloud.

"B.W. doesn't come cheap." Todd speaks as if he's finished some sort of sheep-counting boot camp. His new messiah's week's wages are more than I take home after a month of teaching English to yawning teenagers. "But she was worth every freaking penny," he declares, sounding cheerful and well rested. They say that money doesn't buy happiness and that people who brag that they sleep like a baby usually don't have one, but somewhere a woman with a Mary Poppins accent, carrying a folding cot, a white-noise machine, and a pocketbook full of cash, is proving them all wrong.

Pussy

Just before Christmas, my son, London, started saying the word *pussy*. As a seasoned father, I understand that new words stick to two- and three-year-olds like toilet paper to the bottom of your shoe, yet this instance of ideogrammic discovery struck me as different from the others. The first time London uttered this word we were sitting at the dinner table—me, Lala, the boy, and his seven-year-old sister, Poppy. London had just declared that he had finished with his meal and, not restricted by the rules of eating that the rest of us subscribe to, he ran around, *Thomas the Tank Engine* stuck in the dark and sticky tunnel of his closed hand. "Pussy!" he yelled, Thomas above his head weighting his fist like a roll of pennies.

Lala and I looked back at him in unison, not dropping our forks but definitely halting the chew. "What was that?" she mouthed at me, careful not to alarm the daughter that this word had some thorns.

"Hey, London," I called as casually as I could. "What did you say?" I forced a phony smile to throw him off the scent.

"Pussy." He cocked his head and waited.

"You see a cat somewhere?"

"No."

"What's a pussy?"

He searched around the room, trying to find an object to attach to the two syllables. My wife is a folk artist, and there were many objects among our many collections for him to choose from—bottle-cap men, ceramic cars from Mexico, strings of red chile lights. He spun around and then pointed at me. "You," he said gleefully. "You are a pussy."

I suppose in retrospect, we paid far too much attention to an otherwise harmless word that I'm sure would have faded like all the other stray sounds that my son gives voice to during any given week. *Pussy*, however, captivated us. As a writer and teacher, the music of the word alone grabbed me, not to mention its myriad meanings. (I had just bought a meat mallet, and I could not stop saying those two words together: *meat mallet*. I said it at home, in my classroom, in my car: "Where is my meat mallet? Who stole my meat mallet? Have you met my meat mallet?") For my wife, it was her love for all things taboo. A two-year-old with that word in his mouth was deliciously naughty. Because we gave London the third degree over this one term, he soon realized its power and said it even more frequently than I mentioned my new flesh hammer. And, as my wife and I secretly hoped, though never admitted even to each other, this word refreshingly complicated our lives.

A former student of mine who is now in college visited us one afternoon to tell of her upcoming trip to the town of Hana on the Hawaiian island of Maui. The road to Hana is famous for its twists, turns, waterfalls, and potential for carsickness. Since we had experienced this firsthand the summer before, we spoke of Hana in great and nauseating detail. London darted in and out of the living room during our chat and then sidled up to my student, Thomas now replaced by Buzz Lightyear, and asked her, "Hana pussy?"

My student, who is OK with children but does not have any glowing fascination or love for the younger versions, tried to be polite and asked London to repeat himself, which he did but now with a more affirmative statement: "Hana pussy. Yes, Hana pussy." She sized us up (I was her high school English teacher, after all) and asked sincerely, "You guys watch a lot of porn around here?"

Pussy is a funny word because its taboo or profane meaning is slang and not definitive. Its beauty is in the eye of the beholder. Since I teach teenagers, I see these reflexive moments every single day. One kid tells another that his fly is open, and the one with zipper attention disorder says accusingly, "Why are you looking at my crotch?" These moments are stupid, but they are also funny until you are maybe twenty-four or in an adult locker room. A simpleton would say that since London does not know the profane meaning of the word or the feline meaning either, anyone who thinks he's uttering an obscenity is perverse, but if you hear *pussy* out of context and out of a young boy's mouth, most people cannot help but be offended, intrigued, or both.

My older brother, Rich, and his wife, Mimi, recently split up, and my sister-in-law is quite wounded from the separation and impending divorce. I phoned her to offer my ear, and as is the habit in my family, I put Poppy on first to say hello and tell her aunt about her busy suburban life of spelling, tap dance, and horseback riding. She then passed the telephone on to London, who shouted enthusiastically into the receiver: "Hey, you big pussy!" I snatched the phone away, which sent him into hysterics, and was prepared to start the long explanation to Mimi about the word, our fruitless investigation of its origin, and our subsequent embarrassment, but Mimi snapped. "What did he just say to me?" she asked, and then wept like La Llorona.

London had evolved into a short and scurrying time bomb. Lala and I take our children everywhere, and London, loaded with that one lexical bullet, ticked along to birthday parties, various parks and playgrounds, and the grocery store. And he lived up to Chekhov's rule of drama: if you have a shotgun in the first act, it has to go off in the second. London hitched otherwise mundane modifiers to his new linguistic engine. He called our butcher "stinking pussy" and his playmate Augie "Robopussy" (after a terrible Alvin and the Chipmunks video); even my father became the benevolent "Grandpa Pussy." Most people thought our anxiety around the word stemmed from a future nightmare of our son becoming a foulmouthed sailor at preschool, dropping the F-bomb, smoking Lucky Strikes, and drinking mouthwash. I hesitate to admit I kind of loved the anticipation of the adult reaction to my little Don Rickles: the double take at him, the PC glare at us (the careless parentals), then the pat questions about leonine friends at home or perhaps overhearing our bedroom TV blasting videos you can only rent with a photo ID after midnight.

Pussy made the boring dinner party tolerable, the dance recital closer to a punk rock concert. *Pussy* broke the structure of our soccermomstrumental week. The part I didn't foresee was the discomfort people felt even discussing the meta-fact that London had become this punning linguistic prodigy. That a metrosexual father of four, dressed in $200 jeans and designer eyewear, would march away as soon as I let the word loose. We were at a holiday party, and I was thinking about all this: language, meaning, interpretation, and the profane. One of my current students' parents also attended this festive get-together, and the couple asked me about writing and teaching. The "How is our son doing?" conversation had dried up so they wanted to know what I was working on. About eight people huddled in our wine-slurping circle, eating imported tomatoes that had been de-moisturized in some Etruscan sun. I hesitated telling them, but I figured we were all enlightened liberal adults. Besides, the point still remained: London did not know what the word meant. It was just a *fa* in his song, a narrative scrap blowing in his mind's dust devil. So I said: "I've been thinking a lot about *pussy*." The chewing stopped; mouths held the wine a beat longer before swallowing; the glances no longer seemed casual or mildly flirtatious. I let the sentence linger longer because I was my son's father and because I wanted to experience fully what London could only feel: the power of a word.

Crying in America
(in Three Parts)

I

The last time I cried I was sitting in my Daihatsu Charade in the parking lot of Wood Gormley Elementary on Booth Street in Santa Fe. I had driven to the school for two reasons: to talk to Ted, the wiry PE instructor, about swim lessons, and to surreptitiously purchase two valentines for my daughter, Poppy. The playground buzzed with kids high on recess, and before I exited my car, I scanned the monkey bars and jungle gym for Poppy among the parkas, heavy coats, and hats as they zigged and zagged across mud and blacktop. I caught my daughter right outside the green play structure, standing with her towheaded friend Claire. The two girls stood still while a gang of second graders scurried frantically, trying to escape the tagging hand of a drooling boy named Geno. I could see half of Poppy's face; she was watching the crowd intently, her mouth open just enough for me to make out the two top teeth that would fall out soon. She didn't appear especially happy or sad; her skin shone white in the overhead sun, nothing on her seemed forced or posed in response to someone else's viewing. I experienced a potent mixture of joy and despair and started to weep. I saw Poppy anew as a creature who superseded any ideas or notions I had about who she was or who she could be. From her ardent look, I also understood that she was, in a sense, growing away from total dependence on her father and toward an autonomy that will both amaze me and cleave my heart in two. It was almost film-like, feeling moved as Poppy was moving away.

I then realized I was this shabbily dressed man, alone, watching kids on a playground, crying in his pathetic three-cylinder automobile. I thought, *Don't be the sad teacher in his sad clothes sitting in his sad car.* So I got out and walked to the tot lot, waving to the teacher on duty to assure her that invoking Megan's Law was not necessary. I called Poppy's name. So marvelous to say: *Pop-py*, those two *p* sounds exploding lightly from my lips. I could have crept up behind her, scaring her as I do so often, but I summoned her instead to see how she'd react. Her face bloomed into a smile that I recognized like my best friend, and she called back to me: "Da-da!" I wished for her to run into my arms because I knew that someday she would not. One not-so-distant afternoon she'll turn her head—not her whole body, just her noggin—and nod at me, finish her conversation with some stupid boy, and then, when she feels like it, saunter over to my (hopefully better) car, where I stand waiting. I wonder if it will be harder for me in the future to watch my children without them seeing me, void of the excuse of a play or dance recital or stopping by to talk to the PE teacher about overpriced swimming lessons. How would I have felt as a teenager if I'd caught my mom or dad spying on me outside my Intro to Western Civ class as I discussed some rule, law, or lost cause? What if I'd caught them weeping?

II

On Wednesdays at four-thirty I stand in a tiny lobby with twelve women, all of us waiting for our daughters to finish their Jazz I dance class. This group of seven- and eight-year-old girls has been practicing the same dance number, "I Won't Grow Up," from the musical version of *Peter Pan* for about eighteen weeks now, and most of us parentals could probably slog our way through the whole routine. In the cramped vestibule of a faux granary, we pace and bump into each other, rereading the bulletin board about the $50 costume fee for three minutes of stage time, dreading the week in June that this one brief dance number will destroy. I usually lurk near the empty water cooler, the only male presence in a world of toe shoes, leg warmers, and tight-fitting leotards. Students and parents often look at me as if I took a wrong turn and got lost after a drag race or bare-knuckle brawl. After it's clear that this strange man isn't going anywhere, the females happily ignore me.

Most of the mothers know each other through these types of tarrying moments—by the school fence at three o'clock, the corridor of the Assumption church after Brownies, on the edge of the soccer field on Tuesdays and Fridays at five. Since they aren't friendly outside extracurricular activities, each week they must reintroduce themselves and then identify through their children: "Oh, you're Sally's mother. Riiiight." No one seems to grow weary of this *Groundhog Day* experience, and it feels somehow mandatory given that your face is only inches from Polly's mom's. If you tire of this shallow social custom and decide that you just want to dart in, grab your kid, and dart out, the mothers will not forgive. One salutatory oversight and all those well-bred parents will sully your good name: "I've seen that woman every week for a year. She knows who I am. The least she could do is wave."

After niceties are exchanged, some new topic is broached and discussed very briefly, since most of us have leftovers to reheat, baths to run, and homework to monitor. A few weeks ago, the women were discussing Jim Sheridan's semi-autobiographical film *In America*, the moving story of an Irish immigrant family trying to make it on the mean streets of New York City. Actually, what the women were really talking about was crying.

"That *In America* was a real tearjerker," a heavyset woman said, trying to kill the awkward silence. She worried the strap of her dumpling-shaped handbag, squatting on the bench next to her.

"I know, I cried the whole way through it," another mom agreed, stroking the hair of a non-dancing daughter who sat beside her reading a book called *Junie B. Jones and the Stupid Smelly Bus*.

The group moved through the plot and characters, reminding us all if we'd seen the film or preparing us if we hadn't (bring your Kleenex, ladies, a whole box), how sad each aspect of the film was. "That poor mother," the big woman sighed, swinging her handbag onto her lap.

"Her husband loved her so much," the *Smelly Bus* mom added, and the group formed a circle to weigh in on the communal recollection.

"The dead child. Can you imagine?" an older woman remarked. "I blubbered like a baby." It was obvious from the silver

in her hair that she had gotten a late start on this whole child-
bearing business.

According to the mothers, every element of that movie was
downright depressing: the acting, scenery, props, and soundtrack, even the titles. Then a voice rang out from a thin woman in
running clothes, defying the conventional wisdom: "I refuse to
pay seven bucks to go sit in some movie theater and cry." She
crossed her sinewy arms and shot her frowning glance outside
where our rounded minivans waited to ferry us home. You could
tell from her fatless frame and expensive haircut that she was
battling the frumpiness that often accompanied the soccer mom
role, yet her face couldn't hide the puffy and lined effects of
family fatigue.

"Oh, but it's a good film," Handbag defended. "It's won
awards and it's based on a true story."

"Too depressing," said the jogger. "I get enough of that in my
own life. I like uplifting films."

"Like what?" someone asked earnestly, hoping for a serious
recommendation. Maybe some foreign film none of us had
heard about. A few mothers reached in their bags for pens.

"*Finding Nemo,*" she said, nodding.

"That was a good movie," everyone agreed.

"Well, I saw *In America,*" said a striking woman with hair and
lipstick the color of blood oranges. Unlike the rest of us, her skin
was as tight as a drum. There are some women who seem almost
timeless in their appearance, as if they could be either thirty or
fifty years old. This mother spoke with her hands, which opened
and closed like they were spreading pixie dust in the air. "I was
going out to dinner with Bill that night, full hair and makeup, so
I couldn't cry. I wanted to but I held it all in. Almost caused
damage. The next day, Saturday, I went back to the matinee in

sweatpants and glasses instead of my contacts, and cried like a baby. The movie hadn't even really started and the waterworks were turned on full blast. It felt so good, I can't even begin to tell you."

"I only cry in movies," *Smelly Bus* proudly confessed.

"Me too," someone else added excitedly, as if she had just discovered they shared the same father.

"Some TV shows can get me going," an earnest woman said while poking her Palm Pilot with a tiny pen.

"Commercials too," another chimed in. "That one for the cell phone where the kids are stuck in the rain and the line is busy? Gets me every time."

"How about the one where you sponsor the orphan? You know, African kids with flies on their lips? I think it's Christian."

"Do you sponsor one?"

"Hell no, but I sob like mad. Got my girls crying too now."

As the women spoke, I realized that the dark, sticky-floored caverns of movie theaters had become safe and justifiable places to emote. I wondered if theaters would soon realize this new trend of emotive therapy and market films by their sentimental content. You scan a menu, color-coded for each sentiment, and say, "Huh. I feel cancer-sad, let's go see *Terms of Endearment*" or "Melancholy is for me, one for *Lost in Translation*, please." Each seat would have tissue boxes or stress balls or pistol grips embedded in the arms of the chairs.

In the pause between the end of the conversation and the spillage of children out from the dressing room door, the jogger eyed me warily, as if to say *What the hell are you smiling about?* I thought about my own reaction to seeing *In America*. Even though I often felt like crying during those 103 minutes, I didn't. In fact, I often avoid television shows or films—usually involving death or harm to children—that I know will make me want to weep. I grew up in a family of men, and my father, a Manhattan banker for thirty-five years, was never big on showing emotion. After a painful breakup with my high school sweetheart, her new suitor ribbing me about our split, I came to my father in tears. He was in our laundry room trying to tackle the trash cans full of his sons' soiled whites and colors.

"Never let them see you cry," he shouted at me, and after that I didn't. Not at funerals or weddings, car accidents or fistfights, not even with torn ligaments, broken arms, or a fractured neck.

My amusement with the women in that congested waiting room evolved into envy. How lucky these women were to have a place to truly let loose and feel sadness, even if stirred on by artificial means or manipulation through images, music, and a director's deft hand. What difference did it make what triggered the emotion if the sentiment was real? Maybe, I thought, I should see *In America* again. I could wear waterproof clothing, bring a few handkerchiefs, and cry my little repressed ass off. In terms of weepage, I had a hell of a lot of catching up to do. I could flood the fucking joint.

III

"Are you as scared as I am?" my sister-in-law Becky asked, and I was. We were facing each other, Lala in her hospital gown lying between us, each of us holding one of her tightly clenched hands. Things were not going well. Lala had been checked in many hours before, IV'd, induced, epiduraled, and started the pushing process, and we were getting nowhere. The head would emerge, then scoot back, appear, then disappear, and although the doctor, nurse, and pediatrician, who was standing by to siphon the meconium from the baby's mouth, nose, and lungs, all said it was normal, I wondered what the hell the baby was doing. Could it really just fake us out, play peek-a-boo a dozen times in a row? The doctor, a thin, usually well-dressed woman named Lynore Martinez, serenely asked the nurse to get the vacuum, a machine that was used during the birth of our daughter, who after some initial resistance came into the world quite healthy, thank you very much.

Our hospital had recently renovated its delivery rooms, which are fairly luxurious compared to, say, the emergency room with its bulletproof glass, bolted-down furniture, and signs prohibiting any form of human behavior other than sitting. Everything you need is in those delivery rooms—bathroom with a shower, reclining chair for the father or partner, crib, and an area set into the wall for the doctor to perform the post-delivery cleaning, weighing, measuring, and testing. The only thing missing is a wet bar. Our small team was joking about getting out in time for some television show. Dr. Martinez was speaking calmly to my wife, encouraging her to push while she tested the vacuum's hoses. The assisting nurse seemed almost bored with the routine, while the amicable pediatrician chatted away to no one in particular. The vacuum sounds and acts exactly like its name. A plastic suction cup is attached to the baby's head, and then the pressure is increased slightly until the doctor has a good grasp and the baby is pulled out. Although the whole idea of this birth-by-giant-tentacle freaked me out, I had seen it work before, so I was close to mollifying myself. "It's any minute now," Dr. Martinez said, and I believed that in a few I'd be cutting a cord, capturing the first cries with my handheld tape recorder, taking pictures with my disposable camera, and holding the new addition in my arms.

Then everything changed. Something was definitely wrong. Four nurses charged in, pushing Becky and me forcefully to the head of the bed. Each pair of RNs grabbed a leg, yanking Lala's knees to her ears. Two different nurses started pounding on my wife's stomach in what seemed to be a brutal attempt to force the baby out. Becky and I were surrounded by an unreal amount of activity. It was as if my wife were a car in the middle of an Indy 500 pit stop and she was losing by ten laps. Eight people were working their hands on and in her, while four more waited anxiously nearby. There was a distinct sense of hysteria in the room, topped off by the nurse next to me crying. I don't know much about medicine but I know if a trained and licensed nurse begins to weep as your wife attempts to deliver your child, you don't need a chart to know that things pretty much suck. Our baby was in deep shit.

My son had what they call shoulder dystocia, and so his delivery required, in addition to downward traction and episiotomy, specific maneuvers to deliver the protuberances below his neck. In other words, when babies are born, they usually twist and dip a shoulder to exit, the way you slip through a hole in a chain-link fence to sneak into the county fair. My son tried to come out straight as a board and his broad ledges got stuck. My wife normally weighs around 100 pounds, and our son tipped the scales at a whopping 9 pounds 12 ounces. It hurts just thinking about it.

Dr. Martinez quickly performed Wood's screw maneuver, the application of pressure to the anterior surface of the baby's posterior shoulder. She had to pull my son out before any of a number of things went wrong, including asphyxia, a broken clavicle, a broken spine, brachial plexus injuries (damage to spinal nerves), paralysis, or Erb's palsy. The list goes on.

According to the nurse who'd helped deliver our first child, the reason for both panic and tears by the normally stoic nursing staff was the loss of a child to shoulder dystocia earlier that year. We didn't know what to do with that information other than to feel lucky, but our fortune soon turned when Lala couldn't move her legs the next day or the day after that. In fact, she wouldn't be able to walk for the next four weeks, her pelvis and pubic bones having dislocated during delivery.

By the time my son was wrenched free, my toes had locked in a curled position, tears were sliding down my face, and Becky and I were deep in some sort of terror stare, each searching for hope in the other, afraid that if one of us looked away, things would end as badly as they possibly could. The baby emerged huge and white, my little Moby-Dick, and while Dr. Martinez (my Captain Ahab) tended to Lala's bleeding, the pediatrician asked nicely if I wanted to cut the cord.

"Make him cry, damn it," I yelled.

And he did. Like a little man.

Problem Pair

There is a small hippie school I know of that divides children into three categories: fearful, flexible, and feisty. I usually resist such simplistic ways of viewing complex humans, even the wee ones, yet this sorting method seems to work well for the cowards, dullards, and biters that have gotten the boot from every other program in town. With my friends Harry and Grace's two boys, however, they'd have to add a new classification, far beyond even the feistiest set. A few years ago, Harry and Grace moved Mark and Mikey to Santa Fe, trading the short pants and Peter Pan collars of Eton for the looser-fitting chaps of southwestern cowboy couture. That, and to escape the future tangles with Scotland Yard that the dangerous duo would undoubtedly experience.

We have a fairly large enclosed backyard behind our home,

and in the summer Lala and I often invite families to bring over meat, booze, and children and let them all mix together in the blood-red light of the setting sun. The steak goes on the grill, the margaritas in the blender, and since we have accumulated so many secondhand toys over the years, the kids get to run their own little anarchistic day care. Everybody is happy.

Harry and Grace might be the most charming couple we know. Harry is Cambridge-educated and a well-seasoned travel writer; if prompted, he will recite Homer or Plato in Greek or discuss the details of his recent trip weaving baskets with the Cuna Indians on the remote San Blas Islands. Grace is tall and elegant, her manners and accent inherited from parents who are on a first-name basis with the queen. Like any such swanky couple, they are consistently late, and by the time they arrived at one of our barbecues, Mark and Mikey in tow, the other kids had already set up shop in the Little Tikes playhouse and were slipping down the slide or cruising around in the Power Wheels Barbie car. Unlike their parents, Mark and Mikey are not ones to stand on ceremony, so it wasn't long before they threw off whatever fearfulness and flexibility they may have had to embrace their boyish belligerence. Mikey, the older of the two, immediately carjacked the Barbiemobile, slammed it into gear, and started chasing the other kids around like Lizzie Grubman outside a crowded nightclub in the Hamptons.

"Fasta, fasta," he squealed in the Artful Dodger's accent as he slammed his leather-clad foot on the pedals. Those Europeans do make damn nice footwear even for vehicular homicide. Mikey is petite, with delicate hands, hair that stays plastered to his head, and pointy eyebrows and ears. He looked a bit like a crazed nancy boy tearing down Christopher Street in his pink Jeep with purple floral decals. Mark followed close behind, laughing and shaking his fist like a soccer hooligan after his team just won the FA Cup. Mark has a large bumpy head, very little hair, and a strong, stout body that could push my real car if it needed a jump start.

I suppose since I don't like people telling me how to parent my own kids, especially in public, I hesitate to discipline other parents' offspring, no matter how unruly. None of our tiny guests had received an injury worthy of a trip to the emergency room, so I left the boys to chase the straights around the yard. I figured Poppy would learn some evasive maneuvers that might come in handy in the future when she had to outrun a bobcat or Johnny Law after shoplifting a few sticks of Bonne Bell lip gloss. After a good fifteen minutes of Mikey's vehicular vehemence, the smarter kids found refuge up in our fruit trees and on top of the plastic-shingled roof of the playhouse. A seasoned criminal, Mikey knew better than to target the adults, who would confiscate his wheels, so his grin drooped a bit as he set his sights on knocking the kids from their perch in the apricot tree. Once the pink plastic grille struck the thick bark and kids started dropping like swollen fruit, he was back in hog heaven.

Like any good party, we had our share of nudity. Mark, who looked years older than the other diaper-wearing sissies around him, ripped off his Depends-sized Pampers and ran around the yard Carmen Electra style. Lala and I like to think we are open, accepting parents, so we thought nothing of naked kids until we saw Mark in all his massive glory.

"Jesus. He looks like one of those guys in *The Full Monty*," Lala told me much later, after we had cleaned up all the broken furniture and glass.

When Mark started to freeball, I was trapped behind the grille, trying to sear the haunches of one beast while braising the flanks of another. Lala, freed from the solitary confines of her art studio, gabbed incessantly like a speed freak to Harry and Grace, who stood holding cocktails with perfect posture. After a few minutes, Poppy left her playgroup, which now seemed a lot like *The Lord of the Flies*, and sidled up to me grillside.

"Dad?" she asked, a serious look draining the blood from her face. "We've got a problem."

"Honey," I said, trying to control the numerous flare-ups spurned on by excessive animal lipids. The grill was so hot, I could feel the enamel on my teeth start to bubble. "I'm kinda busy right now."

"It's Mark. I think you better see this." Like her mother, her hands moved naturally to her hips; there was indeed something wrong.

I called over to one of Lala's childhood friends from Wyoming to man the grill. The guy was so pickled I worried that his breath might catch fire, but I had no other choice.

Poppy took me by the hand and led me to the slide near the back of our yard. There, in the middle of the slick white surface, sat a turd that looked as though it'd come from an NFL linebacker after digesting his huge pregame meal.

"Oh, my Lord," I said, and stepped back as if the excrement could grow legs and embrace me. "Did Mark really do this?"

"Yes, Dad. He really did," Poppy said with a note of sadness. She'd never use that slide again.

"Well, maybe it was an accident," I said, but soon realized my gross misjudgment. Only a few feet from the crime, Mark and Mikey jumped up and down on the seats of the now-dead Jeep, laughing like those lovable dickheads from the television show *Jackass*. "I can't believe it," I said, shaking my head.

"Oh, believe it," my friend Nell said from behind me. She

was holding a paper plate of roast chicken in her hands. The wino from Wyoming was doing a damn fine job after all. "They did it at Ray and Doreen's too. Poor Grace dropped her skirt over the mess and stood in the same spot for an hour until Ray and Doreen left the room. It's like their calling card."

"When did you get here?" I asked Nell, my head reeling from all this new scatological imagery that was sure to poison my dreams.

"Just now. I heard Mark and Mikey were coming. I love to watch them run amok," she said, and dislodged a shred of chicken from between her teeth with a fingernail.

Pretty soon a crowd of adults and children gathered around the mini-man manure as if it were some rare artifact or oddity like that piece of toast with the Virgin's face on it. Behind me, a parent with a digital camera took photos from all angles. "My mommies' group is gonna love this," she said, snapping away.

"Oh, my God. I am so embarrassed," Grace said, running toward the slide and scooping up her son's calling card with a shovel. She then wandered around the yard like a zombie looking for a garbage can big enough to hold the stool sample.

Sidling up next to me, far more relaxed than his wife, Harry enjoyed a Mexican beer with a lime stuck on the rim of the glass. "Why didn't you tell us, old man?" he asked, clapping a hand on my back.

"I didn't have the heart," I said, and realized that I needed to rethink my philosophy about not parenting other people's kids. If I didn't do something soon, my yard would be just one big toilet for Harry and Grace's boys.

I've been in close contact with rock stars, major felons, and CEOs of Fortune 500 companies, and these larger-than-life individuals can really change the energy and dynamics of a room, but none come even close to Mark and Mikey. Whenever I am with these urchins, my dramatic expectations are so great that I feel as if I am suffering a mild yet unending heart attack. I went to visit Harry one day at the house they were renting in a historic section of Santa Fe. When they moved in, Harry had taken all the art from the walls and removed anything remotely breakable and placed the lot in a "safe room" that he nailed shut. The rental home was so bare it looked as though a sect of monks lived there. When I arrived that afternoon, Harry was literally pulling his hair out as Mark sat in a corner sporting a gauze bandage taped to his forehead. Mikey looked on from the couch, laughing to himself like a hyena high on nitrous oxide.

According to Harry, he had been in the kitchen preparing lunch for the boys. The CD player was set to repeat Kylie Minogue's single "Can't Get You Out of My Head," otherwise known to the boys as the la la song, due to the monosyllabic chorus that appeals mostly to creatures incapable of abstract thought. Grace had escaped earlier for an art class, her only freedom from her chaotic world where the inmates do in fact run the asylum. When their father was out of range, Mark and Mikey started slam dancing to the la la song, and by accident Mark bumped into a pane of glass in the French doors that opened onto a stone patio. Realizing the endless possibilities, Mark head-butted each square of glass even though his new hobby had sliced open his head. Mikey, his partner in crime, picked up each shard, named it, then slipped the jagged piece into the driver's seat of a Brio train car. When Harry came in, a plate of food in each hand, he saw Mark bleeding and laughing as he crashed his line of sparkly trains into his brother's.

No matter how Harry tried to boyproof his house, his kids outdid him. I spent one afternoon helping him create a holding pen by wrapping chicken wire Christo-style around one side of the second house he rented. Within two days, Mikey had tunneled under the makeshift fence using Mark's top teeth as a hoe. Not to be outdone by his bro, Mark stacked rakes, rusty barbed wire, and old lawn mower blades into a makeshift ladder, hopped over, and escaped into the woods. This pair was unstoppable, and it was beginning to wear on Harry and Grace.

Harry decided that our two families should get out of town and see some Native American ruins. He figured such a spiritual place would have a calming effect on the boys and help slow the growth of his ever-increasing damage deposit. We caravaned a few hours south and west to the Acoma Pueblo and stayed at the nearby Sky City hotel and casino. Besides running away in the crowded buffet, the boys seemed distracted enough by the flashing lights of the one-armed bandits and the sight of more real Indians than bad Hollywood films could ever produce.

The day after our arrival, we rose early and rode the van up the mesa to the oldest continuously inhabited pueblo in the United States. On the guided tour, we learned that this huge rock was the sight of one of the bloodiest slaughters of Native Americans by the Spanish in the history of that infamous conflict. I could tell by Harry's face that he hoped the boys wouldn't get any ideas from the gruesome details relayed by our guide. After each stop on the tour, an inhabitant of the pueblo sold fry bread, jewelry, or the thin-walled pottery Acoma was famous for. At one stand, Mark and Mikey crept up to the display and each grabbed a bowl; they were about to bring their pottery together in a celebratory toast when Harry inserted his hand between the two, saving face and about $150. Both our families could tell the boys were getting bored, so Harry tried to move the tour guide along. We needed to get back into the van and down off this mesa, which didn't have fencing or chicken wire to keep the boys from throwing something or someone off.

The last stop on the tour was the San Esteban del Rey Mission, located next to an ancient burial ground. On the steps of the church, our guide told us that the graveyard was the most sacred spot in all of Acoma. She pointed out that since the mesa is all rock, the Acoma people had to carry up many many cubic feet of dirt just to create a place to bury their dead. She also mentioned that since space on the mesa is so limited, the elders of the pueblo had to bury their people one on top of the next. Since they stopped using the burial ground years ago, no one had set foot on this most holy place. After a moment of silence, she led us out of the sun and into the cool darkness of the church, asking us all to remove our hats and maintain quiet.

"The timbers on the roof are forty feet long and a foot square," she told us, her voice echoing off the thick mud walls. "The Acoma men carried each one from the San Mateo Mountains, over twenty long miles away. As there were no building materials available on top of the mesa, all the smooth rocks and mud for adobe bricks were all carried up the steep rock stairway."

"What? No Home Depot near here?" some idiot joked. No one laughed.

The group moved back to the church steps outside and gathered around our guide as she prepared to wrap the tour up. She wasn't a tall woman, yet had the commanding presence of someone much larger, uglier, and fonder of prison tattoos. She wore a string of antique turquoise around her neck that stood out against the clean white backdrop of her western-style dress shirt. Opening her mouth to speak, she began trembling as if she was experiencing a stroke.

"Are you OK?" a man in a cowboy hat asked, his accent straight out of Bush country.

All she could do was point her shaking finger at Mark, who was in the middle of the burial field trying with all his might to pull a grave marker from the ground. Horrified, we all watched the demon seed grunt and groan, unable to unearth the ancient whitewashed cross.

"We are so going to hell," Grace said, grabbing Mikey as he struggled to join his brother and Harry ran across the holy dirt to retrieve his baby boy. I gathered my family and herded them quickly into the safety of the van. I didn't want any cases of mistaken identity when the massacre of white folks began.

Jump in the Pool

In March, my family reunited to celebrate my father's seventy-fifth birthday. The four of us Wilder brothers flew to Florida with spouses and children in tow and gathered with thirty or so of my father's friends in the courtyard of the Sarasota Classic Car Museum, annoyingly located on the busy intersection of the Tamiami Trail and University Parkway. Beside an overstocked bar, a light buffet of chicken wings, conch fritters, and cocktail franks was served in front of Jackie Gleason's '69 Lincoln limousine. The wind was incessant that day, blowing Xeroxed photos of my father in various stages of his life around the patio tables. Faces of my dad in his previous roles as banker, smoker, irate citizen, and boozer ended up in potted ferns, under our feet, and as coasters for our much-needed drinks.

I had written a speech that poked fun at my father's obsession for bargain hunting and price comparison, as well as his reverence of Sam's Club and all things bulk in nature. I pretty much shouted the whole piece, thinking I needed to be heard over the gusts, but Lala later told me I'd overcompensated and sounded as if I thought the whole congregation were deaf, which may have been true given the average age. A few of my dad's friends from the geriatric gym rose and recited a poem in rhyming couplets that presented my father's duality. The Dr. Seuss–sounding epic praised my dad's neighborly generosity and ribbed his argumentative nature, especially when it comes to current events. According to the poem,

> He'll welcome you home with a cake or a bun
> But his politics are to the right of Attila the Hun.

My older brother, Richard, offered a few words. He was followed by my younger brother Tom, who, having suffered a recent tragedy in his wife's family, grew tearful as he thanked my father for raising him basically alone. Finally, my youngest brother— "Crazy Eddie," as people are known to call him—exploded onto the makeshift stage with what looked like the scrap paper box stolen from Kinkos.

Eddie is thirty-four, with a Chihuahua's energy, a young boy's head, Baby Huey's body, and the sensibility of someone who should have opened a smoke shop on the corner of Haight and Ashbury in 1966. Consider the opening of his voice mail message: "Hey, fellow rockers and beautiful babies of this most luscious galaxy, you've reached Crazy Eddie..." The greeting then pounds on about the caller having a glorious day and living in peace and love now and forever, or at least until the beep sounds. Stranger or loved one, when you are with Eddie, this message never ends. He rarely rests, which makes him the world's best uncle and the most exhausting member of a long drive. Eddie is the kind of uncle who, after doing a forty-five-minute song-and-dance routine for his nieces and nephews and is asked to "do it again" by one of the grinning little ones, actually repeats the performance in its entirety without any trace of bitterness. Later that night, after the party, Eddie and I walked from our dad's place to a Mexican restaurant to decompress about the day's family drama. During our mostly one-sided conversation, he had to remind himself out loud to let me speak. It was something he'd been working on, he told me, and then smiled like I was his dentist checking his teeth.

Eddie's verbal barrage is peppered with pirate jokes, vaudeville puns, children's songs, digressions, tangents upon digressions, and a frightening forensic memory. As an actor for Disney World, the stage, radio, and local television, and now as a middle-school drama teacher, his life and work have always been improv. While my speech had been written, revised, and rehearsed, Eddie's bits sprang instantaneously from props he had lugged from his happy hippie home. His box contained photos, ticket stubs, programs, and news articles from my father's adult existence, and what Eddie attempted to do was re-create the old show *This Is Your Life* using bits of paper instead of people. What he hadn't planned for in this world of 60-inch plasma screens and PowerPoint presentations was that many of his photos and printed matter were too small for any of us with normal eyesight to see, not to mention those in the crowd who changed their prescriptions weekly. What Eddie didn't comprehend was that most of his recollections, although poignant and quite precise, were understood only by my father, who guffawed in a rented plastic chair beside him. The rest of us Wilder brothers have shitty memories from an experimentally misguided youth, and the larger circle of aunts, cousins, nieces, nephews, in-laws, fellow condo dwellers, and water aerobicists was lost in these verbal sprints down memory's superhighway. Eddie, unfazed or unaware, undulated on, and we all tried to follow as best we could, taking our cues from my father—when he chuckled, we chuckled; when he seemed melancholy, we tilted our heads back and gazed toward the hazy Florida heavens. The adoration Eddie had for our father was both apparent and contagious. My brothers and I shot each other a look that said *He's rolling now*, and we lovingly let the little guy have his day.

In one of his musings, Eddie dredged up a credo that my father developed (and he developed many) when we moved from Long Island to Connecticut in 1977. The family, six then instead of five, left our small beach cottage for a split-level ranch, an acre of land, and a neglected swimming pool. For us boys, suburban Connecticut was the sticks, and the pool, although swampy, held almost magical promise. The pool was a standard kidney shape with a springless diving board, all bordered by a loose brick patio. What we didn't see that day, climbing out of our Ford LTD station wagon, were the future hours of testing (chlorine = yellow, pH = blue), skimming leaves and dead moles, vacuuming, backwashing to gain pressure, vacuuming again, covering, uncovering, draining, painting, and filling (but never heating). I won't even mention the yard work or Dad's ambitious projects within the confines of the self-shutting fence, as required by law and the often-invoked insurance company. But a pool it was, and there's nothing like a clean, blue body of water to fill those humid summer days. There's also not a better setting for a teenage boy to convince a teenage girl to take off her teenage clothes.

"Landscape shapes culture," Terry Tempest Williams writes, and my father is proof of that. He taught his sons how to cut grass in an enclosing square shape with the chute facing out to spread the clippings away from the center and therefore avoid the dreaded clumping. We learned when to use a lawn broom rather than a rake; how to repair a rock wall; the best way to split and stack wood; and how, after six hours of hard work in the muggy Connecticut August fueled only by powdered iced tea, to lean on our tool, wipe the sweat out of our eyes, paw the hair from our forehead, sigh, and say, "Now, that looks better," as we gaze at our handiwork. But as Eddie reminded me amidst hallowed automobiles once owned by celebrities like John Lennon and Paul McCartney, my father's teachings had a more philosophical side. The grass in our yard grew rich with white clover, and the brothers, feeling our country bumpkinness, pushed the mower in cutoff jeans and nothing else. Invariably, we would step on a feeding bee, which woke us violently from our shearing-induced haze. I recall hobbling to my father, who was grunting in our vegetable garden on the north side of our property. Bent over, his back broad and brown, gray hair sprouting from his temples, he eyed my upturned foot and thought for a second before saying "Jump in the pool. Make you feel better." I obeyed, shambling along the dirt and patio, avoiding anything green that might hide those vicious insect warriors. Leaping in, I felt the shock of the cold chlorine cocktail, compressing the stinging pain. The old man was right after all.

"Jump in the pool" became my father's prescription for anything that ailed us. Sticky from a melted Popsicle? Jump in the pool. Hay fever? Poison ivy? Blackheads? Jump in the pool. Hatchet wound? Jump in the pool.

It wasn't terrible advice. In terms of disinfecting, chlorine kills bacteria and other microbes, including waterborne diseases like typhoid, cholera, dysentery, and gastroenteritis. As for the therapeutic benefits, this rebaptism gave me pause and reminded me why people enjoy bodies of water in the first place: they surround, support, and give freedom of movement unattainable on dry land. As we entered the Grimm forest of adolescence, our problems became more complex but my father's advice stayed the same. Failing geometry? Jump in the pool. Got cut from the basketball team? Jump in the pool. Calling from the police station? Jump in the pool. Think your pot was laced? Jump in the pool. Your girlfriend is late? Jump in the pool.

My father was from the "move on" school of emotional counseling. Something hurts, you feel pain, and then you either cut that part off (even if it's your heart) or ignore it and move forward. The pool served as the Pavlovian cue to forget the old and begin the new. Keep the best and deny the rest.

In 1983, our mother was diagnosed with cancer and died within four months. That jump-in-the-pool advice didn't hold water anymore. Nothing much did. Even though we were expected to carry on with algebra, select soccer, and wheelbarrowing wood chips, trauma such as this couldn't be washed away with a simple dip, even though we wished Ben's remedy could still cure. In *The Great Gatsby*, just before he dies, Jay Gatsby asks his butler not to drain the pool even though it's the beginning of autumn because, as he laments to Nick Carraway, "You know, old sport, I've never used that pool all summer."

Recently, Poppy came to me when I was in the middle of fixing dinner. Lala was at the gym, and I stood lost in thought while sautéing pork loins in the narrow confines of our kitchen. Poppy was having social trouble at school and asked me if excluding someone was a mean thing to do.

"Not necessarily," I said, creating a mental checklist of all the people I work with whom I'd never invite to parties.

"But what if the girl starts to cry?" Her face held the same earnest expression as famous do-gooders Jane Goodall and Mother Teresa.

"Well, then," I said, stumbling for the right way to handle this quandary. I believe firmly in freedom of association, yet I didn't want my daughter to end up living the bitch role from the film *Mean Girls*. The electric frying pan started to smoke, and Poppy grew anxious for my reply.

"Dad, are you listening? Is it mean or not?" She crossed her arms and scrunched up her face.

London wandered in as I was yanking the battery from the smoke detector. He pulled his two middle fingers from his mouth and said, "Let me get this straight," his new randomly chosen sentence that week. One day he too would come to me with a moral question concerning self-defense against bullies or some gender dilemma about wearing his sister's hand-me-downs. I wasn't ready for all this complexity. Not yet, anyway.

"Grab your suits, kids, off to the Chavez Center. We're going swimming," I said, pulling the frying pan's plug from the wall outlet.

"But, Dad, it's dinnertime," Poppy said, half excited at the idea of such spontaneity from a man usually so tethered to habit and routine.

"I know it is, but a quick dip will make us all feel better."

London shrugged, then scanned the room for obvious signs of sadness or pain. "I feel fine," he said, and jammed his fingers back into his mouth.

Snowman

I

The Birth of Frosty

As a teacher at a fairly affluent private school, I am strongly encouraged to attend a few fund-raisers every year. I usually bring along my reluctant wife to these benefits, and we fool each other time and time again into believing we can successfully outbid the other revelers and secure an item in the silent or not-so-silent auction. We always end up being outbid by people whose car cost as much as our house, or we lug home the crappy items no one else wanted like a Day-Glo painting of a crying Indian or a do-it-yourself liposuction kit. When I first started attending these giving galas, partygoers signed their names on the cards next to the offered dollar amount until shameless faculty like me started writing "Don't outbid your son's teacher" in red ink next to my name. Lala and I came home with some decent booty that year, but the school didn't raise enough to cover the cost of the banquet hall. They've gotten smart and assigned everyone a bidding number with the explicit instructions not to reveal your code to anyone dressed in tweed or with a haircut that looks like it cost less than a hundred bucks.

Last winter, Lala and I were bored to tears, sitting at a folding table draped in a white tablecloth. The fund-raiser was a thinly veiled gambling night where people bet on which numbered ball would be pulled last from an old popcorn machine. I had already slurped up all our free-drink tickets and fought the other attending teachers over the single baron of beef that the skimpy buffet offered. The silent auction had the usual spa packages, hotel stays, and hideous sculpture by some wealthy and talentless artist who had slept with all the gallery owners in town. In the corner, strung up on a coatrack, stood a full-body snowman costume, complete with a top hat on his head and red scarf around his puffy neck. The retail value was $250, and the bidding started at half that. Both amounts seemed ridiculous, not because of the quality of the item but because of the practicality. Most of the parents in attendance had children over the age of thirteen. Unless one of the couples was into serious sexual role play, this item was the true white elephant of the bunch. That meant it was perfect for us. We assumed no one else would bid, so our plan was to wait until the bidding was over and then offer the PTA $50 cash. We figured the kids would love it at Christmas and I could don the costume at the occasional holiday party or class visit—or to freak out our neighbors at 2 A.M., the ones who kept stealing our recycling bin.

A minute before the auction closed, I strolled by the coatrack and was shocked to see the president of the board's name boldly written where his secret code should be. I knew the guy had two boys, ages fourteen and fifteen. What the hell did he want with our costume? I scanned the room and found him surrounded by other men dressed in wealthy casual attire— cashmere sweaters, wide-wale corduroys, and leather driving shoes with those black nubs on the bottoms to keep their feet from touching the mortal earth. While neither of the prez's sons had been in my class, I knew him from our faculty/board retreat in the fall, where we all participated in a game that attempted to analyze and classify our personality types. Ironically, we were both in the "smart-ass, slightly overweight white guy" group. I waited until he was alone and approached him in what I considered a genteel manner.

"Hey, Prez," I called to him. "What do you need a snowman costume for?"

"How the hell do I know?" he said, rattling the ice in his glass. "My wife felt like we needed to bid on something and it was the cheapest thing left. Just another thing to clutter up the garage." He took a drink of his scotch, then eyed me. "Why?"

I told him about our scheme and added orphanages to the list of places I planned to visit. Community service is the new black for rich folks.

He shrugged like a gangster. "Just take it."

"Really?"

"It'll save me from hauling it to Goodwill in the spring when my wife goes to Palm Springs with her girlfriends."

Just then his wife walked up. She was dressed from head to toe in red like a garish tree ornament.

"I'm giving the teacher the snowman," the president said casually.

"What?" she asked.

"We don't need it. Tell her what you plan to do with it," he said, pointing his well-fed finger at me.

I repeated my story and added that in Poppy's eyes, old Saint Nick had nothing on Frosty. I tried to appear sweet and cute, but it probably looked as though I had gas from eating too much rare beef.

"Tell you what," the first lady said, screwing up her face in thought. "You can take it, but if our sons graduate, you have to wear it to the commencement ceremony."

"Deal." I smiled at her, enjoying the fact that she had a sense of humor about her kids. Besides, given the odds of her boys graduating and me getting fired, I figured it was a safe bet that Frosty would never don a cap and gown.

I've only worn the snowman costume two times. The initial launch occurred shortly after we brought the suit home and hid it in the hall closet. I called Poppy's teacher ahead of time and asked if Frosty could come to her class and hand out candy canes. She thought it was a great idea and agreed to keep the visit secret, even from Poppy. I have to confess that I was vying for Father of the Year, maybe the decade. I'd go in, hand out the peppermint, and then reveal myself to my daughter, who would declare her love to me now, next year, and even when I followed her in our minivan on dates. The event almost went as planned. I parked my little car in the staff parking lot, slipped on the suit, grabbed the basket of candy, and headed toward the school. The costume is made of thin polyurethane foam that appears padded because of the way it is gathered, draped, and sewn. I had dressed in a white long-sleeved turtleneck and gloves so that Poppy wouldn't recognize my hands, which are a little on the delicate side for a man. I also wore white sweatpants purchased from Wal-Mart and tennis shoes to try to get as snowy as possible on the fashion scale.

I encountered two unexpected hazards while inside Frosty. The first had to do with limited vision. The eyeholes are about the size of quarters and are covered with a fine mesh material that has the dual purpose of hiding human retinas and giving off a nice matte shade of coal. The holes do not allow for any sort of peripheral vision whatsoever. It is not unlike making goggles out of your hands and putting them to your eyes. Like many politicians, you can only see straight ahead.

The second problem was of a stuffy nature. Petroleum plastics are not big breathers, so I stewed in my own juices. Worse, though, was trying to get vital oxygen from my own coffee-scented carbon dioxide, which hung around my mouth and nose like filthy punk rock groupies. I was light-headed before I even entered the doors of the school. This tunnel vision, accompanied by dizziness and nausea, reminded me of a party in college where I was served "whippets," hits of nitrous oxide, by the handsome son of a famous jelly manufacturer. The party was full of strange combinations, ending in my own when I laughed hysterically while projectile vomiting.

As soon as Frosty entered the building, the kids sensed it. One long line of first graders passed another string of older kids going to PE class in the gym.

"It's Frosty!" one kid yelled, and they all struggled not to run over, checking with their teachers, who made it clear that single-file lines in silence were of the highest virtue, winter character or no winter character.

I waved and utilized the myriad moves I had practiced in the mirror the night before, based loosely on mascots from professional sports. I showed them the hands over the mouth in mock surprise, the fingers covering the eyes à la peekaboo, the "I can't hear you" cupped-hand-near-the-facial globe. The kids ate that shit up, and even the pair of spinster teachers cracked a smile on their otherwise concrete faces.

Poppy had no idea it was me when I entered the second grade classroom. She was hunched over her desk, busily writing a story about ponies that make it onto MTV without sleeping their way to the top. The teacher introduced Frosty, and I shook hands and gave out most of my candy canes to the second grade students. When the lovefest had run its course, I slipped into the cloakroom and came out looking like a condom, long and white and wet. Poppy's face lit up.

"It's my dad," she said, not to me but to her pals, who nodded to her in agreement: her father was indeed the coolest in town. That made all the nausea and vertigo worth it. I was basking in the oxygenated glow of the moment, when Poppy's friend Dennis, an ADHD kid in training, asked, "Hey, where's Frosty?"

"Yeah," another boy echoed. "Where is he?"

"He's resting," I said, rubbing my back. To get the eyeholes lined up correctly, I had severely contorted myself. Now that the costume was off, my back and neck burned. During college, not long after the whippet party, a drunk driver hit me, cracking a vertebra in my neck. My doctor didn't advise me against wearing mascot-type attire, but maybe he should have included such activities on his never-to-do list.

"We don't want you," a girl yelled, her lips a swirl of peppermint. "We want the snowman."

"Get the snowman!" another demanded, shaking like a spaz.

I gave the teacher the can-you-help-me-out-here eye, but she just smiled vacantly, like every other fried educator in December. Poppy looked around at the groundswell of public opinion and asked me quietly, "Hey, Dad, put Frosty back on, OK?"

I had a rare moment of clarity where I knew enough was enough and slipping back into Frosty would end badly for sure. That clarity vanished when I saw Poppy's pleading face, and I was eager to drink again from the overflowing cup of a young daughter's love. So I slinked back into the cloakroom and emerged again as the snowman. It felt far worse than the first time. Even though the suit was brand-new, the inside already smelled of BO and wet rubber. The light-headedness returned quicker this time as I waved a last goodbye to Poppy and her sticky classmates. So as not to fall and risk embarrassment, I steadied myself by leaning against the door frame.

At the entryway, I was greeted by two dozen waiting school-children. Public school classrooms are interrupted more often, especially around the holidays, than members of the McLaughlin Group. The news had gotten out about Frosty being on campus, and the rabble had tracked him down.

"Where's our candy?" they cheered, not unhappily.

I handed out the last remaining peppermint alpenstocks and went through my series of pantomime gestures, hoping to ap-pease those who still remained empty-handed and for me to make a clean getaway. A litter of truant kids followed me down the hall, past low-hung water fountains and a dizzying poster project on the dissection of snowy owl vomit.

"Who's in there?" an older girl called from behind me.

"I bet it's Ted," someone answered. Ted is the beloved gym teacher at my daughter's school. His approval rating always hov-ers close to 100 percent.

"It's Mr. Q.," another guessed. Obviously a woman wouldn't be foolish enough to walk around an elementary school dressed like a giant marshmallow.

"Is that you, Ted?" I felt a sharp poke in my rear end.

"Ted, where's our candy? You're not being fair." One kid actually started weeping into the back of the costume.

I wanted to ask why they weren't in class, where their teachers or parole officers were. Where the hell were those baton-wielding security guards everyone wanted nowadays? These children were being left behind and I couldn't say a thing. All the great mascots and costumed characters were silent, and since I decided to join their hallowed ranks, I had to keep the code. Through my peepholes, I couldn't see any kids, yet I could feel their tiny feet making the ground tremble like a herd of stampeding bansai buffalo. The crowd grew larger in number, more intent on finding candy and the secret identity of the moving holiday icon. It was like a scene out of *The Crucible Before Christmas*, the angry mob ready to melt the snowman who couldn't prove he was not Ted, the candy-hoarding PE instructor.

Toward the end of the school day, the crossing guards block off the street in front of the main building so the buses can pick up their load safely. To get to my car, I had to travel through the playground. Like most public schools where ketchup is considered a vegetable, recess is an AP class, and the playground that day was just lousy with kids. Little creatures maniacally ran from one another, hung from steel bars and beams, and swung violently on strips of rubber held aloft by thick metal chains. When Frosty appeared, it was like George Lucas surprising the hordes of nerds at a *Star Wars* convention. The little monkeys all dropped, jumped, flipped, and sped from their various activities and tore toward me like the filthy Huns on the Capital One credit card commercial.

"Frosty!" the boys screamed.

"Snowman!" the girls yelled.

"Christmas tree!" the special ed kids cried.

I couldn't see the dual ring of children hugging my legs or the mob behind me. Some urchins were content just to be in Frosty's presence, yet others who were learning critical thinking skills in science class tried to dissect this most strange and puffy object through precise and violent methods. When I was doing research on my mime-like moves, I skimmed the parts about how often mascots are injured, figuring I was performing at an elementary school, not some ballpark where they served 42-ounce beers to unemployed teamsters. According to one source, half of all mascots are stricken with heat-related and lower-back injuries. One-fifth have knee damage, and mascots' overall injury rate equals that of male gymnasts. These lovable goofballs are routinely punched, tripped, body-slammed, spat upon, groped, and showered with both hot and cold beverages. Since my crowd was about waist high and Frosty's midsection lined up with my crotch, my 'nads were taking a serious beating. By placing my gloved hands over my mouth, I thought they'd get the picture that their pummeling was naughty, but mime has no effect on the lower species of mammals. I shook my index finger back and forth in a "no, no" gesture, but that didn't work either. I started running. After stumbling over the defensive line of kindergartners, I hit the open field. I am desperately out of shape, but on any given day I'm good for a decent twenty-yard dash. I saw my black turd of a car in the distance and moved my legs as fast as possible given the constraints of the suit. If I could only make it to the parking lot, which was out of bounds for these conditioned drones, I would be scot-free. That's when I stepped into a prairie dog hole, twisting my ankle and dropping Frosty's ass hard on the drought-ridden dirt. Shock waves of pain ran from my tailbone up my back, into my neck and down my arms. I wondered about possible paralysis as I threw up in my mouth.

"Ha ha!" The kids laughed, thinking that my spill was all part of my slapstick routine. They pounced on me WWF style, hitting and kicking once they landed. I rose gingerly, brushing them aside like rats. I needed to get to my car, which had never seemed safe until now.

"Look at his butt. Frosty went poop," a boy said. I couldn't see it then, but later I would discover a skid mark of dirt streaking the undefined section of Frosty's rear end. Oh, the humanity! I limped over to my vehicle and for some reason huddled behind my car to maintain the illusion. I slipped off the costume and threw it in the open rear hatch. I figured Poppy's love had better last well after my death from asphyxiation and the numerous injuries sustained by the treacherous and unrelenting mob.

II

Frosty's Revenge

The *Lord of the Flies* episode on the playground soured me on character cross-dressing for close to a year. Halloween is the national holiday for children and gay people, and my students and family reminded me this October that I hadn't dressed in costume in years. Some teachers go all out in full hair and makeup, exploring their transsexual side with the full support of the school community. This educator has been happy to hide behind his children as they extorted giant pails of candy, all paid for by precious tuition dollars. As my wife and I were searching our storage unit for last year's jack-o'-lanterns and motion-sensing skeletons, I came across Frosty. He was sadly bent over in a garbage bag, tucked under boxes of the children's artwork that were not good enough to be hung on the fridge. I figured I could take him for a spin around the DeVargas Mall, where we'd start our trick-or-treating. Like a gigolo, I'd be in and out of him in about thirty minutes, just before we had our dinner. Again, the initial response at the mall was a good one. This time, my three-year-old son, London, dressed as his favorite colors, was the one bragging to all the devils, ghosts, and padded cartoon characters that it was his dad inside the snowman suit. From the time Frosty appeared, people surrounded me as if I were running for office. I hugged old ladies, kissed babies, and posed for pictures with hordes of small children. I felt happy and a bit more comfortable since I wore a T-shirt underneath the chamber of heat. This is why we got the costume in the first place, I recall thinking as I waved to my adoring fans, their faces as bright as any holiday lights across the land. Then, like Adam and Eve after the fall, something shifted. Instead of the Garden of Eden, my knowledge arrived against the bleak landscape of Hastings Video, Ross Dress for Less, and Osco Drug.

"Did you fart?" Lala asked me as we walked.

"In this suit? Are you kidding?" I admit I am as flatulent as the next guy, but to let loose in my personal gas chamber would be suicide.

"Something is really rank," she said, waving the air in front of her nose with her hand.

Then I realized that it was the suit. In my halcyon haze of spreading joy to the sugared masses, I ignored obvious and foul odors of the darkest kind. I hadn't cleaned Frosty since I hid him in the storage shed close to a year before. The BO odor that I'd cultivated had fully fermented. And the night before Halloween, Lala and I had celebrated our anniversary by going to a Japanese-style spa, where they conned me into a salt rub followed by a facial that uses nightingale shit as a cleansing agent. I was told by my husky Austrian aesthetician that I should not bathe or use soap for twenty-four hours. I regrettably complied. I smelled like a locker room for professional homeless men. All the toxic aromas mixed inside the suit, and I felt and smelt as if I were decaying.

"I need to get this thing off me," I said, feeling my heart rate speed up.

"One more store," Lala said. "Just stop with the farting."

"I'm serious. I need to shed Frosty." I could taste the bile rising in my throat.

"Just Panda Express, then we'll go. Get into the spirit, will ya?"

I grabbed my kids' hands and marched to the flashy Chinese takeout place, staffed by Hispanics who tried to pass as Asian. I was feeling nasty, rotten, and very angry. I'd heard that most mascots go bad once or twice in their careers and end up kicking pregnant women or getting into a fistfight with Tommy Lasorda. I let my kids loose to fetch their goodies at the steam table while I fumed in my suit. In the sights of my tunnel vision, I spotted an ex-student seated next to a fellow skater kid at a bistro table on stilts. This former pupil, who no longer attends my school, had been particularly unpleasant in my English class, destroying any hope of a serious discussion and teasing the other kids if they tried to cobble together an education. I had tried talking to him, his academic advisor, and his parents, but nothing worked. The boy seemed to derive pleasure from spoiling my attempts at teaching. Something got into me when I locked onto him in his sideways baseball cap and baggy jeans. I recalled all the ways he'd ridiculed the other kids and me, and decided a bit of harmless Halloween revenge was just the trick. I pointed my finger at him in a stern manner. I came closer to his table, my finger wagging menacingly. My family was already off to beg at the next shop, so I was free to act like a nutcase.

At first he smiled, thinking the mall employed Frosty, but as I crept nearer, he reevaluated his feelings.

"Dude, who's that?" his friend asked, putting down his chopsticks.

"I have no idea," ex-student said, lines of worry forming on his pimply brow.

"Seriously, who is it?"

"I'm telling you, I don't know." He held his hands out in a rare sincere gesture.

I shook my fist at him and then feigned martial arts punches and kicks: Frosty meets Jackie Chan. Frosty Chan.

"Get away from me, man," my ex-student said.

"How do you know it's a man, dude?" his buddy asked. "Look at the hands, they're kinda small."

"Shut up," ex said to his buddy. "Go away!" he yelled to Frosty Chan.

I crept closer, until Frosty's belly was pressing against the lip of their table. I positioned my hands as if I were about to wring his neck.

"Freak! Freak!" the two of them yelled as they grabbed for their cell phones.

Whom were they calling, I wondered, the mascot police? I closed my fist, then freed my pinky and thumb so my hand formed a phone. I brought the symbol to the side of Frosty's head. I mimed talking on the flesh phone while swinging my hips from side to side in a playful dance. Then I pretended to throw the cell to the tiled floor, where I smashed it under Frosty Chan's skilled weapon-like feet.

"Asshole!" the ex-student screamed.

"Freak! Stalker!" his friend added.

I raised my dainty fists in the air like Rocky and goose-stepped out of the restaurant, smelling the sweet aroma of victory and the sour stench of my own rancid body.

Flattery

"Poppy, why does everyone say you are cute?" my nephew, still dressed in garish rash guard and board shorts, asked my daughter, who was seated next to him.

"Because she is," I joked from the front seat. Truth be told, I often wondered about the same thing.

"Yeah, but everywhere we go . . . sheesh," he moaned, and turned his head away.

I was driving an Excursion full of my wife's family back from windsurfing camp on the island of Maui. My nine-year-old nephew, Kipling, posed an earnest question to my daughter, who is a year younger than he is. Kipling couldn't fathom why so many strangers felt compelled to flatter my daughter, a cousin he could easily outrun, outswim, and outeat. I understood his struggle. Flattery is something we are told to dish out generously but receive with great reservation, like birthday gifts purchased at the dollar store. I should say in Poppy's defense that she is petite, slightly smaller than her peers, and has fair skin, and on this day, leaving Kanaha to go to the surf beach of Launiupoko, she had just lost a Chiclet-sized front tooth and her hair was dyed bright pink. Her windsurfing teacher called her pixieish, which is like calling RuPaul slightly overdone. When we visit Kipling's family on Maui (his mother is Lala's sister), Poppy dresses in elfin bikinis, bright floral cover-ups, and tropical skirts and tops, and no matter how much we marinate her in sunscreen she gets this blushing red tone about her face. Because of her small frame, people often mistake her for a kid far younger. So when she parrots words her PC teacher taught her, like *commitment* and *metacognition*, knows the sitting president sent troops to Iraq, or sings the lyrics to a Damien Rice song, adults mistake her for a prodigy straight out of *Spellbound*.

Poppy has received these types of accolades since she was born, starting with her unique name (which I am sure will get her in trouble in middle school or the first opium den she stumbles into). For a long time, I didn't know how to handle such seemingly undeserved compliments. One Sunday, she and I were enjoying buckwheat griddle cakes and huevos rancheros on the outdoor patio of the Cowgirl Hall of Fame restaurant. She was barely three and wanted to dress like a cowgirl, so she had on shitkicker boots, a denim skirt, a bandana tied around her neck, and a light pink cowboy hat. After breakfast, she danced for a while to the slight talent of a one-eyed banjo player named Patches while I gulped the rest of my chicory coffee. Some old friends of my wife's had started their drinking early that day, caught Poppy's spastic attempt at the Virginia reel, and were nice enough to yell how sweet she was over the chorus of "She'll

Be Coming 'Round the Mountain." Busy paying the check and making sure I didn't forget all my child gear, I thanked them with a wave and we left.

Santa Fe is a relatively small town, and it got back to my wife that I was arrogant, a snob, and far too proud of my daughter and myself. I don't know what the gaggle of stray dogs expected—maybe another round of Bloody Marys with sides of tequila to thank them? So I changed my compliment-reply tactic from silence to what all those obnoxious bumper stickers had advertised to me: I would practice kindness of the not-so-random variety. A few months later at her preschool open house, a man I had never met saw Poppy acting out the role of grocery store clerk in the dramatic play area. She had on the standard dress-up garb: adult glasses, oversized lab coat, pink feather boa, and high heels donated from some reformed ex-hooker. Reminded me of Dennis Rodman when he started his fall from what little grace he had. Poppy was muttering something unintelligible when the father said: "Is that your daughter?"

"She is today," I answered good-naturedly. He shot me a soft and confused look. From his fuzzy sweater, comfortable shoes, yoga pants, tortoiseshell spectacles, and hair like a toy poodle's, I could tell he was one of those overly sensitive Santa Fe males.

"She is very precious, you know," he said, as if passing on some odd snippet of trivia he'd just read. "And articulate. So very clever."

I landed my new approach: "Thank you so much. You are very kind to say that. Very kind." Which he was. I thought it would end there, and I could go home and tell my wife that my reputation in this town was changing, yessirree Bob. Soon they'd be calling me Humble Hank. Surprisingly, Poodle Man grabbed me by the shoulders and stared deeply into my eyes. I was worried he would start either shaking me or kissing me very soon. "I'm not being kind," he demanded. "I'm telling the truth. I know children." He recounted his expertise in character judgment (he was a shrink) and how he grew up with Mikey from *Life* cereal, a wunderkind if he'd ever seen one, and would I please acknowledge my child's greatness? If he reacted that way to a girl playing dress-up, I mused, what would he do at a chess tournament for children, speak in tongues?

When Poppy started kindergarten, her cuteness didn't fade the way I'd secretly hoped. She was a teacher's pet—taking attendance and carrying notes to the principal like a runner for the mob. It also didn't help matters that on Free Dress Fridays, my wife and Poppy would conjure up some outfit that looked like a cross between Paris Hilton and Carmen Miranda. Like many other public schools in the country, Wood Gormley Elementary has a standard dress code, which is as close to a uniform as you can get without saying Gestapo. The citywide rule was written to stop gang influence and economic bullying, but if the West Side Locos are interested in jumping my kid, I haven't seen it. Poppy hasn't asked me to trade her Hilary Duff CDs for 50 Cent, and as of today she hasn't called me "dogg" once, asked Santa for any bling-bling, or flashed finger-contorting gang signs to her homies at recess.

One Friday I was waiting for Poppy to be released from school. The K-through-3 mothers and fathers linger at the Parentgate bordering the playground, gossiping mostly about forever-adjusting kids, too strict or too lax teachers, and new diets and haircuts that make you look as if you are enjoying your thirties and forties. Poppy exited the door and hugged her teacher goodbye. My daughter sported a pink coat with a fur collar and a pricey patterned dress that the rich side of the family had given her. My wife had glued matching fuzz on Poppy's clogs the night before. She looked like a midget female pimp. The mothers near me oohed and aahed and said how Poppy always dressed with such style and how they were all too exhausted even to think about such trivial things as clothes with pigments. Then one mother said slightly bitterly, "Well, Poppy is famous around here." That was it, I thought. I had tried being quiet; I had employed the altruistic approach; now I would slip back into a realm that had served me well as the younger brother of a weapon-carrying wannabe thug: I would once again assume the role of Johnny Wiseass. I turned to the group and said in my best Dorothy Parker voice, "It's true. She is cute. Now, if she'd only give up smoking." The bitter mom laughed politely but uneasily, her mouth pinched like a pickled octopus's ass. Surely Poppy wasn't actually smoking, yet cancer-causing addictions aren't the usual fodder for humor so near the monkey bars. The self-deprecating barb freed me from feeling guilty for having an overpraised child and stopped anyone from shaking me in search of my admittance that my daughter was the next Gary Coleman.

At Poppy's recent jazz dance recital, my Gatling gun lay fully loaded. I had seen the rehearsal, and the whole number rated quite high on the saccharine scale. The group of twenty or so little girls performed "I Won't Grow Up" from the musical version of *Peter Pan* in wee Tarzan outfits, fountain-pen-sized daggers strapped to their waists with toupee tape. Poppy was one of the smallest of the flock, which meant she was in front most of the show, and the choreographer had given her a lot of Shirley Temple mugging-it-up moments. I love my daughter, but she was not even close to being the best dancer onstage. That's all I'll say for fear of her seeking revenge or expensive therapy later.

After the 150 minutes (147 of which my daughter was not on-stage), I felt like a contestant on some type of rapid-fire game show, and the hosts were all these parents lobbing me the same cue: *Poppy was so cute!* Here were some of my replies:

> Her clubfoot doesn't seem to slow her down, does it?
> We find that a small shot of gin helps with her nerves.
> We told her if she didn't embarrass us, we'd put the door back on her room and sheets on her bed.

My wife doesn't agree with these wisenheimer answers, even though she turns away and laughs into her wrap when I deliver them. What she doesn't admit is that I am her human shield when it comes to these types of social scenes and because she's supposedly "shy," she usually waits for me to answer any sort of question or comment first. Since I am the initial line of defense, I feel I have the right to choose the response. Further, as a teacher, writer, and now renowned snob, I give these issues more thought than she does. For instance, I realize that flattery for our children is not going away anytime soon, and as they grow older, exaltation can turn even uglier.

At Poppy's school, they don't give grades on the ABC scale. Instead, in an effort to avoid competition and grade grubbing, and to confuse the hell out of parents, they give O (outstanding), S (satisfactory), and NI (needs improvement). I knew Poppy's school wasn't perfect when she told my father on the telephone, "O stands for *awesome!*" The teachers also tack on pluses and minuses to their O's and S's, which make those letters just like traditional grades anyway. I have outlawed grade comparisons in my own high school classroom but at the Wood Gormley Parentgate there are no such rules. On report card day, one overly driven dad turned a statement into a question, hoping to elicit a response. "Poppy must get all O's?" he wheedled. Before my conversion to Johnny Wiseass, I would have answered that she didn't, and why the hell are we discussing grades when these kids can barely read a road sign? This father believed his son was a genius, destined to solve Rubik's Cube through mind control. Such parents are never satisfied, the comparisons never over until we all die horrible deaths, so I said, "Poppy's kind of slow, so they don't even bother with grades. They just draw her pictures."

Receiving flattery is something like a stiff drink: it feels good going down at the time of ingestion, but too much can leave you sick, guilty, and feeling like you owe your laudators something but you can't recall what or why. I guess the other thing I do when I repel flattery is prepare myself for the inevitable heartbreak when Poppy becomes an adolescent. People may see her now as demure, diplomatic, and polite, and she is mostly those things, but she will someday evolve into a creature far more complex, dark, smelly, and brooding with a voice like Moon Unit Zappa's in *Valley Girl*. Since I get paid (very little) to spend too much time with teenagers, I have seen those lovely butterflies turn into slimy caterpillars who sneak out at night and wreck the family car. Two of my closest friends have a daughter named Ginger, who, when younger, was a lot like Poppy: a sweet, kind, fair-skinned girl who rode ponies with silly names and could play with her younger brother without smacking him or forcing him to wear a dress and makeup. Once Ginger turned thirteen, however, she tried to live the movie based on her age. Over bowls of wine margaritas at the Guadalajara Grill in Taos, New Mexico, her mother bluntly gave me a glimpse of what I was in for.

"Does Poppy like to stay up late?" she asked coyly, fingering the salted rim of her glass.

I nodded.

"Potential runaway." She slurped the jade-colored slush set before her. "Play dress-up?"

"Guilty," I admitted.

"Think Christina Aguilera in a hot tub full of boys."

Temporary tattoos forewarned future permanent ones and multiple piercings. "Good with younger kids" meant my daughter would be cleaning up all her friends' puke in jail after being arrested for hiding Handsome Hunk's eight-ball of coke in her panties.

Ginger received multitudinous compliments when she was younger—some hurled upon her by me, now that I think of it. Looking back, all that praise must seem like ancient history or the lickspittle calm before the real shitstorm. "Parents are doomed," a wise friend of mine once said, and he was right. I guess there's nothing for me to do but get comfortable in the audience of my daughter's twelve-year-long talent show and think of the next snappy comeback.

Thunderbox

On eight consecutive Saturdays this summer, London and I attended toddlers' swim class. My friend and colleague Marla and her boy, Calvin, joined us each week at a local cavernous pool. Calvin and London have a symbiotic relationship. Calvin is the puckish instigator, London the dramatic snitch. Marla's son will poke, pinch, or pretend to bite, and my son will come to me screaming that his pal jacked him in the face. Calvin has been suspended from preschool; London carries around a mohair sweater for comfort. You get the picture. Both boys, however, feel the same way about large bodies of water as I feel about movies starring Ben Affleck, so Marla and I signed up. The fact that the price of each lesson cost less than a breakfast burrito worried us a bit, as did the general reputation of Mommy-and-Me classes in Santa Fe: they usually included some sort of yoga, strange breathing techniques, and past-life regression therapy.

Two very different instructors who alternated teaching each week shared the class. The first Saturday we had a wiry and energetic woman in her seventies named Mamie, and the next greeted us with a lifeless and hungover teenager with a soul patch who I believe was named Kurt, though I'm not completely positive since he communicated mostly through grunts. On Mamie's week, parents and kids would circle in the hibernal water and dance around while singing children's songs with vaguely aquatic terms thrown in for relevancy. In "Ring Around the Rosie," we substituted *fishes* for *ashes* while Mamie in her blue swimming cap, thick glasses, and false teeth urged us to "sing louder, OK?" and to dunk our kids under the water whenever they weren't looking. Mamie kept a waterproof clipboard near the edge of the pool and referred to it often by holding the thin plank so close to her face that it bent the tip of her nose. Even with the heavy spectacles, the woman who was in charge of our aquatic safety had the sight of a blind cavefish. No one noticed or cared. The icy water changed our parental instincts to more basic ones of avoiding shock and hypothermia, and Mamie left only one girl near drowning in the deep end.

On Kurt's Saturday, he teetered on the lip of the pool, drank orange juice from the carton, and pointed to the far end, belching, "Again!" as we held our kids like kicking two-by-fours in our arms. Marla and I both work at a private school and are probably a little oversensitive about edification, so we quickly left Kurt's zone of negligence and started singing Mamie's songs and inventing our own games, which included impossible scenarios like swimming dump trucks, robots that do the backstroke, and rude diesel trains that love to blow bubbles. No matter how hard we tried to distract our duo, Calvin still spat on London, who cried to go home and take some mohair fuzz from his sweater and rub it under his nose like an ether addict.

On the third Saturday, I noticed Calvin wearing Bob the Builder underpants without a diaper. Calvin is three months younger than London, and although our son had shown some interest in potty training—oddly enough, in the men's room of Mexican restaurants—my wife and I decided to wait to complete training until the end of the summer, after we had twice traveled on holiday and I had gotten over my hangover. Marla told me that they had indeed started Calvin's initiation into the world of sanitary ware by the now-normal and enlightened methods: buying a potty seat, cartoon underwear, and a training chart with accompanying motivational stickers ("Way to go!"). I could tell that they were in the initial stages of their journey, since Marla asked Calvin pointedly if he had to go to the bathroom every three minutes. Calvin happily waved his johnson at us, finding the tool of his new trade quite compelling as of late. When London and Calvin were dressed and dry and Marla was busily packing up towels, mini Tupperware, and dripping suits, Calvin padded over to me. I was sitting in a white plastic chair with the Corona logo painted in blue on its back—an odd sponsor for a public pool. I remember thinking, Calvin looks a bit like London, though he's a shade fairer, his hair is neatly cut, and you can see he's got a great set of teeth when he bares them.

"I want to eat your penis," he said, and stared deeply into my eyes. I've had this phrase said to me by a man twice—in a fraternity house and at an after-hours party at a cabaret restaurant—but never from a child.

"Calvin," Marla called from the table, "potty talk in the potty only."

Calvin is a sharp kid, bordering on devious, and had moved quickly from the poopoo-peepee poetry to the powerful syntax of the sentence I received, which he had recently lobbed over the coyote fence to his neighbor, a man older and far more sensitive to language than I am. The neighbor told the young boy that such a sentence was a terrible, terrible thing to say to someone, which isn't necessarily true at office Christmas parties or in sad-boy magazines like *Maxim*. Calvin realized, as all toddlers do, that taboo words make people pay attention. Marla's solution to this issue was not to censor the language and thereby feed it more force but to restrict the words to their point of origin. I knew what she meant. Saying "holy mother of Jesus" was acceptable during mass at St. Luke's when I was an altar boy but not OK on the playground with your hand down your pants, especially when Sister St. Ignatius was within ruler-striking distance. After telling London that he had a penis, with London flatly denying it since so far he hadn't been that interested in anatomy, Calvin went home with Marla carrying the bags behind him.

There is much published on how to tell if your child is ready for potty training, steps to success, and the difference in tactic and technique for boys and girls; there are even methods to train your children as soon as they are born (a creepy practice called "tickle treating"). You can buy a kit online that helps you achieve your goals while traveling in the comfort of your automobile. Most of the discussion around the language of toilet training has to do with familiarizing the child with the process of recognizing the need, dropping the trousers, using the john, and washing the hands. Some parents even make a game out of it, substituting what my dad called "potty mouth" to familiar songs: "This is where we poop and pee, poop and pee, poop and pee. This is where we poop and pee, we do it in the potty." Great songwriting aside, there's never much discussion on what to do with the accompanying vernacular in grocery stores, the DMV, your church or synagogue, or, as Calvin found out over dinner one night, with your befuddled grandmother:

"Nana, can you say *penis* and *bum*?"

"Yes, but why would I want to?"

The Saturday before my family flew to Hawaii, a place where these swimming lessons were supposed to come in handy, Marla escorted Calvin to the bathroom near the entrance of the complex. London watched them and a minute later said he too had to use the potty. One of the bullets on the *Is My Child Ready?* checklist says that kids like to imitate others' bathroom habits, so I dutifully led London to the doorway. In most public locker rooms and bathrooms, sound reverberates, echoes, and amplifies, and before we even stepped off the carpet and onto the tile, we heard Calvin's rapid-fire Tourette's-like rant:

poop	penis	peebum
pee	bum	poopmouth
poo poo	bumpenis	pottypoo

My son and I paused for a moment, the nearby automatic sliding doors blowing hot air on us as fitness buffs came in to claim a treadmill or play pickup basketball in the gym next door. Calvin's harangue evolved from words and phrases into complete sentences:

> I have a big penis, Mom.
> You don't have a penis, Mom.
> Eat my penis, Mom.
> Do we take our penises out at the table?

Then he ended with a song reminiscent of Mamie's musical stylings but with an added gay overtone: "Row, row, row your penis gently down the bum."

London gripped my hand and peered up at me, his face confused. He could sense the darkness inside that restroom, and the way Calvin was shouting seemed a departure from their usual train/dinosaur/backhoe speak. London wasn't ready to enter that door just yet. He absentmindedly patted his Custom Cruisers, *Sesame Street* characters smiling dumbly—sans diapers or genitalia—on the superabsorbent front flap.

"Dad, do I have a penis?" London asked once he was safely strapped into his car seat. He was happy as a relapsed alcoholic, having found a bloom of sweater fuzz on the floor of the minivan.

"Yes, you do, son," I boomed in my best fatherly tone. "And hopefully someday," I added, "a very nice girl will want to eat it."

Mister Mom

My feat wasn't anything heroic; it was selfish, actually. I wanted to attend my twentieth high school reunion in Connecticut and then spend a week with my college buddy Drew and his family in Southampton on Long Island. Lala's folk art orders had piled up when we were away in June, so she couldn't come with me. For the first time, I took my two children on a trip alone. I wasn't very worried. Poppy is old enough to wash, brush, dress, and entertain herself, and I hoped London could be placated with ice cream, the mohair sweater he carries around for comfort, and twenty-seven toy trains stuffed into a Spider-Man lunchbox.

A man traveling alone with two children unfairly gets far more props than a mother completing the same junket does. While we were waiting to deplane at JFK, a woman in a hempish-looking dress lightly squeezed my unimpressive biceps and said,

"I just want to say I admire your parenting." I thanked her, felt proud for a minute, then realized that my son London had slept half the flight, and Poppy was quite happy watching the in-flight movie and gulping sugary soda we rarely allow her at home. It really was no big deal, but I didn't admit that to Rainbow Gathering Gal.

At my reunion, I continued to receive acclaim and raised (and plucked) eyebrows for my three's-company tour from either women who had yet to marry or wives whose husbands would rather build a deck from scratch, starting with cutting the trees, than fly coach alone with two small offspring. I happily rode the wave of fatherly hauteur all the way from Connecticut into Southampton since, as any person married longer than three weeks knows, flirtatious compliments in one's own home are harder to come by than paintings by Vermeer.

Seeing our first great beach day on Long Island, my family and Drew's lugged towels, sand toys, sunscreen, diapers, swim diapers, wipes, hats, cover-ups, snacks, and drinks in boxes to Little Plains Beach, about a mile from the place where I was freeloading. (For a two-week stay, the house Drew and his wife, Sue, were renting cost about as much as the yearly starting teacher's salary in New Mexico.) Minutes after we set up our mini-compound, my friends had to take their son, Eden, back to the house. Eden is allergic to just about everything, including dairy, soy, legumes, nuts, seeds, most fruits, and, like Icarus and Michael Jackson, the sun. Allergy Boy had to exit early even after his parents had dressed him in a full-length, UV-blocking bathing costume with a bell-shaped hat that made him look like a gay Amish child. Their departure left me with my two kids plus their five-year-old daughter, Dayna. It wasn't a big deal. Poppy had recruited Dayna early on to be her personal assistant and surfside Gunga Din, and London was content making cupcakes out of wet sand and then eating them.

A fatherless family arrived and parked themselves near us, a bit closer to the pounding surf. The mother had a very dark tan, her private parts barely covered by a yellow bikini that was smaller than Poppy's. Oversized sunglasses shaded her eyes like two black saucers, and platinum and diamonds were inserted into her earlobes and curled around her fingers. She was one of those well-kept mothers who didn't work but worked out. A woman I guessed to be her mother-in-law unfolded fancy beach blankets and padded chairs with cupholders, and a little girl stared at the ocean, while High-Maintenance Mom checked the messages on a cell phone the size of a sugar cube.

"Dad, could you make us into mermaids?" Poppy called.

"Huh?" I choked. I was staring at HM Mom's rippled six-pack just above her tonsured bikini line. "Sure. Let's start digging," I said. Making mermaids is a tradition started by my wife and her artistic sisters, who've spent hours burying our kids and shaping long, elaborate tails adorned with hundreds of hand-carved scales and waistlets fashioned from seaweed, shells, and live hermit crabs. The little girl left her mom and wandered over to what must have seemed like more fun than an outdoor office where your boss ignores you. She had brown curls that bounced off her shoulders and a polka-dotted bathing suit with the Neiman Marcus price tag still attached.

"What's your name?" I asked her, still digging. It freaks me out when kids just silently gawk at you. Reminds me of *The Shining* or the photos of missing children on the post office wall.

"Maddie."

"Maddie, who's Maddie?" London popped up and chirped, deeply confused whenever two people shared a name. He already had two cousins named Maddie. I knew that without photos to help me explain, I was in for a lengthy family tree discussion that night.

I invited Maddie to merge with our hoeing and tilling team; she eagerly joined but only tentatively executed, as if the sand were made up of millions of live insect heads. I had all four kids sit on a ledge and as I prepared the burial, the Yummy Mummy strode over and squatted on her well-defined legs. I wasn't prepared for the strong Long Island accent out of such full lips. She said her name was Rachel and she lived in Manhattan but loved coming out for six weeks in the summer to "escape all the people she knew." I was impressed. She had single-handedly developed her own high-society witness protection program.

Like a well-mannered gravedigger, I buried Maddie first and with great flourish, trying to flex any dormant muscle left over from my mediocre high school athletic career. She squealed at first with delight but then wailed with horror. I wondered if she saw the ghosts of dead Maidstone debutantes.

"Maddie, what's wrong?" Rachel asked her daughter, who by now had jumped out of her foxhole like a scared soldier on D-day. "I don't think she's ever been buried in sand," Rachel told me, searching her memory.

"Oh?" I was surprised. "How long have you been taking her to the beach?"

She shrugged. "All her life."

I envisioned a series of prior vacation photos of Rachel talking on her cell phone to her personal trainer in Austria while Maddie flopped around on the beach in search of a net.

I finished burying my two mermaids and one merboy, and my tails were as formless and misshapen as a trio of swollen whale tongues. "I want hipples," London said, and pointed to his chest. Poppy laughed at me knowingly.

"Not today," I said, and thought to head to the surf to chug seawater.

"I want hipples," London moaned, and I realized if I didn't heed his request, his even demeanor on the trip might be blown. Sometimes kids' emotions are as fragile as a house of cards. One false move and we'd be on the next flight home.

"OK," I sighed, and gathered sand for two breasts. *Hipples* came from *nipples*, which came from the mammary gland, a body part always included when my wife and her sisters made mermaids. The last thing I wanted to be doing in front of a squatting hottie was to create, shape, and form two round boobs on my three-year-old son. My embarrassment and anxiety were multilayered. If I made them too small, London would complain, drawing more attention to the freakish act. Too large or detailed and my fetish would be revealed to this woman and the surrounding children. Then there were aesthetics to consider. Pointy like Madonna? Overflowing like Anna Nicole Smith? Neat and tidy like Kate Moss? With nipples or Barbie-smooth?

Either I took too long or London grew weary of his breccia bosom, but when he rose, I felt a great sense of relief. Without comment or segue, we moved quickly on to the business of sand castles, which, the last time I checked, involved no breasts, vaginas, or asses unless you attend a Dungeons and Dragons sex party. Rachel chatted away as I coordinated the workforce with a series of orders, veiled threats, and suggestions for the sharing and swapping of tools the color of crayons. It turned out that Rachel's husband was a corporate lawyer who came out only on weekends. During the week, Maddie spent her days at camp, in private swimming lessons, or fully ignored on the beach. From what I could assess, Rachel checked her cell phone for messages, worked out, and avoided her friends from Manhattan. When I told her I was from New Mexico, a state she'd vaguely heard of, and was traveling with my kids alone, she was very impressed. "I can't believe how you handle all these children," she whispered, and actually touched my skin. Then she examined her manicure to see if any sand had rubbed off.

Intoxicated by her praise, I told her all about my trip and how, at my friends' rented house the night before, I had prepared swordfish with grilled vegetables, with burgers for the kids. "I even did the dishes afterward!" I squeaked like Opie on the *Andy Griffith Show*.

"Oh my gawd," she said, the Long Island equivalent of "golly." She called me Mr. Mom and touched me just above my knee twice. I could have died.

I imagined her husband, an overweight, balding man who spent too much time at the office, leaving his wife all alone on the island without friends or body fat. A man, if you could call him that, who had never played Stewardess Barbie or visited the stylin' salon at the Polly Pocket mall with his daughter.

I, on the other hand, could cook dozens of hard-to-pronounce dishes and scrub pots afterward; I knew most of the *Thomas the Tank Engine* trains by name and postwar attribute and could change shitty diapers in a turbulent airplane bathroom. So when Rachel asked if she could sit a spell, I told her to go right ahead and relax. I had everything under control. While she was still within hearing distance, I sang out, "Come on, kids, let's go play." My voice boomed like Dudley Do-Right's.

"But, Dad," Poppy replied, "we're not finished."

I grabbed her arm and yanked her from her grainy drum

tower, then gathered up the three remaining small people in an aggressive game of tag starring me. I bobbed and weaved around the reluctant participants like a drunken Pied Piper as Rachel and her mother-in-law looked over in bemusement. I sang, danced, told jokes, and did impressions of forgotten television celebrities like Rodney Allen Rippy and Mason Reese. I swung all kids for equal amounts of time (under their arms to avoid dreaded nursemaid's elbow). A few other tots joined us, wanting to know what the crazy camp counselor was smoking and could they buy some? I shoved the rookies into the conga line and ordered them to smile and march by the blanket with the bronzing woman wearing Bono's sun spectacles.

I was sweating like a pro basketball player after a night of Stoli and Red Bull by the time Sue returned from bathing Eden in pricey hypoallergenic products made by robots in labs near Iceland. As we packed up, Rachel called from her chair that she hoped to see us at the beach again soon. I told Sue of my many educational and healthy activities for the kiddos and how impressed Rachel had been with my expertise handling of so many of God's creatures. Sue, a veteran of the city-island experience, glanced back at the cocoa skin, firm body, diamonds, $300 shades, and the watch I had missed that must have set Lawyer Man back a cool grand.

"Sure, she's impressed with you now," Sue explained, "but wait until she sees your paycheck. No gym, no personal trainer, no nanny, no private school for the little contessa over there, forget the vacations in Aruba ..." The list grew longer than any mermaid's tail I'd ever seen. I started to understand what she meant as we entered the parking lot. My Chevrolet P.O.S. rental from Hotwire.com cowered next to a Hummer, a Porsche, a fleet of SUVs, and what looked like Sean Connery's Aston Martin convertible. I did further inventory. At home, I drove a three-cylinder Daihatsu Charade with a hole in the floorboard. The T-shirt I donned had lasted through four graduations and had juice stains on the front in the pattern of Gorbachev's birthmark. I earned less in one year than the price of any of these cars in front of me. Feeling like a roadie for my children with all their crap in my arms, I stuffed the little gossoons and ten pounds of sand into the Hertz bargain.

"No dinners at Nobu, shopping at Citarella's...," Sue droned on.

Pulling out, I saw a tan silhouette rise over the white dune like a burnt match. It was Rachel waving her arms. *She'll tell Sue how special I am,* I thought, *how making a crustless cheesecake after giving the kids a bath is worth any other man's millions.*

"Hello again," I said, trying to deepen my nasal voice into a velvety purr.

"You left a sippy cup on the roof," she said flatly, and handed me the Playtex Insulator crusted with sand, juice, and kid spit. I thanked her, adjusted the crotch of my wet bathing suit, and drove away, the long corridor of manicured hedges steering me back to the hamlet called humility.

Kidalgo

People who forget they were once children have been getting me down lately. I avoid adults who, upon seeing a child, wince, complain, or recoil as if these smaller versions of themselves are really tiny lepers with bad haircuts carrying the West Nile virus. Don't get me wrong. I don't believe that everyone has to adore the younger species by running up to little Jimmy or Susie, speaking fluent baby talk, and handing out Baby Bottle Pops by the case. In my view, kids deserve the same mild respect we give the elderly or ineffective comedic actors like Tim Allen. Even though our nation is supposed to be founded on family-takes-a-village values, and the topics of children and education are currently the "it" girls who give politicians a stiffy, I've witnessed a fair amount of anti-kid behavior lately that has ultimately led me down the nefarious path of revenge.

Just before I left Santa Fe with my two children to head back East, as they say out here in cactusland, my family visited one of the few truly kid-friendly restaurants in the City Different—the Cowgirl Hall of Fame. Most upscale bistros in our adobe-colored town try to avoid toddlers by refusing to stock high chairs or spoons that weigh less than two pounds. The Cowgirl not only tolerates kids but also lures them in with bright colors, barbed wire, pictures of grinning cowpokes, and a holding pen for children, which is aptly named the Kiddie Corral. This toddler turnout offers weary parents an enclosed area with swings, play-houses, rocking horses, and ring toss games so adults can eat a meal while it's still hot or get hammered on cheap beer and not have to duct-tape their son to a telephone pole outside the bar. The Cowgirl is like Disney meets Westworld, so instead of your tyke sprinting to shake Mickey's hand, the goal is to run away from the slurring drunks in ten-gallon hats.

Lala, the kids, and I took a break from playing in the carnival atmosphere of the Kiddie Corral and ate our dinners on a picnic table near a party of six adults celebrating some minor victory at work involving office supplies and a fresh 401(k). My son spilled his glass of water, which crept over to the shoe of a woman laughing about some office hijinks that included heavy-duty staples. When the harmless liquid kissed the sole of her black Payless boot, she jumped as if the fluid were molten lava laced with Asian bird flu. "Jesus Christ!" she screeched, and dabbed frantically at her feet with a wad of napkins yanked from the dispenser.

"Sorry 'bout that," Lala called over. "Don't worry, though. It's only water." A busboy getting baked behind the gate to the corral heard the commotion and stumbled over to her table to investigate. The woman pointed her typing finger accusingly at

London. "He ruined my shoes," she declared for the whole corral chorale to hear. This caused our son to duck under the table in shame (and for cover from the scary woman dressed in a patterned tent). I don't know why—maybe it was the grand gold margaritas or the sight of happy children throwing rocks from the roof of the playhouse onto the overloaded tree swing—but I held Lala back from dismembering the office supply sow. Her motherly instincts boiled inside her as we paid our bill.

"Those boots are not even leather," Lala growled as we left.

One week later, my kids and I were in a very chi-chi boutique on Job Lane (either way you pronounce the name, it's ironic for this hamlet) in Southampton on Long Island. We were visiting my friend Drew's sister, who worked there selling cubic zirconia replicas of fancy baubles to socialites who were either too frightened to travel to New Jersey with their authentic ice or hadn't found a man lonely enough to buy them the real thing. Two older women with wide-brimmed hats wandered in separately, each with designer dogs in tow. One dragged a teacup Chihuahua by a piece of blue dental floss, while the other sported a canine that looked like Phyllis Diller's wig. The women kissed the air near the gallery owner's Botoxed cheeks, and London placated himself by pulling the fur from a $500 pillow and sniffing the plush clumps. One dog must have said the other bought his sweaters off the rack because they started a posh pooch fight near a display of necklaces made from red coral and the teeth of baby hippos. London dropped his vestal animal hair and bolted out of the store into the cobblestone alley outside. He crossed the path of a short, squat woman who moved like Gertrude Stein with a malt liquor hangover.

"Watch!" she barked at my boychik. No subject, no direct object, no *please* or soft terms to cushion the harsh imperative

command. London and I checked with each other, and I am sure
that we thought the same thing: *Barren-ass beeaatch!*

My kids are seasoned air travelers. They understand not to pack
Fiskars, pickup sticks, or magic wands in their backpacks lest
they be confiscated by security. Poppy and London know how to
load the X-ray conveyor belt with their gear and to place their
arms in the flying position for a full-body search. We carry
plenty of ATA-approved snacks, toys, games, and sedatives, and
I am happy to sacrifice a watch or cell phone for an uneventful
flight from JFK to Phoenix. Traveling alone with my two offspring, I felt thankful that America West is one of the enlightened airlines that allow adults with small humans to cut in front
of the other child-free passengers. Walking the aisle, I grabbed a
few extra pillows and blankets to aid sleep and in case I had to
muffle cries. Poppy buckled herself in by the window, plugged
her headphones into the arm of the seat, and searched for a station that offered voices powered by helium. London, in the middle, checked out our tray tables, which on this flight were
decoupaged with ads for a cable travel channel. To keep him occupied while other passengers boarded, I made up stories about
smoking poodles in Paris, same-sex teddy bear couples in San
Francisco, and fishes crossing borders in Miami. Two adults sat
in the shortened emergency exit row in front of us and giggled
conspiratorially about the extra leg room they received for
agreeing to save our lives. London wasn't so lucky. Being a vertically challenged guy in a grown-up seat didn't allow him to bend
his legs. Therefore, the soles of his Buzz Lightyear sandals rested
against the San Francisco tray table when it was in its upright
and locked position. While waiting for the plane to taxi, he

hummed the proletarian anthem from *Bob the Builder*, lightly tapping his feet, almost in time. The balding man seated in front of him turned around and popped up so we could see most of his face.

"He's kicking my seat," he explained to me, smiling that phony smirk London surely recognized from the great villains of his milieu like evil Uncle Scar in *The Lion King* and that sexy canine-seamstress Cruella De Vil in *101 Dalmatians*. I apologized profusely to the man and dutifully pointed out to London how his tapping foot might bother the passenger.

The plane took off and, as promised to my wife, the three of us held hands so that if we went down, the coroners would declare upon examining the carnage, "Those Wilders sure were a happy and well-adjusted family!" The beverage service and in-flight movie arrived concurrently, which excited both my kids and made my strapped-in life a bit hectic. London cried out for cranberry juice, and I allowed Poppy ginger ale, a drink usually reserved for tummy aches and Daddy's brown bottle flu. As London fumbled with the male/female anatomy of headphones and jacks and I lowered the Golden Gate Bridge, his little trotters brushed the seat back just above the pocket that held an *America West* magazine, emergency instructions, and a barf bag, an item any parent worth his salt knows is really twenty minutes of puppetry waiting to unfold.

Chrome Dome unbuckled, stood upright, and faced us. "He's kicking my seat again," he sang angrily, rolling his eyes. The lady in the aisle seat with a cabasset of black hair rose also and peered at me through cheap drugstore glasses. "I've got a bad back," she declared. London frowned and began to cry. The pair remained unmoved. Poppy unsheathed her ears and patted her brother on the arm.

"I heard you," I said through my teeth as the notebook-sized screens lowered and the movie *Hidalgo* began. I did my best to console and distract my three-year-old even though I was fuming inside over these awful passengers (still talking childsmack in their seats). What London had done with his tiny feet had far less impact than what adults do all the time on flights with full-sized legs, knees, and pointy laptop computers. It was clear they were attacking him because of his age and size. If an obese senior citizen or restless college basketball player was bumping into them, they would say and do nothing.

I wasn't happy. Besides causing my son to cry, they had also spoiled the only film without puppets or cartoons I would be allowed to view in months. I did catch an early scene in *Hidalgo* where cavalry rider Frank T. Hopkins with his Vidal Sassoon haircut decks a man for insulting Hopkins' famous horse. Here was a guy who defends the honor of a wordless animal while I hadn't done jack shit for my innocent son against enemies far uglier and more poorly dressed than the vaguely Middle Eastern actors in the film. I started to entertain thoughts of retaliation and revenge, issues I explore deeply every year when teaching *Hamlet* to teenagers who eagerly cheer on actors like Vin Diesel in his quest for payback and better intonation when delivering his lines. The fate of Prince Hamlet should teach all of us, I explain, that revenge is an act that only causes more damage. Yet, trapped in this Boeing 737, a far cry from my chalky classroom or the Arabian Desert, evil King Claudius and whiny Queen Gertrude within striking distance, I decided to ignore my own advice. After all, what the hell does a gassy windbag of an English teacher know about settling a score?

On the newer airplanes, the jets and lights above your seats rotate a full 360 degrees. Trying to turn down the air above my head, I pushed the little spouter a bit too forward and realized I could point all three geysers at the pair in front of me. Anyone sensitive enough to feel the brush of my boy's tootsies would surely notice three streams of cool air showering down upon him. I opened the floodgates and let them flow.

"Dad, you be this guy," London ordered, handing me the only unnamed train in his traveling railyard.

"Can I call him Orestes?" I asked innocently. "Or George Bush the Younger?" I even suggested *The Bride* after Uma Thurman's role in *Kill Bill*, but London never liked Tarantino—too self-referential.

When the flight attendant came by to collect trash, the lady with the psychic sciatica in front of me whined, "Can I get a blanket?"

"Sorry," she answered, "they were all handed out at the beginning of the flight." I glanced over at Poppy, who had constructed a *beit al-sha'r* tent out of our half-dozen airline coverings.

"I'm so cold," Bitchy McFrumpass cried to Baldy McAsswipe.

"Try to get some sleep," he advised his partner in misery.

That was my cue to turn on all three of our lights and swivel them toward the object of my karmic lesson. Her seat area was so bright I could see corpuscles of blood moving through the veins on her temple. I have to confess, unlike the noble and surprisingly celibate Frank Morgan in *Hidalgo*, that I got a tad drunk on revenge. Light and air were not enough for me. I lowered and raised my flat Chicano City a bit more often than was necessary. I swatted imaginary flies. London and I clumsily visited the restroom about four times. I wasn't just doing this for my son, I figured, or for my own guilty enjoyment. I had a cause. My rebellious behavior was for all the parents who worked hard to keep their children from annoying adults on any mode of public transportation and were still persecuted for it.

The woman moaned and complained to her man, who said, "I know, I know," like a congested turtle. But every time they peered back, London was either on his knees like an altar boy, or the Lilliputian legs that had done so much damage earlier were harmlessly crossed.

"Miss, can I move my seat?" Wailing Woman called to the attendant, who informed her that the plane was full. "Can you arrange a switch?"

Visibly annoyed by the barrage of requests, the purser answered, "No, but you may ask your neighbors if you wish." She then moved her gaze to our aisle. My daughter peacefully slept with her head against the window while London quietly connected Thomas and Percy in a safe and nonsexual manner. "You have the sweetest, most well-behaved kids," she said to me and smiled.

"Thank you. I know," I answered, and kicked the seats in front of me.

For the Children

It wasn't anything I planned on but one Saturday afternoon, while studying the army of fire ants claiming our driveway as their nation-state, I noticed how splotchy my car's paint job had become. Hailstorms, sun damage, and the nighttime barrage of eggs and paint balls from irate students (and their parents) had turned my 1990 Daihatsu Charade's finish from sexy black to grandma gray. My car, a two-door, three-cylinder P.O.S., is not worth much in terms of Blue Book value—less than what my watch costs—but it still gets me to school and back, is worry-free when it comes to theft, and it provides hours of fun for family and friends to tease me about.

While rummaging in our house for paint, I came across some Chalkboard-in-a-can, left over from one of Lala's many projects. I figured what the hell. Over the ten years of owning the

Charade, Lala, my kids, and a few students where I teach have treated my car as a community bulletin board on wheels. They attach Post-it notes, farting magnets, and embarrassing bumper stickers with catchy slogans about feeding my inner rainbow and "I'd rather be masturbating." It's not uncommon for me to have a student during first period congratulate me on getting married.

"Huh?" I reply like a midwesterner at an authentic Chinese restaurant. Then I walk down to the faculty lot to see that my wife and her friends have hitched me to someone named Moonbeam in car-friendly spray foam.

In my driveway that Saturday, I shook the Chalkboard vigorously, enjoying the *ping ping* of the ball inside the can as I evened the viscosity of the paint. I covered the car in the flat black spray, and to me it looked cool, like a Civil War bullet or a stealth table tennis ball. Sunday was the last day of summer and the day before Poppy's best friend, Sierra, was moving south to Albuquerque. We invited Sierra over, and I told Poppy to fetch the tub of sidewalk chalk if her brother wasn't busy eating it. I led the two eight-year-olds to the driveway and told them to have at it.

"Are you kidding?" Sierra asked in her usual forensic questioning kind of way. She's a kid who needs everything at face value.

"You can write anywhere but the windows," I instructed them. "Oh, and watch the tailpipe, I used dental floss to keep it from dragging."

"Oh, man," Sierra said excitedly. She grabbed a hunk of blue and scrawled a moon on the driver's side door. Then she scurried back to Poppy's side and waited for me to tell her it was all a joke and she was in big trouble.

"Looks great," I said. "Now you just need to draw some yellow stars and green clover and we'll go on the road to sell Lucky Charms."

"Dad, you're being stupid again," Poppy reminded me.

"Have fun, kids," I called over my shoulder, feeling like a superdad, and went inside the house in search of ant napalm. Half of my entire home has been sacrificed for the supposed happiness of my children. The duo currently occupies three rooms—bedroom, playroom, and an art room, which I suppose now technically extends into the driveway and onto my vehicle. Since Lala and I grew tired of twisting ankles on diesel engines with faceplates in the hallway at night, we recently surrendered the territory formerly known as the living room to my son's three-by-five-foot train table. Pitching the coffee table, we now place our feet and cocktail glasses on any unclaimed patches of the island of Sodor, between the roundhouse and Cranky the Crane.

My car a black metal canvas, Poppy and Sierra happily drew rainbows and sunsets in yellow, pink, and blue chalk. In order to escape the invitation for my vehicle to be the clown car in the gay pride parade, I asked the two girls to create self-portraits on the hood. Sierra drew herself as a lopsided angel, and Poppy traced a longboard under her feet and transformed into a tiny surfer girl. As a note of thanks, she wrote "Dad stinks" in street-sign yellow just above the back bumper.

The reactions to our family project were mixed. The head of maintenance at my school asked me if I knew the punks who'd tagged my car. The Saab-driving trust fund teachers scoffed at such immaturity and lack of respect for my investment. Most of my students when they arrived on campus that week wished their parents had done something like that when they were little. Then they asked me where they could get a good deal on chalk before final exams.

Most parents wouldn't advocate turning their Subarus into finger-painting easels, but all moms and dads do crazy things out of love for their children. I'm talking beyond the daily sandwich making, ass wiping, and I'm-my-kid's-roadie chores and responsibilities. I think of my friend Jim, a former gymnast with bad knees, who took up skateboarding at forty so his son wouldn't feel lonely among the stoners at the skate park. Dads dress like Santas every year; moms who can hardly walk without getting breathless run a mile for school-sponsored charities. Otherwise intelligent adults who can successfully manage a major financial portfolio or treat fifty patients in a day act like fools for their little kiddos, and we do it over and over again.

For a few weeks in September, Santa Fe celebrates "Fiesta," a commemoration of Don Diego de Vargas' peaceful reoccupation of the City of Holy Faith in 1692. One of the highlights of the final weekend is the Children's Pet Parade, or *Desfile de los Niños*. The last time my family entered was 1998, when Poppy was two and there wasn't a train or bulldozer in our house. Like my students know now, my wife then came to realize that in my quest to win Father of the Year, I had unwittingly become the village idiot. That year Lala adorned a toy car with a dozen of Poppy's stuffed animals, dressed her in a white fiesta dress and striped beret, and hung signs on both sides of the car that read "Cruisin' Together," which she thought would appeal to both lovers of animals and low-rider aficionados. She even hung a birdcage off the handle of the car and crammed a reluctant stuffed parrot inside.

"There's something missing," Lala said, circling the colorful wagon. This single sentence is her life's motto. She repeats it each week, hits a tag sale or flea market, and returns to jam another piece of folk art or redundant furniture into our already crowded house. Makes me want to live in a desert monastery, naked.

"What?" I eyed the Dr. Doolittle mobile. It was our understanding that she would decorate and I would push Poppy on the two-mile parade route and throw cheap hard candy to the crowd in a traditional gesture of joy and toothaches.

"You need to dress like an animal," she said.

"Hold on a minute," I said.

"It'll look so cute. The big animal and all his babies."

"His babies?" Did scientists discover a male mammal that bears children? "No way."

"Do it for Poppy," Lala said, invoking the "for the children" clause, which is hard to veto. We see it everywhere—it's why former box office draws like Alec Baldwin or Sylvester Stallone agree to appear in low-budget cartoons or Claymation videos. Why professional and college coaches quit teams that rudely offer them a salary of $3 million instead of the family-friendly $7 mil. Oftentimes, it's why we invade countries or take hostages. So who was I to deny my daughter another sturdy layer of cuteness that might earn her a certificate and savings bond that would be worth $20 when she finished college? We needed the boost anyhow, Lala added, since we were going in at a handicap for not having a live pet.

After trying on a turtle costume made from a refrigerator box and a fox outfit that looked too similar to a cavewoman's vagina, we settled on a rabbit. I strapped on floppy ears, a cottontail, and a pair of woman's bunny slippers two sizes too small. With an eyeliner pencil and some year-old Halloween makeup, Lala drew on arched eyebrows, whiskers, and a pair of huge buckteeth. I felt like Hugh Hefner's bad dream.

Participants in the Pet Parade gather in a large parking lot behind the St. Francis Church, close to the historic plaza. The folks who run the show assign you numbers and divide you into categories based on the type of animal you are yanking around and the effect you are going for. The teacup Chihuahuas in tutus for world peace are separated from the long-haired guinea pigs dying of heatstroke for voter registration. People from all over the state haul many kinds of birds and beasts from dusty barns and pens. Appaloosas march proudly in front of a minnow sloshing around in a cup no bigger than a shot glass. It's a sight to see.

It's still hot in New Mexico in early September, and the air was thick with odors of seventeen types of animal dung, grease-paint, and parents like me sweating in costumes made of wool and thick cotton. Poppy was lounging in her bucket seat, watching the pink pit bulls growl at the llamas with dreadlocks from Taos, all under the atonal tent of the underfunded Ortiz Middle School marching band. Even though my costume registered ten notches hotter than the 80-degree air temperature, I stood tall and proud, my painted overbite stretching into a smile. Damn, I was a dedicated dad.

A whistle blew, we started moving, and the honeymoon ended. The handle of Poppy's car curved lower than I remembered so I had to stoop to push the bloody thing. The parade snaked for two miles along the main streets of downtown Santa Fe. The slippers from Wal-Mart were void of arch support and offered no protection from the ever-warming blacktop. It was as if I were walking on two slices of Wonder bread. Within a block, my feet burned and my back throbbed. Land mines in the form of animal crap started to appear every ten feet or so. I'm no animal husbandry expert, but once we started walking, all of God's creatures felt the urge to let loose feces reminiscent of Jackson

Pollock's paintings. Poppy and I had stumbled onto a slalom course, only instead of poles or gates, mounds of guano marked our trail.

Sweat poured from under my bunny ears, running down my face, streaking my whiskers and teeth. In front of us crawled a family of pugs dressed in dark suits and shades like Will Smith and Tommy Lee Jones in *Men in Black*. Behind me marched a group of twenty-five Christians in animal masks, white robes, and halos carrying a sign that quoted a line of scripture that connected ranch animals, the denouncing of Satan, and becoming born again. Their leader, a striped tiger with a whistle, was desperately trying to keep his hoofing flock in the shape of a cross.

I wasn't faring well. The birdcage had slipped from its perch, so I tried to hold it in place on the handle while steering around the shit humps. I had to stop every few minutes to change my grip or stop my slippers from coming apart at their haunches.

"Please keep it moving, sir," Father Feline called to me. I ignored him, but I couldn't ignore the crowds of kids waiting for us at the next corner. My wife had stuffed about ten pounds of sourballs in a messenger bag and slung it over my shoulder just before we launched our maiden voyage. On the flap she glued a "Cruisin' Together" sign, just in case the judges missed the first two on the car. All the entries in front of us—diapered monkey on biker guy's shoulder, spray-painted Labradors with the Waldorf School, potbellied pigs with polka dots—started tossing their candy to the mob of youngsters just off the curb. In anticipation of the Hershey-happy hooligans, I put the handle and birdcage in my left hand and flipped the flap of the messenger bag with my right. The bag had a zipper under the flap that was a bit stiff, so I stopped to address the jam.

"Halt!" screamed the prophetic tiger to his holy varmints.

Then he growled at me: "Sir, will you please keep moving? This is a parade, not a statue garden."

"Clever for a Christian," I called, still fumbling.

"Sir!" Tiger Boy shouted.

"Will you hold on? There." I freed the clenched teeth of the zipper, tore open a plastic bag of candy, and tossed the pieces to the frenzied kids, who scurried after them like sand crabs. The candy was still grouped in its individual bags, so after I emptied the first, I stopped briefly to open the second.

"Sir! I told you—" the minister began.

"Will you shut up?" I yelled back. The cage had started to slip, so I threw a handful of sourballs blindly into the waiting hordes and hit an old lady in a folding chair in the middle of her forehead. "Ah," she cried, and clapped her hand on the knot that was sure to form.

"Sorry!" I called back, feeling like shit, and then I stepped into a puddle of it. Horse diarrhea engulfed Mr. Bunny Right Foot and seeped into the open heel, forming a layer between my bare foot and what was left of the sole.

"Oh, God in heaven," I cried.

"That's right," the preacher said.

"One more mile to go!" a cop with a plastic pig nose said, popping a sourball into his mouth.

The parade just got worse. A staple on one of the candy bags sliced my finger, so I unintentionally threw bloody suckers until my stash ran out. On the last quarter mile, my messenger bag thankfully emptied. All the other participants had run out too. The crowd hadn't thinned, but it had grown ugly from lack of sugar.

"Where's *our* candy?" the toothless kids cried, shaking their fists. The "sorry, we just ran out" sissy excuses didn't cut the mustard. In a state where cockfighting is still legal, you don't want to get on the wrong side of an angry mob, even if they're under the age of thirteen.

"Get some more sweets, bunny fag!" some Goth kid yelled at me.

"You smell like shit, bucktooth," a little girl in pigtails called, pointing at my now-gangrenous foot.

"What about *our* children?" an angry dad in a leather vest demanded.

I shrugged, so he threw a penny, hitting me square in the cottontail.

We have a picture that Lala snapped in front of the judges' stand, only a hundred yards from where I would collapse in a heap of sweat, excrement, and humiliation. In the photo, I am so bent over that my bunny ears point straight into the ground. My eyes are closed, and there is an oily film on my skin that reflects the blazing sun. Poppy, however, is standing in her carriage, all two feet of her, waving like Queen Elizabeth to the judges. A beret topped by a ladybug Lala glued on at the last minute covers her little melon head. Poppy's smile is as wide and curved as my body. She ended up winning a prize for best costume in the hysterical category.

It's been six years since we entered the Pet Parade, but Lala thinks it's time London throws his hat into the ring. Her plan is to dress Poppy as Frida Kahlo, the unibrowed Mexican artist, and London as Diego Rivera, her distinguished-looking husband with the double chin. She wants me to pull the kids in a fancy garden wagon on sale now at our local Home Depot.

"There's only one thing missing," she says as she makes sketches of the costumes on a pad in the dining room.

"What's that?" I ask dumbly.

She takes me by the hand into the living room, where a framed print of one of Kahlo's most famous paintings hangs. Behind the artist's striking face sits a devious-looking monkey with a bandana around his neck. His eyes are as black as death.

I rub my lower back in anticipation.

"It's for the children," she says.

Little Latina of My Loins
(Crescit Eundo)

When I moved to New Mexico from Manhattan over fourteen years ago, it was more to escape the East than settle in the West. I was twenty-four, fresh out of the advertising industry, and starting a family was the furthest thing from my mind. I would have never imagined getting married in a shiny suit on Canyon Road in Santa Fe and raising two children who would, by default, become New Mexicans. Life, or in this case reproduction and rearing, happened when I wasn't looking.

Poppy's skin is as white as George Washington's wig powder. She has chestnut hair and slight features, and until recently her accent honored the fast tempo and dropped *R*'s known to those who inhabit the more lockjawed New England states. I'm just starting to understand that Poppy, through a selfish choice I made over a decade ago, is becoming a Spanglish-speaking, taco-chomping, coyote-loving New Mexican.

My first glimpse of Poppy's regionalistic allegiance came two years ago on the shores of North Carolina. Our family of four was on vacation on the lower Outer Banks after surviving a week with my father, three brothers, and their families. After seven days with the Wilder clan, my wife and kids joined me on a series of ferries headed south toward the quaint city of Beaufort. Back north, with the Wilders, we all ate communally, enjoying each brother's signature dish: Rich steamed mussels in garlic butter, Eddie boiled then grilled his famous barbecued ribs, I marinated flank steak, and my brother Tom, who lamentably lacks the family cooking gene, ordered a damn fine pizza. On our own in a small time-share condo in Beaufort, Lala, the kids, and I opted to eat out most nights. A seafood lover by nature and nurture, I relished the bounty that a coastline town could provide. If it had scales, gills, or tentacles, I was all over that shit. During the middle of our weeklong stay, we ventured along Route 17 and found a beat-up old crab shack hidden in some overgrown beach grass.

"Doesn't this look great?" I chirped like cheery Chevy Chase in a *Vacation* movie. I've always associated squalor with low prices and authentic regional cuisine. My wife, on the other side of the rental car, held other visions that involved botulism and staph infections from felons who don't wash their scabby hands.

Inside, picnic tables stretched along the width of the crumbling building, four or five deep. All we could see were backs huddled over the carcasses of cracked crustaceans. Like a trial judge convention, people rapidly hammered claws with wooden mallets, bits of crab flesh spurting onto walls, water glasses, and faces that didn't bat an eye.

We were lucky, in my opinion, to snag benches near the window so we could watch an adopted family of otters pick through white buckets of the remains of the last seating. The place felt "down home" to me—from the beer served in sweaty bottles to the cluster of condiment choices set near an ashtray full of half-smoked menthol cigarettes. Lala is from Wyoming and is generally afraid of creatures from the ocean unless they are so heavily deep-fried that you can no longer guess the species. The plastic menu had many battered items for her to choose from, so I settled in and ordered a beer from the portly man who seated us. Poppy and London would undoubtedly choose the Landlubber's Chicken Tenders from the Mini-Mariners menu. I was ready to feast.

Our waitress was a classic salty dogette, beehive hairdo with pencils lodged in the silver nest every which way. The white apron she wore over her gray uniform looked as though it had just come from some seafood killing-floor. Her shoes were built for both comfort and stealth, as if after twelve hours on her feet she could still kick the shit out of a customer who stiffed her. Barbed from years of smoke and dirty words, her voice sounded like a cross between those of Brenda Vaccaro, Harvey Fierstein, and Darth Vader. Like most career waitpersons at places like this one, she arrived at our table forty seconds after we were seated, guest checkbook open to a new page, pencil poised and freshly licked, her foot tapping in anticipation of our decisiveness.

I went first, since my choice was easy—everything in a bucket: gallon of crabs, pail of fries, and did they serve beer in anything larger than 20 ounces? Lala played it safe with the fried heart attack on a plate, and then all eyes turned to Poppy. She glanced at the sheet of paper covered with crude drawings of a parrot pirate, then rolled her eyes toward the sky. At first I thought she noticed the asbestos hanging from the ceiling next to the dusty fishnets and buoys. Then I recognized the pensive look; she was searching that odd part of our brain that tells us, as they say in the South, what we are a-hankerin' for.

"Do you have any quesadillas?" she asked.

"Huh? K say what?" the waitress grunted like Junior Samples from *Hee Haw*. "What did she say?" she asked me. I was so scared of being exposed as a tourist that I pretended to be hard of hearing.

"What did you want, darling?"

"Um, a quesadilla?"

"What the hell is that?" the waitress spat back.

Flustered, Poppy quickly thought of something else. "How about an enchilada?"

Diner Diva just glared at us over her mustache.

"Burrito?"

Turning her head back toward the two lifesavers mounted on the bathroom doors, the waitress called out to the man who had seated us. By his moist white shirt, dripping apron, and rain boots, it was obvious that he doubled as the dishwasher.

"What's this problem?" he asked all of us.

"This'un here," the waitress said, pointing at Poppy with her pencil. "Say what you said 'gain."

Poppy repeated her initial order.

"Nope. Ain't got none of them," the dishoster said, and clomped back to his post.

This moment of West meets East, or Santa Fe meets southern Gothic, alerted me that, unlike her father, Poppy was not being raised on crustless cucumber sandwiches on Wonder bread dripping with Hellmann's mayonnaise. Upon our return home to Santa Fe, I started paying closer attention to the Chicano cuisine that my child longed for—the quesadilla plate at Felipe's, the barbacoa tacos at El Parasol. Even McDonald's made a breakfast burrito that Poppy could wrap her little hands around. My daughter might have the skin of a *blanca*, but her heart (and stomach) was *en fuego*.

Poppy's best friend, Sierra, is a Rodriguez, one of the cuchara land-grant families of Santa Fe. They are called the cucharas since the King of Spain honored them with a silver spoon and vast plots of land in the 1600s. When Sierra turned seven, we drove across town to her grandparents' home to celebrate. They live in a traditional New Mexico adobe house on the last remaining plot of the original land grant, now surrounded by a bus depot, municipal parking lot, and city office buildings. Except for the urban blight bordering their chain-link fence, you feel as if you could be in a small town in Mexico or Spain. Dozens of people, most of Hispanic descent, attended the party, bringing six-packs of beer, guitars, and presents for Sierra. In the kitchen, bowls of posole, beans with red chile, carne adovada, tamales, and menudo crowded tabletops and counters. It was like a commercial for Taco Bell, only better.

I felt like a spy in this world that had things like culture, rituals, food with flavor, and songs with names like "Las Mañanitas," "Los Flores," and "There's No Tortillas." I tried to think of the soundtrack of my life growing up on Hillandale Lane in Westport, just a block away from that poor Martha Stewart, and I could only recall my three brothers and me singing the theme songs from *The Brady Bunch* and *The Partridge Family* in our wood-paneled Ford station wagon. At the party, Lala and I sat off to the side, eating just enough to be polite. The food was delicious and there was plenty of it, yet it felt somehow wrong for me to enjoy this trespass too much. Maybe I overthink things, but I didn't want to be the steal-the-culture guy I see around town wearing phony ghetto clothes and bling-bling or a full Indian headdress and beaded moccasins.

Amidst the music, drinking, and fiesta-ing, I turned to locate my children and there was Poppy, learning the words to "De Colores" on the knee of some man in jeans and a denim work shirt. Later, I caught her stamping her feet and clapping her hands above her head like a midget flamenco dancer. She felt none of the inhibitions I did and was eager to truly immerse herself in the food, songs, and mother tongue of her homeland.

This past September, Poppy decided, albeit unconsciously, to fully jump into the Latin culture gang of her hometown. Every autumn, the city celebrates the reoccupation of Santa Fe by the Spanish in 1692 by holding a two-week-long fiesta. On the Thursday before the final weekend, the Fiesta Council visited Poppy's elementary school, and while a sixteen-piece mariachi band played, the king, queen, and their court danced with the schoolchildren. The council visits my school annually too, and it's definitely a festive affair (and a "cultural" reason to cancel classes), yet for Poppy this year, the royal court's entrance could be rivaled only by the King of White Guys coming down the chimney three months later.

"Dad, it was so exciting," Poppy said while I drove her home after school. London rode next to her, happily focused on a male-gender toy from McDonald's. "You should have seen *la reina*," she said.

"Reindeer? What reindeer?" London asked, turning his attention from his Happy Meal motorcycle toward the window, expecting to see Rudolph steering the Subaru next to us.

"*La reina*, not reindeer. It means 'queen,'" Poppy explained in a condescending tone. "*Dios mío!*" she exclaimed like a grandmother, the back of her hand pressed dramatically to her pale forehead. "Anyway, she wore a crown and a white dress. And Don Diego—"

"Tiego? I know Tiego," London said.

"How do you know Don Diego de Vargas?" Poppy asked in an accent that reeked of Corinthian leather.

"From *Dora the Explorer*. On TV, silly." He was referring to Diego, the vine-swinging boy on one of those cartoons that attempts to make kids multicultural through the painful use of repetition and catchy jingles.

"*Pobrecito*," she said, patting London's knee. "That's not what I'm talking about. Don Diego resettled Santa Fe in 1692 without shedding one drop of blood. Pretty good, huh, Dad?" she asked, looking at me via the rearview mirror.

"No blood for a conquistador is pretty damn good, I must admit," I answered, and tried to hurry home. I didn't want to inform Poppy that all these foreign words made crackers like us nervous.

Saturday was Poppy's coming-out party for her "down with the brown" debut. My daughter and the rest of her Junior Girl Scout troop donned colorful fiesta dresses, placed freshly cut flowers and colorful ribbons in their hair, and wrapped paper roses around wrists and ankles. The half-dozen girls led the Children's Pet Parade, each holding an American flag except for my daughter. She had lobbied the Girl Scout leader to hold the flag of her home state, a yellow square with a striking red *zia* symbol—stolen from an Indian tribe—in the center.

Lala, London, and I found a patch of sidewalk in front of an art gallery on Palace Avenue, parked the stroller, and waited for Poppy to arrive followed by a troop of older Scouts and your run-of-the-mill off-key high school marching band. We could hear the music coming from the plaza, highlighted by the chirps of sirens from cops on flashing motorcycles. About a half block away, I could see the white lace of the fiesta dresses glow against a colorful backdrop of banners, costumes, and the fur of various household pets.

"Here she comes," I called to Lala and London. My wife had the camera poised, ready to snap the photos we would send to family all over the country, furthering their idea of Santa Fe as a mystical city that is both child-friendly and happily ethnic. A place where a kid like Poppy could lose some of the whiteness that kept me so naive and sheltered most of my childhood and young adult life. As the troop approached, I spotted my daughter proudly holding the state flag, marching with the carriage of *la reina*. Her back was perfectly straight, her head was erect, and a regal smile covered her face. Every five steps (I counted), she would release her right hand and wave majestically to the crowd.

"Hold on. I want to get closer," Lala said out loud in an odd bit of self-narration. Luckily I knew her sentence really meant "Make sure London doesn't pick up dog shit and eat it." She muscled her way off the curb onto the street. "Poppy!" Lala called, waving frantically, as our daughter grew closer. "Hold on a second. Look over here." It was as if Poppy had no idea that the *pinche gringa* in short hair and baseball cap shouting her name was the person who had given her life. Our daughter did not stop, slow down, or break the pace that she set from the beginning of her promenade. All Lala received was an up-close view of the screw-in-a-lightbulb wave that queens employ when dealing with their adoring masses.

"What the hell?" Lala called, shooting me a look.

"You mean *dios mío*!" I said, blocking London from a Great Dane's recent colon catastrophe.

The way Poppy's going, I think she'll get sick of living with us ethnocentric Anglos and will move out of the house by middle school. I can see her now, far more culturally aware than I was as a teen in Connecticut surrounded by cake eaters in plaid pants and shirts with alligators on them. My little Nueva Mexicana, dressed in a Che Guevara T-shirt, a dog-eared copy of *The Words of Cesar Chavez* tucked under her arm, will bust my white ass by asking political questions like whether the raisins I bought for London came from union grapes. Sitting in front of the *telenovelas* on TV, she'll whine about her *vida loca* of algebra, geography, and New Mexican history. I will only half listen as Poppy will mention her new boyfriend, someone named Puppet or Little Puppet. Instead, I'll lean back on the couch and think how wonderful a cucumber sandwich would taste right now.

Burning Questions

I'm driving London to the Bicentennial Pool for one last swim before they close for the season. I anticipate we will be the only parent/kid combo in the tot pool, since other toddlers have started preschool, day care, or playgroups, so I do not race over the newly installed speed humps on our little *paseo*. While New Orleans braces for transformation from the Big Easy into the Big Squeegee, Santa Fe is having a classic Indian summer, with afternoon temperatures in the low eighties. The only hint of autumn is crispness in the morning and the overnight invasion of a Halloween aisle in my local grocery store.

London, neatly tucked in swim diaper and suit, sings happily to a surfing CD we picked up on Maui when we visited Lala's family in June. Even our minivan soundtrack reeks of a lingering summer. Near the intersection of Paseo de la Conquistadora and Camino Alire (try spelling those names to AT&T customer service), we spot a single tennis shoe dangling from a telephone wire.

"Da-da," London calls from the backseat. "A shoe!"

"Yes, it is a shoe. Good eyes," I say, shooting back the positive parental retort.

"Where's the other shoe?" he asks.

If London were my first kid, I would have conjured up a story of a magical sneaker that becomes disenchanted with the whole cross-trainer movement and heads to Niketown to find CEO Philip H. Knight and ultimately his true sole mate. Or I'd ask London open-ended questions about where he thought the absent footwear might have gone, stimulating his own sense of inquiry. Maybe I'd string together a rap, rhyming *shoe* with *doo-doo*, humor that would slay my audience of one. But I don't attempt any of these things. I just stare at him in the little child-view mirror clipped to the visor over the dash. My mouth hangs open like a lobotomy victim. I'm paralyzed because I've been down this road before with Poppy. My son is about to enter the who-what-where-why level of development known to my friends as the "little investigative reporter" stage. With that one question, the summer of innocence is now over and the fall of interrogation has begun.

Some adults say the hardest thing about parenting is the questions their children ask. "Why is the sky blue and the sunset red?" shocks us all the first time (hint: it has to do with colored light, wavelengths, and electromagnetic forces), and these inquiries get even more complex, ranging from the origin of our species to existentialist matters such as what God wears to bed and why gerbils so happily eat their young. Then there are the more personal and frightening queries of where babies come from, when Daddy will die, and the whopper Poppy unloaded on me recently: "What is rape?" Makes you want to cut out your own tongue with infant nail clippers.

Many moms and dads are at a loss as to how to appropriately respond to these unending lines of questioning. How do we deliver answers that won't oversimplify the issue, offer information impossible for their minds to comprehend, or keep them up all night waiting for the Amber Alert to sound? Since we don't want to get the anti–John Kerry "flip-flop" cheer from our own vertically challenged constituency, parents usually find one narrow philosophy of retort and stick to it no matter what happens. Here are a few response categories I've noticed as a parent and teacher:

Forensic experts answer every question based on the most recent scientific research and spend hours on Google locating the precise terminology in pursuit of empirical truth. Their children are usually pencil-packing Myrons who, at the age of four, speak a lot like George Will. Since manners or social graces have been ignored in favor of higher truths, these kids don't know that one doesn't comment on Auntie Ruth's constant consumption of Seagram's until after she has passed out.

Forensic potty talk goes something like this: "I need to unzip my trousers, retrieve my penis and testicles, and urinate into the nearest sanitary ware."

Fairy-tale spinners try to cushion the blow of cognitive and social development through the creation of intricate and magical stories. Their children commonly dress like wood nymphs well into their forties, ask pears for permission before eating them, and end up driving cars with birds' nests and crystals glued to the dash and bumpers plastered with stickers announcing belief in magick, angels, and *Star Trek* as a religious calling.

Potty talk: "My inner dragon needs to fly from his toothy cave and spit golden blessings upon the marble waterworld."

The **rest of us** wallow in the middle ground, trying to meet each question on its own terms with a blend of honesty, caring, and relativity. What that means in my family is that my wife is too busy to read Freud or use the Internet to find the names of every mountain in New Mexico. And me? I don't want any answer to get in the way of my love for a good steak and a shot of tequila. So our responses are not unlike those of a hungover teacher who forgot to prep for class. We offer a lot of awkward silences, "What do you think?" and "I'll get back to you." Children, in my case London, aren't so easily swayed by our ineptness, even in the face of fire.

Santa Fe is host to one of the largest pagan rituals in the country. On the Thursday night before the final weekend of Fiesta, forty thousand people descend upon Fort Marcy Park to watch a fifty-foot-tall effigy named Zozobra, or "Old Man Gloom," burn. The tradition started in 1924 when a man named Will Schuster gathered fellow artists and friends in his backyard to celebrate the end of the summer and to get rid of any bad feelings or thoughts before the beginning of autumn. He based his flammable idea on a Mexican Indian tradition of burning an effigy of Judas with firecrackers, which, in this age of 12-step programs, would be too unforgiving for a guy who really made only one mistake.

We've skipped the last few burnings of Zozobra since London was born three years ago. Lala and I didn't like the mix of an infant, massive crowds, and pyrotechnics. Oh, and someone was fatally shot after the celebration a few years back, which sobered our enthusiasm a bit as well. This year my daughter, Poppy, begged us to attend, even though the festivities would take place after soccer practice and would cause her to stay up very late on a school night. She's really been enjoying her New Mexican up-bringing lately—marching in the *Desfile de los Niños* in a colorful fiesta dress, cooking corn in the *horno* with her Hispanic friend Katarina, and boldly requesting tamales in Italian chain restaurants.

We loaded kids, a stroller, and a bag containing flashlights, snacks, pepper spray, drinks, and extra clothing in our minivan and drove a mile to the parking lot of a nearby shopping center. As soon as we got out of the car, I could feel that the City Different was in a party different kind of mood. Santa Fe is a major tourist destination, and the population can swell to over four times its usual size during the summer months, when Texas gets too torrid and the only entertainment available in the Lone Star state is watching cows and armadillos explode from the heat. In September, when Fiesta takes place, the Santa Feans feel as if they are owed something for putting up with gridlocked traffic, the infestation of big hair, and the constant mispronunciation of street names and menu items. Zozobra is like Mardi Gras with a serious grudge.

Hoots, hollers, and the anthem *"Viva la Fiesta"* echoed in the jammed parking lot. Most people dressed in black even though Fiesta is an otherwise colorful celebration during the day. The attire reflected the tonal combination of rock concert and funeral procession that Zozobra encourages. Yet, as any parent knows, wearing black at night is just a nonverbal cue for a car to hit you so we chose white. Everyone in Santa Fe has their own agenda, a friend of mine once told me. On our walk toward the burning of Old Man Gloom, a gangbanger in an Oakland Raiders shirt marched next to a slight woman advertising that President Bush is a "chump ass punk." Militant Christians stood at a red light with lesbian trapeze artists; punk rockers rubbed safety-pinned shoulders with aides from Governor Richardson's office. You'd think that these disparate groups marched together in search of peace and solidarity, but, like our foreign policy, they were only united in the future destruction of a common enemy.

I pushed London in his umbrella stroller while he gazed at the glow sticks and light-pulsing necklaces hawked by unlicensed vendors. Poppy marched ahead with Lala, eager to catch the pre-burn show of "Glooms"—kids dressed in white sheets representing the worries or bad feelings that burning Zozobra will make disappear. We decided to split up—invoke man-to-man defense—since trying to navigate a stroller in the dense crowd near the stage was like a Louie Anderson trying to pedal a tricycle in a Tokyo subway car during rush hour. Lala and I naively took Poppy into the throng when she was barely a year old, and I spent the whole time covering her ears and deflecting the bottles, falling drunks, and wine-colored vomit that cascaded our way.

The female side of our family melted into the crowd while London and I pushed on toward the northeast gate of the park to watch with the other protective parents, claustrophobics, and cheapskates who didn't want to cough up ten bucks to the Kiwanis Club, a group that still lists the Golden Rule as its highest virtue. Our vantage point offered a profile view of Zozobra, the fifty-foot ghost with a nose like Karl Malden's, Groucho Marx's eyebrows, and thick red lips like two bloodworms. We ran into one of London's friends, Malcolm, who was there with his mother, Debra, and her other two children.

"Will London be afraid?" Debra asked me, stringing a green glow necklace around Malcolm's neck. Her other two kids had run to the hurricane fence, stuck their fingers into the holes, and started shaking it violently in anticipation of the burning. Debra is a reputable attorney in town and had posed a good question, one I hadn't had a chance to consider during my week of faculty meetings, Brownie gatherings, and other hurried child activities. Only an hour before, I had coached Poppy's soccer team, and the bulk of our practice time had been spent learning proper names so they would stop calling each other "fat kid" and "butt-munch" before they passed the ball.

I guess I looked as stupid as I felt, because Debra offered a lawyerly follow-up: "Don't you think you should prepare him for what's to come?"

"I guess you're right," I said. Just then, the initial volley of fireworks exploded, shooting long strings of orange and red into the sky. The Kiwanis Club's puppet master tugged on Zozobra's wires so that his hands, one molded into a fist and the other making a peace sign, seemed to be flashing gang signs to the already pumped-up crowd. His head rocked slightly from side to side the way my dad's does when he's trying to fit in at a rock concert. London jumped a bit after the detonation, so I picked him up and held his body close to mine. "Did that surprise you?" I whispered into his ear, not inviting the word *scared* into the conversation until necessary.

"Uh-huh," he said, nodding.

"You see that guy?" I said, pointing to Old Man Gloom. I could tell Debra was listening to my handling of the topic, since her son had already been briefed and was busy biting his necklace. "Well, you see, he's not really a guy. He's a puppet."

"A puppet. Whose puppet?" London asked, referring to the hands-up-the-ass style of *fantoccino* we practiced at home.

"Well," I explained (knowing that when I start my sentences

with *well*, I am in deep shit), "he's not really a puppet. Um ..." I was losing my train of thought. "He's just not real, OK?" I prayed London would magically or stupidly accept my answer. I wondered if having a slow kid had its advantages at times like these.

"His hands, Dada." London gestured toward the stage. For a guy who wasn't alive, Zozobra's mitts sure were gesticulating wildly. "He looks real," London said.

"He's not, though," I said weakly. Then the moaning started. As the fire grows closer to Old Man Gloom, he groans loudly. As any decent pyromaniac knows, it's not as much fun to burn something if it doesn't cry out in agony. It's all part of the fun.

"He's crying," London said.

"He's not really crying," I explained like Johnny Dictionary. "He's moaning, actually."

"Huh?" He didn't recognize the word.

"It's like crying but it's different."

"Why is he boning?" he asked.

"Not boning, moaning," I said, and stifled a laugh. Debra, in her silver Nike shoes and Juicy Couture velour, eyeballed me. "It's because he's gloomy," I explained.

"Gloomy?"

"Like a ghost."

"A ghost? Like Casper?" Two fireballs erupted near Zozobra's feet. "Fire!" London yelled, then went back to our subject. "I like Casper, Dada. He's nice."

"He's not like Casper. Zozobra's not real."

"Is Casper real?" London's face squished like a dishrag. He was thoroughly confused now. I was doing a fine job.

"No, Casper's a cartoon. On TV." I thought I'd have to explain about cathode-ray tubes, electron beams, and what's inside a Teletubby, but luckily Zozobra saved me by kicking it up a notch.

"He's boning louder now," London said.

"I know he is." Old Man Gloom rocked like a giant Joe Cocker, his moans turning into wails. Debra studied me intently, her short professional haircut framing an obvious scowl. I needed to hurry. "That's what I want to tell you. They are going to light him on fire."

"Why?"

That's a good fucking question, I thought. "Because people feel better. After the gloom burns, everyone is happy."

"Why come?" This expression was something Lala and I adored and even used ourselves. London had combined *why* and *how come* into his own unique and—I'll admit it—cute query. Sometimes after an enigmatic passage in *Hamlet,* I've even found myself asking the class, "Why come?" Last year, they all wrote on my evaluation that I should stop rocking the ganja.

"Because," I explained rationally, "all their worries and sadness are inside the puppet." The folks around us grew impatient and started suggesting that the burning begin. On the stage, two fire dancers twirled flaming batons, teasing the crowd by creeping closer to Zozobra, then backing away as if they had forgotten to turn off the oven at home. Since we were in the family section, I noticed all the little Beavises and Butt-Heads shaking their fists and mimicking the angry refrain. I started worrying about the unguarded blue-tipped matches in the drawer right next to our stove at home. "But you know, London," I said, "you shouldn't burn things, right?"

He had nothing to say about that.

All around us friends, coworkers, mothers and daughters, and fathers and sons chanted, "Burn him! Burn him! Burn him!" London's pal Malcolm, sitting atop his mother's shoulders, his mouth now stained with the glowing green liquid from his necklace, eagerly joined the chorus. Even Debra had surrendered to her inner pagan. Every January, in honor of Martin Luther King Jr., I teach eleventh graders about Emmett Till and the terrible history of lynching. There is a photo I pass around of a woman in a housecoat holding up her baby so that the child can see a black man burn. Even though Zozobra is not race-based and the ritual is designed to let go of negativity, not create it, my hands trembled as I hoisted London onto my shoulders. And when those two words burst from his lips, I felt as if my heart were the thing being torched.

We caught up to Lala and Poppy in front of the Masonic Temple on the corner where the Christians used to gather to shout at us for partaking in such a heathenistic party. This year they were noticeably absent, replaced by vendors yelling for us to buy their crap before the phosphorescence wore off. Lala and I instinctively changed places; she pushed London ahead and peppered him with questions: How did he like it? Was it too loud? Was he scared? I closed my hand around my daughter's and we walked side by side down the busy street.

"Look, Dad, I got this necklace." She held up a three-dimensional star amulet, hanging from a piece of purple string. A spectrum of colors pulsed and sparkled in the dark night, illuminating different parts of Poppy's glorious face. Behind us, the ravages of the ritual still lingered on. We could hear the jubilant voices of revelers whose night had only just begun and whose answers would be found later in a bottle, a pipe, or the arms of another. The air was thick with the smell of smoke and beer and sweaty bodies.

"That's cool," I said, cradling the amulet in my cupped palm.

I felt totally spent, fully exhausted from the event, yet I didn't want my daughter's curiosity for the world, or mine for that matter, to end. "How do you think they can make it do that?" I asked her, referring to the colors blinking in my hand.

"Dad," Poppy groaned. "You always ask the hardest questions."

We've Got a Runner

My friend Tom and I recently went out to dinner with our families to celebrate his new teaching job at a high school. We also gathered to commiserate over the fact that this new opportunity would force Tom, his wife, Katie, and daughter, Halle, to move sixty miles south to Albuquerque. The seven of us opted to dine at the Cowgirl Hall of Fame restaurant, and our largish group was seated in the back room, away from the crowded main floor and the smoky noise of the bar. Lala, Poppy, and Katie huddled around one end of the table, discussing Katie's new haircut and the stylist they all share, a guy named Jimmy who, after regrettably never making it as a rock star, channeled his theatrical talents toward a career even more snippy in nature. Jimmy, who cut my hair a few times, dresses like he just got bounced from Studio 54—satin shirts open at the chest, hip huggers, Beatle boots. His trademark move is to blow on his comb like it's the smoking barrel of a pistol before he shoves it into the custom leather holster he wears on his hip for "his ax, baby."

On the other end of the table, Tom and I manned the real kid duty. I always fill London's diaper bag with toys to amuse, distract, and confuse, just so I'm able to sit down for a half hour and enjoy 12 ounces of liquid Prozac. London's good for at least twenty minutes if you don't mind flying Harold the Helicopter around salt and pepper towers with your left hand while your right pours Lone Star down yer gullet, as they say out West. Halle, with her light hair, big head, and rosy cheeks, is worse than London when it comes to sitting still in restaurants. She'll stop moving for maybe nine minutes before it's clear that she's got somewhere else to be.

"Yeah, they gave me three thousand dollars as a moving allowance. Can you beat that?" Tom said, dipping a chip into the monkey dish of Texas caviar—black-eyed peas drowning in a spicy jalapeño salsa. Tom is originally from Athens, Georgia, and although he's six foot four, he has the voice, demeanor, and higher education of someone far less imposing. His goofiness has made him the most popular teacher wherever he's worked. One year he didn't have a costume for Halloween and his students kept bugging him about being lame, so he grabbed a ruler, pressed it to his scalp, and told everyone he was Crazy Ruler Head in a pitch-perfect hillbilly accent. He won first prize in the faculty category, beating all the other teachers who chose that day to reveal their secret love for cross-dressing and bestiality.

"It's odd," Tom said, speaking of his new job. Teachers smell a rat when people pretend to respect them. "They are all so nice to me. I don't really get it, to tell you the truth." While Tom was talking and I was chugging along, Halle crept closer to London, seated safely across from her. Tom and I have always hoped that the two of them would someday entertain each other (without the use of Krazy Glue) so we could finish a drink and a conversation all in one sitting. London saw Halle approaching and quickly gathered his trains into a clump near his chest.

"She's not going to steal your engines," I reassured him, and sure enough, I was right. As soon as Halle got to the end of the table, she tore out of the room like a shrunken purse snatcher.

"We've got a runner," Tom announced, threw back the rest of his Cutthroat Porter, and slid along the wall toward the place where his daughter had exploded out of the blocks.

"Christ," Katie swore from the other side as she watched Tom exit stage right. "Man, I never thought we'd have a child who should be put on a leash. Remember that kid at Christmas? At the mall?"

Everyone nodded, even Poppy. The seven of us had gone en masse to the Villa Linda Mall to get our kids' picture taken with Santa under the big cardboard tree. Lala had scoped out the three St. Nicks in Santa Fe and decided that this one, even though he refused to muss his hair by donning the hat, was the lowest on the creepy-Santa scale—the least likely to overenjoy his job, if you get my drift. Our two families waited in line, grouped the same way as at the Cowgirl dinner. Tom and I held Halle and London, trying to convince them that sitting on some strange old man's lap in front of an angry photographer was a completely normal American holiday tradition.

"But he's got a mushbeard," London said. Somehow in his tiny brain, London had scrambled mustache and beard into one convenient term for his facial hair phobia.

In front of us, a family of three huddled around their fourth, a boy about five years old, who was tethered to a nylon harness that engulfed his upper torso. Once we all realized we had a real live leash kid within touching distance, we couldn't take our eyes off him. Leash Kid pulled hard on his halter, running in circles trying to tangle up his father. The dad/owner had experience with such tether trickery, sidestepping each pass with the ease of a double Dutch expert. Leash Kid then snapped at the hatless Santa, who was busy providing lapness for a toothless girl with pigtails.

"He's like Stitch," London said, pointing at little Harnessed Harry. Stitch is the alien with ADHD who stars in an animated movie set in Hawaii, a place that, at least in this movie, seems to allow the odd and unusual treatment of small creatures.

The line moved and it was then Leash Family's laptime. The dad unbuckled the shoulder and chest restraints while the mother held Leash Kid's shoulders. Dad, holding up one finger, scurried over to the photographer. You didn't need to be Dr. Phil to figure out that he was saying that they had only one chance to get this photo right. Sister of Leash Kid sat on one thigh while her brother took the other; they both smiled, the flash went off, and so did the kid, sprinting off Santa's shelf onto the AstroTurf below. If the North Pole hadn't had a gate, the junior escapee would have been well past menswear at J. C. Penney by the time the hyperventilating father caught him.

When Tom returned to the table, his face was Georgia Bulldawg red. He had little Halle in his arms, and she was crying furiously. "She almost made it to the street this time," he said, which meant she'd navigated through the next room, around barflies seated and staggering, and onto the brick patio.

"She might not make a bad cartographer," I said to him.

"That or a sprinter. She sure is lightnin' fast," he said, trying to calm Halle down by stroking her hair. "I used to think parents who bridled their kids were abusive, but now I'm beginning to see the light."

"Amen," Katie said, ordering a shot of Cuervo Gold.

I can't count any leashers as friends, but I know a fair number of runners, dashers, and wanderers. My brother Eddie's daughter, Marcy, is a wanderer. A few days into our family reunion two years ago, Eddie and I were standing near the water's edge in Corolla, North Carolina. Eddie's wife, Sandy, ironically doesn't enjoy the feeling of her name on her feet, so my brother brought his daughter out to play with her cousin, London, who sat burying my tootsies in two holes I had dug to keep him occupied. Down the beach, Poppy collected shells with my older brother, Rich, and his two daughters. Eddie was telling me about his recurring role on the most popular drive-time radio program in Orlando. He plays a character called Eddie the Shaman, a mystical freak who attempts to educate the conservative host and his lackeys on the finer points of spirituality, transcendence, and the use of essential oils when scolding your inner child in a darkened room.

"So I'm doing this thing about smudging, you know smudging, dude, you live in freakin' Santa Fe, baby. I'm talking about how smudging is the common name for the sacred smoke bowl blessing. The all-powerful cleansing technique from the Native American tradition? And the guys start playing fart noises and cuckoo sounds in the background."

"Fart noises?"

"Yeah, they think it's funny." He shrugged.

"Doesn't that bug you?"

"Nah, it's all good. Don't bother me none, brother. People laugh and then they call the station to hire me to marry them, which is *beaucoup dólares* for me, Master Kai."

Before I could ask why fart noises would make someone want to hire my brother, who is not really a shaman, to marry them, I spotted Marcy ambling down the beach. I checked my kids: Poppy was safely fighting over a silver dollar shell with her cousin Maddie, while London entombed my feet, his face now covered with sand so he looked like a leper baby. It's August and we're on one of the premier beaches in the continental United States. Families have pitched tents, raised canopies, unfolded elaborate reclining chairs, and are now drinking beers, tossing Frisbees, and pretending skin cancer was, like Y2K, way overrated.

"So, dude, check this out," Eddie continued, clapping his hands. "I show up at the Disney Pavilion dressed as Eddie the Shaman—beads, tie-dye—to marry this suh-weet couple, Bob and Linda. Bob is a CPA, but he's seen, like, eleven hundred Dead shows—"

"Eddie," I interrupted, "Marcy's down the beach."

"She does that, the Binks," he said, using his pet name for her. Then he glanced over to the scene of the impending crime. "Hold on. Marcy! Marcy!" he yelled through cupped hands.

Marcy turned back briefly but couldn't locate the origin of the call. She looked up into the sky, spotted a seagull, smiled, and then continued on toward some unknown location.

Nothing fazes Crazy Eddie. "Yeah, so I met with Bob and Linda at their house like a week before and they are so cool, but they've got no clue what they want to do about vows. So, you know what I do?"

"Smudge them?"

"No, but that's a good idea, Einstein. I whip out these other vows I wrote for a wedding I did at the celebrity skeet shoot. Kazaa, baby!" he said, then exploded his palms like Doug Henning.

Marcy, not wanting to mess with a band of Florida State frat brothers gulping beer out of a kitchen funnel, veered left toward the ocean. Without her floaties, Marcy cannot swim a lick. I checked my kids again. London had noticed his cousin's course and was chewing nervously on the sandy head of his shovel.

"Eddie?"

"I know, dude, it's killer. Two hundred simoleons to chill out with all these beautiful rockers. Boo-ya!"

The water was licking Marcy's waist, yet she was as happy as the clams she was about to meet. I estimated her to be about two hundred yards from me, so I prepared myself to run, but London had done a damn good job of fitting me for a pair of wet sand shoes.

"Eddie, look!" To make up for my paralysis, I yelled as loud as I could.

"Oh, shit," he said, and took off. My brother is well over six feet tall and tips the scale after the 200-pound mark. He still has a bit of red left in his hair from when he was a kid. Eddie does nothing in a small way. He tore across the shoreline, knocking people to the side, yelling "Sorry, dude!" as he pushed past. The splash he created once he hit the water equaled the entrance of the entire Polar Bear Club of New York City. London peered at me in disbelief, then walked back up the beach to his towel, away from the Wilder brother madness, into the calm waiting arms of his mother, who has learned over time to keep a safe distance.

Eddie pulled his little Ophelia out of the drink and, like

Halle, she started to cry. I guess she didn't want him to intrude on her right to drown.

"I don't know how you do it," I told Eddie.

"It's all good, dude. It's all good," he said as he hoisted his dripping child onto his sunburned shoulders.

The best runners I've ever seen are two boys named Mark and Mikey. They belong to my friend Harry, who, along with his wife, Grace, hail from England. A travel writer by trade, Harry is always dragging his family and friends on some crazy adventure or another. When his family lived in Santa Fe, he decided that it would be a good idea for all eight of us to travel together on an overnight visit to Acoma Pueblo, 60 miles west of Albuquerque. Known as "Sky City," the pueblo is situated on a 367-foot-high sandstone rock, the perfect height for kids like Mark and Mikey to fall from.

We caravaned our minivan and station wagon and arrived at the Sky City hotel and casino late in the afternoon. Even though it was only 120 miles from Santa Fe, we were hindered by the constant snack, potty, and vomit breaks our kids so enjoyed. When traveling with small kids, a friend of mine once told me, double the time it takes to get somewhere. He wasn't just referring to long trips, either. After his daughter learned to move, it took him two hours to walk to his next-door neighbor's to borrow a wrench.

Outside of Albuquerque or Santa Fe, New Mexico runs on a different time than the rest of the country. After waiting in line for an hour to check into the hotel, the kids were famished, so we opted to eat at the Huwak'a Restaurant's all-you-can-eat buffet, located inside the casino. Mark and Mikey are rambunctious boys, to put it mildly. They are the kind of kids who make other kids nervous. Mikey is the older brother, with dark hair and pointy ears and eyebrows. Mark's hair had yet to come in, and the combination of his bald head and thick body made him look like a mini Telly Savalas. Mikey was the brains and Mark the brawn. Even Poppy, who is pretty even-tempered, would hide her favorite toys before the duo visited. She even went so far as to suggest our childproofing was insufficient after Mark cut up her last copy of *Goodnight Moon* with a steak knife. After a string of broken guitars, plates, and noses, she demanded that we always meet the boys at a neutral location with easy-to-find fire exits.

The line at the buffet was as long as the one at the front desk. It was obvious that the staff couldn't keep up with the hordes of customers. Dirty dishes remained at tables waiting to be cleared. Bus tubs overflowed on gray carts. It got to the point where people who were waiting to be seated started offering to wash dishes.

"I've got to go to the loo," Harry said, and dashed off in search of a bathroom. I cradled London in my arms while Lala held hands with Poppy. Then I saw something that I could not believe. Noticing that his father's absence had changed their parents' defense from man-to-man to zone, Mikey whispered, "Let's go," into his brother's ear. Mark smiled and nodded, and they both started running—in opposite directions. Mikey headed in the direction of the casino floor, while Mark mucked his way toward the rooms of the hotel.

A million things raced through my mind, the beat of my heart matching the manic bells and whistles of the army of one-armed bandits nearby. *This is a parent's worst nightmare,* I remember thinking, *losing a kid in a crowded place.*

"Oh, bloody fucking hell," Grace said in language uncharacteristic of her proper English speech. She did a double take that reminded me of Scooby Doo in the cartoon of the same name. Her husband was gone. Which one to go after? Out of instinct, I dropped London into Lala's arms and pointed toward the casino. As fast as she could in a long skirt, Grace darted after Mark. Deep into the heart of the casino I ran, trying to spot Mikey's little Vulcan ears and worrying about being tackled by beefy security guards just itching for a reason to kick someone's ass.

Harry, Grace, and the boys live in England now, but if they were still here I'd tell them about Digital Angel, a new tracking device designed for "wanderers such as children and Alzheimer's patients." Using satellite GPS systems, mobile communications, and biometric technology, you can now buy a watch that will keep track of your little runners, errant livestock, and even nuclear waste that ends up in Roswell instead of Carlsbad where it belongs, damn it. In the future, we won't even have to worry about Halle, Marcy, Mikey, or Mark ripping off the electronic Big Brother and strapping it to the family dog, since Digital Angel has acquired the patent rights to a miniature digital receiver that allows implant wearers to emit a homing beacon. Now you will always be able to find your little Johnny Mnemonic as he moves from school to the smoke shop and into rehab.

I didn't know that the angels I was praying to that day at Sky City were digital as I bobbed and weaved around old ladies playing nickel slots and cowboys from Old Horse Springs hoping to roll eight the hard way. All I knew was when I caught up with Mikey, he'd be lucky if he only got leashed.

Mrs. Piggle-Wiggle
Hot-Sauces the Baby Jesus

My daughter, Poppy, is close to finishing the Mrs. Piggle-Wiggle series of children's books. The stories, written in the 1940s and '50s by Betty MacDonald, center around a hunchbacked yet friendly spinster who uses creative and sometimes magical solutions to various children's behavior problems. The plot of these tales is usually the same: May O'Toole has a smart mouth, or Hubert Prentis won't clean up his room, so the mother of the ne'er-do-well phones Mrs. Piggle-Wiggle, who prescribes odd and, by our present parenting standards, abusive cures that include scare tactics, mild starvation, and the use of illegal tropical birds. Whether Mrs. Piggle-Wiggle is at her upside-down house in town or visiting a farm, she finds unique ways to get children to eat their radishes, clean their rooms, and freely share their postwar balls and skates. These books are satisfying reads for kids ages six to ten because of their simple problem/solution structure. No cliffhangers, no lingering nightmares, no homosexuals or minorities. Definitely no minority homosexuals. When viewed through the wrinkled eyes of a parent, though, disbelief in this scenario sets in pretty quickly. The only people who could believe in such remedies would be the ones who don't have or know children, or men like my father, who've been out of the child-rearing game since the invention of unleaded gas.

My father, Ben Franklin Wilder, is a kind and generous man who sends all his daughters-in-law cards with checks on their birthdays, Mother's Day, and even Valentine's Day. However, like other men of his generation who survived a few wars, a few presidents, and the hardship-story-producing Depression, he likes to simplify complicated matters in order to (stealing a line from *The Great Gatsby*) have the world stand "at a sort of moral attention forever." He's not unlike Mrs. Piggle-Wiggle in his intent, except my father's cures are far simpler and not very funny, and his hump hasn't fully grown in yet. Years ago, when Poppy was cutting teeth, I called my dad about another matter—an upcoming visit or to borrow money—and he heard his first grandkid wailing in the background. "What's wrong with that child?" he asked, having already digressed from the reason I called to reading me some letter he wrote to the editor of his local paper, offering a solution to the city's parking problem that included senior citizens with shiny badges, helmets, and stun guns.

"Oh, she's just teething. No big deal." Stupidly, I shrugged even though he couldn't see me. That's the effect the old man has.

"Rub a little vodka on her gums," he suggested.

"Are you serious?" I asked. I'd heard about this cure before but thought it went out of style when cigarette advertising was banned from television.

"Worked for you."

There is no way to verify whether he actually performed any of his remedies on the four of us Wilder boys. My mother's been dead for twenty years now, and my older brother, Rich, would have been three when my dad pickled my pink tooth holders with Smirnoff. I don't want to believe him, yet he did have a well-stocked liquor cabinet full of booze for his post-work Beefeater Gibsons and for his Friday night "we're all good Catholics, let's eat fish and get polluted" parties.

In his active parenting days, my father belonged to the school that believed if you yell at something loud and long enough, you can get that thing—child, monkey, waiter—to behave. Big Ben has a booming voice, deep and operatic, which when combined with the profanity picked up in his hometown of Queens and during a stint in the navy makes him a powerful force to be reckoned with. The day after my brother and I decided to try a new word for procreation on the telephone operator, I went to my neighbor's house to play with my friend Chris. His family saw me coming across their yard and gathered at the head of their porch.

"What'd you do this time?" Chris asked, one eye closed.

"Whaddya mean?"

" 'Fess up," his father said, dying to know the whole story. "We heard Ben blow."

My dad was an equal-opportunity yeller and shouted at all four of his boys: Rich for crashing his Chrysler Sebring into a telephone pole, Tom for waking up in the bushes after his own

Friday night party, Eddie for getting caught holding a dime bag when the police pulled over his buddy's conversion van. He'd scream at my friends for mistakes we made and mistakes we had yet to enjoy. My friend Todd burned donuts on our lawn in his Firebird because he figured since Ben would yell at him anyway, why not well relish the sod-kicking ride?

My dad's ultimate solution to our antics was a weapon originally made for stirring sauces. The dreaded wooden spoon had a slightly triangular head and a hole bored on the middle like a great seeing eye. Mostly Ben would just threaten us with the power of pine, but once in a while, he'd take it out of the drawer where it slept with the other more peaceful cutlery and start the whacking. I don't believe corporal punishment taught me anything redeeming about behavior or morality. I learned to use sissy fronts like drama club and Cub Scouts to hide my delinquency. I knew my brother Rich did gain something when I saw him packing tongs and a salad spinner for his upcoming gang fight.

I can only recall a handful of times when my dad spooned our asses, but if you talk to him about how parents today indulge their kids, he will convince you he had us in thumbscrews and iron maidens 24-7. Dad recently stayed with my family for two weeks. Even though I realized such a living arrangement would present challenges, I want my children to know their grandfather in ways I never knew my own. I don't want their memories to be limited to a wooden cane, a bearskin rug, and conversation based on a "don't ask, don't tell" policy.

Things were running smoothly for the first few days of my dad's sojourn. We had given him our bed, and I assigned him daily household tasks so he'd feel useful and to prevent him from finding the time to write letters to the editor of our local paper about making English the official language of New Mexico. On the third day, London decided not to take his nap. Until then, Ben and his grandson had been good pals. The boy showed the old man his fifty-two trains, and Grandpa tried to teach him the mechanical and historical difference between a steam engine and one that ran on diesel fuel.

"Die-sel," my dad would overenunciate to his grandson.

"No, Thom-as," London would correct him, and then point to the shit-eating grin on the train's faceplate.

London is fairly good-natured when he's well rested. He's sweet to adults, has a good sense of humor, and is content with the toys, games, and siblings we have lying around the house. If he doesn't nap, we hide the sharp objects, because that makes him mean, belligerent, and he looks a bit like the possessed doll, Chucky. Around three o'clock, it was clear London wouldn't go down, not even after a ride in the car, a really dull video starring Piglet (a character who, like Joey on *Friends*, should have stayed a sidekick), and my dad's long story about petitioning his condo board to install a new sprinkler system. I denied London something, a cookie or his civil rights, and he tore around the house like his hair was on fire. I'm talking, screaming up and down the hall for twenty minutes. My dad, upon viewing this dramatic display, crossed his arms in front of his barrel chest, plunked down on the couch, and began to stew.

"What's wrong?" I asked him.

"I cannot stand the disrespect," he said.

I explained to him the idea that if you know the cause of the tantrum, in this case fatigue, then the crying is unimportant— it's not deliberate, it's chemical. You don't blame the addict; you blame the problem. Or as my friend Hip-Hop Joe Ray would say, "Don't hate the playa, hate the game." On past occasions like this one, London would run around until he either tired himself out, realized we were ignoring him, or the neighbors called the cops. I didn't tell my father that I often drown out London's cries with the first Clash album or AC/DC's anthemic *Back in Black*— my dad is more of a Duke Ellington fan, so he wouldn't understand.

Ben wasn't convinced by the idea of a sensitive war on misbehavior.

"Unimportant, ha!" he scoffed.

"What would you have me do?" I asked him.

"I'd pour a bucket of cold water on his head."

I left the room and went into the kitchen, where I pounded out my frustrations on a chicken breast with a meat mallet (the wooden spoon stings but does not tenderize properly). As predicted, London sprinted himself into a snot-filled frenzy and then passed out facedown in the bathroom just like a little Courtney Love, complete with a puddle of spittle by his head. The house was now quiet, yet my father had not budged from his nettled nest. His arms were still crossed, and his lips jutted out in a pout. Lala came out of her studio to use the bathroom and saw my dad stone-faced on our couch, then London sprawled on the tile, and delayed her quest in order to question her husband, who was busy banging the shit out of a dead bird's boob.

"I have two questions," she stated calmly.

"Unh," I grunted, and whacked away.

"What is London doing on the bathroom floor?"

"Sleeping."

"What is your father doing on the couch?"

"Sulking."

"Don't you think you should talk to him?"

Now, my wife is from a family of women—she has three sisters, and their mother raised them all. I have three brothers, and we were reared by my dad. It's like *The Brady Bunch*, only without the laugh track, and after thirty minutes our problems are rarely solved. The difference in the ways our families communicate is so vast, it's as if we are two different cultures from two different continents, existing eons apart. My family doesn't "share out our feelings" after an argument. Like other American males, we just stew in our own self-righteousness until a new distraction appears, like a Jets-Miami game on TV, a really loud fart, or the Beefsteak Charlie's all-you-can-peel-and-eat-shrimp buffet. That's how we renew and start fresh. But Lala had a point. I had been trying to work on my relationship with my dad, hence his visit, and I started teaching the next day, so Lala would be stuck with this cigar-store Indian sitting on her sofa.

"OK," I said reluctantly, dropping my hurt hammer and wiping the chicken flesh from my eyes and the face of my watch. I sat on the couch across from my dad and tried to think of something sensitive and strong, but all I could conjure was an image of the bearded hippie Rupert from *Survivor*.

"Can we talk?" These words felt like some foreign tongue tying my lips in knots.

"About what?" my dad asked. Only his mouth moved.

"What do you mean, about what?"

"I have no problems," he said.

"Look at you. You haven't budged." I pointed to his crossed legs. "Your Dockers are developing new pleats." I paused and took a cleansing breath. "About London."

"OK. I'll tell you. I just don't understand how you can sit there and allow that type of noncompliant behavior," he said.

"I already explained to you that it was unimportant. Look at him now." I thought of his head butted against the leaking toilet. "He's sleeping at least."

"What a load of bull."

"What would you have me do?"

"I already told you," he said. "Throw a bucket of cold water on him."

"You must be kidding."

"Worked with you."

Usually when my dad invents memories, like taking us skiing in New Hampshire or toilet-training us in a single day by making us wear horsehair underpants, I let it go. He's trying to keep his life story in a neat little package, and I figure what harm does it do if he exaggerates and moves us around in an ethereal Ford LTD station wagon to places we've never been on his memory's highway? But today was different. We were really talking now.

"So wait. Let me get this straight," I said. "You actually went outside, took a bucket from the shed, filled it with cold water, and poured it over my head when I was two or three?"

He diverted his eyes. "Maybe it was your brother Eddie."

"OK, so you took a bucket from the shed, filled it, and threw cold water onto poor little Eddie Spaghetti? And none of us would remember that?"

"Maybe it was a cup."

"So you took a cup from the cabinet, filled—"

"Will you please shut up?"

I don't blame my father or all the Mrs. Piggle-Wiggles in the world when they try to offer lucid solutions to complex problems. As our world gets harder to understand, we all yearn for the idea of a neat and tidy life aided by plain, no-nonsense answers. Last week in Espanola, New Mexico, just a *Simple Life* episode away from my house, a third-grade student was placed in handcuffs and locked in an adult jail cell because he wouldn't stop crying after some sort of criminal ball usage in PE. And recently I learned that Lisa Whelchel, former child star of the 1980s show *Facts of Life* and one of my first in a series of television crushes (my current is Jennifer Garner), advocates "hot-saucing" your kids if they misbehave. In her book *Creative Corrections: Extraordinary Ideas for Everyday Discipline*, Whelchel, a born-again Christian, says it's not a bad idea to dab your kid's tongue with Tabasco after lying or biting.

It seems to me that my former crush is a New Testament Mrs. Piggle-Wiggle using the Old Testament as a disciplinary primer. I imagine *Creative Corrections: Book Two* will include chapters like "Stop That Nasty Nose-Picking with Loving Locusts," and "Spanking: God's Gentle Nudge." If reading her book is not enough, Ms. Whelchel holds weekend seminars called "Mom Time Getaways" all over the country that combine crop-till-you-drop scrapbook sessions, pajama parties, *Facts of Life* reruns, and practical ways of disciplining your child that God himself used on his only son, Jesus. And look how well that little guy turned out!

I'm calling Mom Time Getaways today to see if my dad could attend one of the upcoming seminars in his area. He may be male and not really a Christian, but he's got this great idea about kids kneeling in gravel as a fail-safe cure for bed-wetting.

Sam, My Dad, and Me

Last Thanksgiving, my father took my daughter and me to Sam's Club, a place I've always been scared to enter. My dad is a loyal Sam's Club member, even though he's lived alone for over twenty years. In his five-room apartment in Sarasota, Florida, he has stockpiled enough food to feed all the people in his building for a month, and most of the meals would include five courses. He's the kind of guy who buys an oil drum of mayonnaise and stores it in his basement because he saw that he could save almost two bucks. When we were shopping for Thanksgiving dinner, he was on a mission to locate the cheapest price per pound for turkey in all of New Mexico. In fact, in the weeks prior to his arrival he sent me e-mails on the fluctuating poultry prices in Sarasota. At first, he'd send phrases like "Butterball 89 cents—how about that?" to which I had no reply. Then these frequent e-mails read like dropping stock quotes: 81, 75, 69, with multiple exclamation points to highlight a truly great price. He also told me that he'd heard (from where I have no idea) that there was a glut in the turkey market and prices would no doubt drop below a staggering 60 cents. You figure you only buy a turkey once, maybe twice a year, and we bought a sixteen-pound bird, so we saved like three bucks, but to my dad it was as if we purchased Microsoft before it went public.

My father is a tour guide at the Sarasota Opera House, and it's the perfect job for him. He talks, people listen. They ask questions, he knows all the answers. At Sam's Club, I was the idiot and he was the expert. He'd walk me over to a sixty-four-roll package of toilet paper, pat it knowingly, and declare, "Now, *this* is the bargain for your family."

"Where would I put all of it?" I'd ask, imagining having to build my children a two-story playhouse out of Charmin extra soft.

Dad waved me off because in Sam's Club, great discounts beat such trivial issues as storage, waste, decay, or arriving home with 51 pounds of cheddar cheese in blocks strapped to the roof of my minivan. Like a wholesale Willy Wonka, my dad showed me freeways of smoked salmon and thick ropes of pork loin, and asked if I needed an underwater TV, a ream of flannel shirts, or a gross of car batteries—Sam's had it all. Plus, since he had nicely gotten me what they called a "complimentary spousal membership," not only was I now married to my own father, a rarity even in New Mexico, but I also had a key to the promised land of savings.

In big stores like Sam's, my dad loves to work the crowd. He greets all the employees in English or poorly pronounced Spanish and comments freely on what's written on people's T-shirts and hats by saying things like "Go Cornhuskers!" or "You know, I hear it's raining in St. Louis." He educates people about the price differential between the Santa Fe Sam's and his home base in Sarasota. "We have the same bagels," he whispered to an overshopped man sweating behind us, "but I think they're a bit cheaper."

"You could call them on the cell and compare prices," I suggested, but he frowned at my joke because I obviously didn't know the good he was doing me. I didn't appreciate the value of Sam's Club, the same way the Native Americans didn't immediately recognize the value of a Christian God. While we waited in line with our bulldozer full of food, my dad spotted a lady about 125 years old who was wearing a hat that stuck to her head like a big droopy wedding cake. My dad left Poppy and me and walked across the slick industrial floor, all the while pointing at the old woman. She looked panicked.

"That is a great hat!" he shouted loudly, and I bet the woman soiled her Depend. I couldn't hear the conversation between my dad and the trembling centenarian, but Poppy and I were riveted by his shock-and-awe brand of friendship.

"I just made her day," Dad said upon his return, and I believed him. He made her day memorable in the way that heart attacks or car accidents often do.

I tell people that it's as if my dad is constantly running for mayor wherever he goes. It's not unusual for him to walk into a store in Santa Fe and yell, "Greetings from Sarasota, Florida," which not only startles the clerk but gives him pause about how to respond to such a vibrant and geographical greeting. I think my dad's passed on this über-gregariousness to all of his sons, and we should thank him for it. This trait has helped my older brother, Rich, amass great wealth and property by charming people into believing that data storage is both virtuous and un-limited. My younger brother Tom, though at first reticent in speech and manner, shows this larger-than-life style by for-warding jokes via e-mail that usually involve midgets and bodily fluids. My youngest brother, Eddie, who lives in Orlando, has perhaps inherited most of my father's dramatic essence by be-coming a star of stage, theme park, and the most dreary of middle-school teachers' lounges. As for me, I know that my stu-dents feel that my theatrics in the classroom make me just slightly less pathetic than most of their other high school teach-ers and slightly more unstable.

The funny thing is now that I have that little yellow card with the smudged picture of me no larger than my thumb, I've started to frequent Sam's. Not every week, mind you, but when the cup-board looks bare, I pass silly little Target and blah Albertson's on my way to the granddaddy of them all. Oddly, when I walk into the huge depository I feel the same mix of excitement and dread as I do when I step into a casino. I realize I'm not leaving without dropping some dough, but the ride just might be worth it. Now, there are some items I buy that even the stuffiest of shirts would agree are great deals: diapers, bottled water, frozen chicken nuggets. But I always walk away with a few things that have my dad's name written all over them and that drive Lala crazy. Sur-prisingly, most of these bargains come in gallon jugs. This last week it was hand soap and pancake syrup. Next week, who knows? Iodine and peanut oil? The possibilities seem as endless as the square footage inside Wal-Mart's younger but wiser brother.

When I drive across town to shop at Sam's, I cannot help but call my dad to bond. He's like my sponsor in AA, the only one who truly understands the valiant nature of my pilgrimage. Dad offers me recipes that will use up all thirty-six eggs before they go bad as well as advice on what new items to be on the look-out for.

"They've got this apple pie there now that would knock your eye out," he says excitedly.

"What?" I ask, still unfamiliar with the lingo of my new cult of consumer consumption.

"I'm telling you, it's as big as a truck's wheel and not so bad-tasting for four bucks. You can feed your family for a week on a pie like that."

Even though I wonder why a single man would have purchased such a large dessert item and whether it makes nutritional sense to force-feed a family sugar, flour, and tinned apples, I am swept away by his odd sales pitch and grab one as soon as I enter the store. I am Luke Skywalker to my father's Darth Vader, and he has convinced me to join the dark side. There's nothing left for me to do but surrender.

"This pie looks great!" I squeal into my cell. "You weren't kidding about the size."

"I know, I know," he says, happy to be passing on his knowledge to his second son.

"What's that music you have on?" I ask, hearing some nice little ditty playing in the background.

"Woody Herman. *Woodchopper's Ball*. You like it? I'll make you a tape."

"That would be great. Now, where were we?" I ask, pushing my grocery sled down the massive aisles stacked high with bags of flour, sugar, and midwestern grains. In the distance I spot an old man with a fedora, the kind you rarely see anyone wearing nowadays.

"That is a great hat!" I say to the man, and after he checks to see that he still has his wallet and watch, he offers me a polite smile.

"Who was that?" my dad asks over the phone.

"Some nice old man," I say proudly. "You should see him. I just made his day."

Dance for Grandma

We are all sitting in the living room filling our faces with pumpkin pie smothered in whipped cream, when London says, "I need to get my guitar," and wanders down the hall. His inspiration came from *School of Rock*, which was playing on the TV—a movie starring the chubbily charming Jack Black as a failed rocker turned substitute teacher. Poppy loves that movie and has watched it so many times that she croons all the songs word for word and can even offer behind-the-scenes gossip as the film rolls.

"You know, Dad," she says while pointing to the penultimate battle of the bands scene, "Robert Tsai, the actor who plays Lawrence, didn't like his hair that way."

"Oh, really?" I ask, not having paid close attention to that essential element of filmmaking reflected in a spiky blue mohawk.

"Yeah, it's true." She nods, bringing a forkful of pie to her lips. "And you probably didn't know this, but Kevin Alexander Clark, the guy who plays Freddy the drummer? He's about to mug for the camera by giving a girl a piggyback ride. See there!" She waves her dirty fork in the direction of the screen. "It's classic."

Lala and I give each other the our-daughter-is-turning-into-a-Valley-Girl look as we listen to Poppy sling around terms like *mugging*, *classic*, and *box office* (as in "that's so box office," referring to a scene where Jack Black crowd-surfs). To make our surreal life that much more "classic," London returns with a guitar about as tall as he is. I bought the instrument at my school's tag sale fund-raiser, and although neither of our children knows how to play, that's never stopped them from pursuing their atonal dreams.

"I've got a song," London says, holding the guitar upright. His hair is tousled, and his costume for this performance is a matching set of fire-engine-patterned pajamas. "Ready?" he asks his audience, and we nod. He strums only the neck of the guitar. "Toys," he sings in a low, somber voice. "You want toys, you need toys." For some unknown reason, he tries to get his eyes to roll back in his head in what he must think is an adult look of seriousness. I guess it takes a worried kid to sing a worried song. At this point, any stranger stumbling upon the scene would have dialed 911 to report a toddler having a seizure. "If you get a toyyyyyyyy, then you'll get a toyyyyyyy," London drones on, moving his head from side to side like little Stevie Wonder.

"Someone needs to see this," I say to Lala. "Who can we call?"

"Just get the video camera," she tells me, even though we both know we haven't used the thing in months. The battery is dead and we have no tape, but we don't want to admit how lazy we've become concerning the documentation of London. As a famous football coach once said, "No one ever remembers number two."

"Seriously, should we invite the neighbors?" I ask, not giving up. "Call Tom and Katie?"

"They moved to Albuquerque," Lala says, reminding me of the relocation of our friends. "And when have we ever had the neighbors over? You can't have someone to the house just to show off your kid. We stopped doing that with Poppy, remember?"

I look over at my daughter, who is sitting on the arm of the couch mouthing the words to an AC/DC song, her fist up in solidarity with the fictional characters on the screen.

What happened with Poppy is that before she was London's age, it was clear that she had theatrical aspirations. Maybe it was my fault. When she was still confined to her crib, I decided to give her a musical education, albeit a limited one at best. Lala would be away all day at the flea market selling her shrine boxes to Texans who needed to assuage their capitalist guilt with something spiritual yet small enough to fit into an alligator purse. I'd grab a stack of CDs and play them loudly on the boom box usually reserved for lullabies at bedtime. I'd hold Poppy's hands in mine and we'd dance maniacally to artists that may have influenced her in a certain direction. Looking back, perhaps I should have chosen Mozart instead of Public Enemy or substituted Raffi for the Ramones, but as Dylan said, it's all over now, Baby Blue.

As Poppy grew, so did her sense of performance. Many of the kids at my school come from affluent backgrounds, and they tend to leave a lot of their belongings at school, knowing that everything in their world can be replaced with a single swipe of a credit card. Right before the maintenance guys haul the truckload of unclaimed castoffs to Goodwill, I pore over the valuable discards to see what would work for Poppy's impressive dress-up collection. Given the annual Halloween bash, myriad history presentations, and quarterly plays and musicals, we have a Broadway-caliber costume department located in our home. Starting at the age of two, Poppy thought it completely natural to come to lunch dressed in camouflage pants, high heels, and a sequined top, wearing a feather boa around her neck and a tiara on her head. And once her aunt gave her a Barbie Fashion Makeup play set, all bets were off.

Poppy's knack for fancy dressing coupled with her love for music and dance made her a natural performer, and as her proud father, I decided that others should enjoy such talent, so our house became the home of toddler dinner theater. Back when we had only one child, we invited friends over for dinner at least once a week. I'd whip up grilled chicken tacos, salsa, salad, rice, and beans, and friends would bring enough wine and beer to wash away the woes of the workweek. After we finished dinner and before anyone could get up to leave, I'd snag my stack of CDs and bring them into the kitchen. I'd already purchased one of those CD players you install on the underside of the kitchen cabinets in order to drown out the vegetarian requests from Poppy and Lala as I was creatively cooking animal flesh.

"OK, Poppy, time for the show," I'd say after the plates were cleared. She'd run back into the playroom to get changed. "You're gonna love this," I'd tell my guests, overfilling their wineglasses. "Her moves lately combine the brilliance of Martha Graham with the urban blight of MC Hammer."

Poppy and I never rehearsed, yet I felt we had the synchronicity of a vibrant creative team. If I surprised her by beginning with Hole's "Malibu," a gutsy choice, she'd eye me warily at first but then embrace the challenge, throwing herself across the saltillo-tiled floor with great abandon. If I switched it up suddenly to the hip-hop pop of De La Soul's "Me, Myself and I," she could bust a move even when weighted down by a furry unicorn costume. In my eyes, our shows were totally box office, giving our unsuspecting guests a fine meal, scintillating conversation, and the best post-dinner floor show outside the Camel Rock Casino.

Lala wasn't so sure. "Don't you think our friends are getting tired of your little numbers?" she asked one night while leaning against the kitchen counter.

"They're not my numbers. Poppy's doing the dancing," I said, cleaning up the soiled stemware. As the social director of my home, not only am I responsible for cooking, but somehow I get stuck with the bottle washing as well.

"Yeah, well, I think maybe we should take a breather from the Wilder family talent show for a while," Lala said, clapping her hands like a dealer leaving the table.

"Are you ashamed of your daughter and her many gifts?"

"No, I'm ashamed of her overzealous father and his infantile behavior."

I feigned shock by stopping over the trash can in mid-scrape.

"Don't think I don't see you pathetically dancing along behind her," Lala said, walking away.

It was true. I couldn't help myself, swaying along to the beat, tapping my toes. One time, in the middle of a screaming solo by Led Zeppelin's Jimmy Page, I caught myself playing air guitar and enjoying the white man overbite. It wasn't until the Wilder family reunion on the Outer Banks of North Carolina that I sobered up to the darkness of making my child prance around like a trained monkey.

It was our first sunny day at our family reconsolidation. The Wilders were all on the beach enjoying the sun, surf, and sand as fine and clean as powdered sugar. I was at the water's edge with my brother, Crazy Eddie, and his two-year-old daughter, Marcy. At that time, Eddie was still employed as an actor by Disney World, a job that he loved and was insane enough to be good at. His sense of theater, especially improv, had leaked into the world of parenthood. My family doesn't get together often, so Eddie was excited to show me all the sides of his marvelous daughter, but what transpired next was closer to vaudeville than casually catching up with Uncle Rob.

"Come on, Marcy, let's pull the curtain," Eddie said, moving his hands up and down an imaginary rope. Marcy followed suit, familiar with the overture. "Introductions," Eddie sang.

"Ladies 'n' genlmen, boys 'n' girrls . . ." Marcy announced, closing her eyes. Eddie watched on, overt pride all over his boyish face.

"Show them your belly, Marcy," he called, and she obeyed like a little Lindsay Lohan, lifting up her shirt to reveal a swath of pale flesh. I got a queasy feeling in my adult stomach watching the mirror version of my own stage-dad treachery. Eddie and I both loved our daughters, yet what the hell were we doing to them? It was like a scene out of the *Showgirls* version of *Pinocchio* with Poppy and Marcy made from wood and dancing for tips, their legs and wrists held up by black strings.

"Circle time," Eddie said, plopping to the ground like a fallen marionette. Marcy sat next to him in the sand, and the two of them began a series of phrases and actions I could not follow. "Where's Mama Esther?" Eddie called.

"Who?" I asked.

"Just watch," he said, giving me a huge stage wink.

Time seemed to speed up as my brother and niece threw crazy-ass gang signs at each other and performed a ritual that looked like a cross between patty-cake and the hand jive number from *Grease*, if Olivia Newton John and John Travolta had done a shitload of speed before the camera started rolling.

"Now, the big finale," Eddie said, rising to his feet and brushing sand from his butt. "At Disney, we call this 'Dance for Grandma,'" he whispered in my ear. I watched in horror as Eddie and Marcy employed many of the same gyrations and cheesecake moves as Poppy and I had thousands of miles away in our own dining room theater. Eddie even enjoyed the same white man overbite during the air guitar portion of his routine.

"Taa-daa!" Eddie shouted, extending his arms like a tall, redheaded Mickey Rooney.

"Taa-daa!" Marcy echoed, and looked up at me for approval.

"Taa-daa," I mumbled, and thought the ocean looked good enough that day to drown in.

As the credits roll on *School of Rock*, I gather up the pie plates and carry them into the kitchen. I think to play the new Wilco release I have waiting in the CD tray, but I refrain. Maybe I've had enough music for one night. I recall something I'd seen on the Internet at work, a new phenomenon called baby blogs. In this virtual Dance for Grandma, parents show off their kids by downloading photos, posting diaries (annoyingly in the child's voice), and recording milestones that range from baby's first bowel movement to how much the tooth fairy coughed up last night. *Is it wrong to show the world something you love so much?* I wonder as I rinse the forks and jam them in their holding pens inside our dishwasher.

"Dad," my daughter calls to me, walking into the kitchen with London. They've both dipped deeply into the dress-up stash. Poppy is dressed like a movie star in a flowing silver gown with long white gloves covering her arms and sunglasses perched on the top of her head. She's got her brother, who is in full cowboy gear, by the hand, and I can tell by the look on his face that they are hatching a plan. "I want to learn how to play electric guitar," Poppy says earnestly. "And Londy wants to play the drums." He nods conspiratorially, holding a lasso in one hand and a six-shooter in the other. "We're going to start a band."

I want to tell her that bands need more than two members, but I stop myself, thinking of The Black Keys, Flat Duo Jets, and The White Stripes, not to mention the old school duos of Steely Dan, Hall and Oates, the Captain and Tennille, and those creepy former Mormons, Donny and Marie. The list is endless. I experience a surge of energy not unlike the way I felt when Poppy and I boogied around her crib, well before MTV had a show with a similar name and premise, where the rock stars act like babies and their cribs are as tacky as air-drying paint.

I bend down and speak in hushed tones, not wanting their mother the buzzkill to hear what I have in mind. "All right," I whisper. "I'll pay for the lessons and instruments on one condition."

"What's that?" Poppy asks.

"What's dat?" London parrots.

"You let me direct the music video. OK?"

"It'll be so box office," Poppy says, flipping her cat's-eye sunglasses over her eyes.

"Knee-ha!" London yelps, and lashes me across the face with his rope.

Blood on the Tracks

Lala and I have been checking out classes for London. He's not the kind of three-year-old who asks for such cultural enrichment; on the contrary, he'd be just as happy staying home hunched over his train table creating industrial accidents for engines with names like Skarloey and Peter Sam. Lala and I feel, however, that London will need the social skills to deal with future friends who are not willing to be rolled around a track, so we've been looking.

I recently dragged London to a preview class for a music program located not far from where we live. When I arrived home from teaching *One Flew Over the Cuckoo's Nest* to high school students who often feel and appear like patients in a mental ward, London was sleeping on the couch. His U.S. Postal Service cycling cap covered his eyes, and his gray Led Zeppelin T-shirt was bunched under his arms. I had to wake him so we wouldn't be late, and as any parent knows, the old saying "Let sleeping dogs lie" could easily be applied to children, especially before unfamiliar activities like dance classes, church services, or trips to the parole officer. On the way over, I had to bribe my son with the promise that he could watch *Trouble on the Tracks*, a *Thomas the Tank Engine* video a friend of Poppy's had outviewed. As her mother put it, upon turning eight the towheaded youngster "finally realized she was a girl."

The busy and overwritten flyer for music class led London and me to a house on a small cul-de-sac ending at the Santa Fe River. Green apples lay scattered under the sole tree in the yard, and I could hear notes of Pachelbel's *Canon* leaking through the open sliding glass doors of a converted garage. "This will be nice," I said to London, inspired by the classical music, as the wind picked up in the promise of an upcoming storm.

"Come in! Grab a name tag!" a chirpy woman in tight-fitting yoga clothes said in the doorway. Her own sticky label said her name was Judith. She appeared to be in her late forties, with tan skin, a few wrinkles, and short hair that had been permed too many times. From what I could tell, there was only one other parent/child combo there: a mom still in her navy blue suit from work and a little blond boy with his name, Kyle, written in red ink on his tag. I name-tagged our chests, and London and I poked around. The open living room had been recently painted in dark reds and purples, and ceramic moons and angels (straight out of the ads in *Parade* magazine) were hung without pattern or design all over the walls. Kyle banged on one of the many mini-pianos sprawled along the baseboards, while his mother, Willa, looked on proudly.

"Everything is for the children!" Judith shrilled, and then

twirled like Julie Andrews on that grassy knoll in *The Sound of Music*. Her motivational-speaker tone and volume freaked out London, who, not usually the clingy type, hung to my leg like an oversized boil. Judith noticed his discomfort and scampered over to one of two large blue exercise balls near the stairs. She straddled the large orb and started bouncing, her buttocks dipping deep into the rubber globe and then springing up again. Everything this woman did was exaggerated and overdramatized. I tried to think wholesome fatherly thoughts, but the sight of this woman grinning and working this ball reminded me of vintage Swedish adult films and the women-romping-on-a-trampoline gag of that guilty pleasure *The Man Show*.

"Do you like to bounce, Lon-don?" she asked, her tongue unrolling from her mouth.

I limped over, removed London from my shin, placed him gingerly on the free ball, and began to bounce him. However, next to Judith's grand range of motion and huge Cheshire-cat grin, our attempt seemed amateurish, so we hopped off.

It wasn't long before I realized no one else would be showing up and I'd have no other parents to hide behind, no human shields. "My ad doesn't come out until tomorrow, so this may be it," Judith told us, "but then again, a whole slew of my regulars may come in late, bringing loads of their friends." Here something revealing happened. She changed her tone from über-happy children's entertainer to a deeper, smoky, almost sinister growl. "I do offer a ten-buck discount if you bring a friend," she said, cupping her hand around her mouth. There were definitely two faces to this euphonic Eve.

The five of us moved into the music studio, a square room lined on one wall with mirrors. Strings of $2 Christmas lights hung just below the ceiling. A stack of keyboards in boxes was jammed between a dark tower of fancy stereo equipment and a shiny black upright piano. On the floor an explosion of stuffed animals waited for resuscitation.

"Everything is for the children," Judith said again, and did the exact same Maria von Trapp twirl. "Except those lights," she added in the gravelly voice, pointing to three freestanding pole lamps. "If they fell, they would split your kid's skull wide open."

Except for vain celebrities, mimes, and failed beauticians, most people don't have full-length wall-to-wall mirrors in their homes. Some manic parents don't even own mirrors, having broken them with the heels of their shoes after too many sleepless nights. So when the four of us—me, London, Kyle, and Willa—saw ourselves, we froze in our stocking tracks. Willa and I were thinking, *Am I really that fat?* and *Do I always look this exhausted?* As he studied himself, Kyle's two-year-old brain wondered, *Who the hell is that new kid?* And London, sixteen months older, pondered existentially, *That's me but it's not me. It's not me but it could be.*

Once Judith had announced that class had officially begun, accompanied by the banging of a Pier 1 gong, she started singing everything, from simple directions to polyphonic prompts to cheerleaderish bullying. If that wasn't bad enough, she tried to make most of her communications rhyme. It was a Hallmark rapfest gone awry.

> "Now that we have banged our gong,
> It is time for our class song."

She played the music course anthem, a trademarked, registered, and copyrighted ditty where the lyrics didn't matter, as they only served as intros to the title of the song, which was shouted and repeated like Pavlov's guilty conscience. This technique reminded me of a *Simpsons* episode where all of Springfield joins a cult but they cannot brainwash Homer because he's too stupid. Finally, they catch him humming the *Batman* theme over and over, and realize that repeating the annoying song with the cult leader's name substituted for Batman's will bring Homer around.

Our song sounded a bit like the music to "Elmo's World" with the words *music class* sung a dozen times in about two minutes. At first I heard:

> "Blah blah blah
> Blah blah blah
> Music class!
> Blah blah blah
> Blah blah blah
> Music class!"

After a few rounds, London's and Kyle's eyes began to glaze over like zombies as they drifted toward the colorful CD and DVD display that showcased the many products one would need to purchase when one signed up. Since the lyrics didn't seem to matter (Judith just sang the chorus), I started making up my own:

> "This is weird
> Judith is a nutjob in
> Music class.
> She's done time
> In the state pen
> Music class."

No one noticed because Judith quickly and without warning changed the track to an instrumental song with a cha-cha beat. She herded us toward the stuffed animals and began a freestyle about the toys:

"Grab your turtle, grab your duck
Let's bring joy, love, and luck."

She nabbed a tortoise and did the tango around the room. Kyle sucked on the head of a rabbit while London sat on my lap not wanting to move. I've taken only one course in ethnomusicology and teach teenagers, not toddlers, but I thought it pedagogically unsound that every time the kids did not respond to an activity, Judith got freakier.

"Come on!
Don't be scared. Don't be shy.
Grab a beast. Rock on. Let's ride!"

She mounted her animal pal and rubbed his fabric shell between her legs. Pressing the turtle into her crotch with her left hand, she freed her right and swung it around over her head as if she were a-ropin' some wild crustacean. London eyed first the turtle in her junk, and then the rabbit's head disappearing into Kyle's gob, and he started searching for rubber gloves and some antiseptic wipes. Not spying those items, or even running water, he pushed all the toys out of our general vicinity. Judith would not give up, though. She plucked an alligator from the mix and had the reptile playfully bite London's toes and then mine while singing:

> "Here's a croc, what a long nose!
> Please let this gator bite your toes.
> Look, he nibbles Dad's toes too.
> I like this game, how about you?"

I'm a good sport most of the time, role-playing in prenatal class and inventing underwater games in toddler swim group, but I expect to be treated a shade above the little kids during these gatherings. When Mr. Alligator went down on my toes, I know myself well enough to realize that my visage was pained, as if someone had let out an awful fart. Judith noticed my mug and scolded me in her own melodic way:

> "Parents, we must model fun,
> So it'll be great for everyone.
> Let Mr. Gator bite your toes,
> And then please let him munch your nose."

She jammed the moist clump into my face, and I inhaled the foul odors of saliva, kid sweat, mold, and sour milk. I held my breath for what seemed like minutes and then bowed my head like a child refusing his cod liver oil. If she was going to treat me like a kid, I figured I might as well act like one.

When animal abuse time was over, Judith dragged a basket into the center of the room and began cleaning up. Willa, as any mother would, guided Kyle's hands toward the mess, gently urging him to join the effort. Sounding like Linda Blair in *The Exorcist*, Judith barked out, void of song and rhyme: "We *do not* touch our children's hands in this class! We *do not* force our children to clean up. They will do it sooner and better if we just model."

Hearing that, a shit-scared London grabbed Mr. Ducky, Ms. Mousey, and Captain Koala and shoved them deep into their wicker cage. Judith morphed back into a manic Mary Poppins and sang:

"If you play the notes on this CD,
Your junior will clean happily.
Repeating notes in such location
Is called proper audiation."

As if God himself were expressing his confusion (was *audiation* even a word?), a huge clap of thunder shook the poorly built house. It came to me that Judith was someone who made her living off children but didn't necessarily like them. She felt the same way about kids that Krispy Kreme employees probably feel about donuts. Judith's mood soured often, yet her face never lost its grin and her limbs never stopped waving. She tried to get Willa and me to shoulder some of the burden by stressing that even if we sang off-key and danced like invalids, parent participation was vital to the success of the program. She asked us to participate in a rhythm exercise where we echoed beats back to her after she clapped them to us. They started out simply: "ta-ta ti-ti ta." We repeated in kind: "ta-ta ti-ti ta." She then varied it slightly: "ti-ti ta-ta-ta." Willa and I smiled at each other in the mirror. *Look at us!* our reflections said. *We're doing great.* Even our kids seemed proud of us; London half smiled and Kyle happily sucked on his foot.

"Oh, crap," Judith growled after a wet gust of wind blew into the studio. "I think I left my computer near the window. Rain will ruin the motherboard." She scooted upstairs. "Ta-ta," Willa started, but without our leader, the effort seemed worthless. We all scowled at our reflections. Our group looked like the product of a low-budget spouse swap reality show on TV.

"Sorry 'bout that," Judith said after she returned, sliding into her place on the floor. "Where were we? Repeat after me." She then slammed out some multilayered Afro-Cuban shit: "ta-ta ti-ti-ti do-do-do bim-bam-boom-chaka skee-dee-daddle doo-wop-a-wop-a-phonic skit-skat-skut." I expected her to shout, "How do you like me now, bitch?" at the end and slap her hip. Willa's and my reflections were on the verge of tears. We couldn't move a muscle. Judith warned:

> "If you do not participate
> Your child will not audiate.
> The program will not work at all
> And you'll feel three inches tall."

I couldn't have felt more like the white guy I am. How could I repeat a rhythm that I couldn't even begin to remember? Willa didn't even try. She just put herself on pause in a way her government job must have taught her. I gave it my Diversity University college try, but even London was embarrassed at my attempt to be the Anglo Scatman Crothers. The sound of my nasal voice attempting to recapture Judith's pattern coupled with my swollen reflection in the mirror and London's I've-got-a-sissy-dad frown made me want to hurl into the wicker world of wadded mammals. Dizzy, I finished with an exhausted single "la."

"Hold that note!" Judith screamed. Leaning really close to my mouth, she said, "That may be London's inner note. See that?" She pointed at London's face in the mirror. My son is usually quite animated, his face a mixture of Calvin from *Calvin and Hobbes* and Macaulay Culkin in the movies where the parents forget their kid and the boy finds happiness and a personality in a split-level ranch. London's reflection at this moment was as flat as the mirror it was projected upon. It was obvious that he had grown tired of the madness. He was bored. Judith went to the corner to consult her manual of metaphysical music. London whispered, "Dad, can we go home and watch *Trouble on the Tracks?*"

"I'd love to tie her to the tracks."

"Huh?" he asked.

"Not yet, buddy," I said.

Judith started her enigmatic chanting:

> "We all have an inner tone
> Find it and you won't be alone."

"What?" Willa asked, growing frustrated. "I don't get it." I agreed. Judith sounded like Dr. Seuss on a meth binge.

"If you sing the tone at home, your child will be a dog *with* a bone," she explained.

"Huh?" Willa rubbed her face. "I still don't understand all this."

"Jesus," Judith moaned, breaking character and stopping her song. "Every kid has an inner tone, a note that, if you find it, will calm them during crying jags, help them clean up, make potty training easier, and improve gross and fine motor skills."

"Will it make him sit up straight at the dinner table?" I joked.

"Of course," she answered, as if I were King of the Dumbasses. "Ever see *Third Encounters of the Close Kind?*"

I said I had, even though I hadn't rented the dyslexic version in quite a while.

"It's like that." She turned away from us and rolled her eyes. She must have forgotten there were mirrors everywhere. "Look at the time!" she yelled, jumping up and running around like Willy Wonka at the end of the film when he rushes Charlie out of the factory and tells him no one will become the new King of Cavities. The lights dimmed, lullabies whooshed over the speakers. London clung to me, and Kyle launched into hysterics. His cries echoed so loudly that London gave up my leg and covered his ears. London and I knew that Judith's lack of warning or transition before turning the room into a kiddie horror chamber had set Kyle off. Judith warbled a different diagnosis:

"Kyle's cries are quite fine.
He believes now it's nappy time."

You've got to be shitting me, London must have been thinking. In the darkness, Judith carried on:

"Mom and Dad, rock your babies
Cradle them, hold them, I don't mean maybes."

Maybes? Babies? London was over three years old and weighed close to forty pounds, so I stalled. Willa gladly obliged, since it was the only thing that stopped a frantic Kyle from pulling the lamps down on his skull. Judith's grin ate her face as she placed her right hand over her left palm, formed a circle with her arms, and rocked an imaginary child for us, just in case I'd forgotten this complicated maneuver. London and I shrugged, him dying to see *Trouble on the Tracks* and me wanting to leave this trouble and make some tracks of my own. I rocked him the best I could, given his length and girth. It wasn't so bad, actually. His body had outgrown my reach, but I do love my boy, and spending a few moments with him in my arms reminded me of when he was first born. Since Lala was laid up after a tough delivery, I was the primary rocker and holder during those opening weeks.

Out of the shadows, Judith emerged playing the flute. She gypsy-danced around us all like Ian Anderson of Jethro Tull—same crazy eyes rolling around over a shiny shaft of silver. What a scene: two parents rocking their oversized boys in a converted garage in suburban New Mexico while a woman with a *Planet of the Apes* haircut blew wind through a metal pipe. I'd thought that when I had children my life would become dull and routine, but this moment was stranger than the windowpane moments I melted through on Uncle Duke Day in college.

"Want to touch my flute?" Judith asked in a creepy voice, like Mister Rogers in drag.

"What?" I asked.

"Does Lunny want to touch my flute?" Lunny? Now she creates pantywaist nicknames for my kid? London was smart, though. He knew she wouldn't back off until he obeyed. He tentatively pressed one shiny key. "Oooh," she moaned. "That feels good." Then she blew harder. And she wasn't leaving yet. London pressed two keys at one time. "Oooh. Audiation," she whispered to me. Sliding across the room on her knees, she offered her flute to Kyle, who had placated himself with the collar of his mother's shirt. All we could see was Judith's hunched back, the rear view of Dr. Seuss' hairstyle, and the zipper on her pants running along the cleft of her butt. She repeated word for word what she'd said to us, and then Linda Blair visited us once again: "We *do not* pull the keys, Kyle, we press them. We *do not* pull the keys on an $825 flute!"

Judith leaped to her feet, Kyle resumed his wailing, and the lights went up full force. Never to be thrown off schedule, Judith dumped fifty-seven instruments on the floor like a farmer feeding swill to his pigs, only with a loud crash instead of a quiet slurp.

"We end as we begin!" she sang, and twirled her way to the CD player to cue up the theme song of our musical Jim Jones getaway. London grabbed some frog maracas so his mouth could remain uninfected, while Kyle sucked on three pennywhistles. The sensory overload of the previous fifty minutes made both Willa and me want to beat the crap out of something, so we grabbed the two widest drums covered in animal hide and a pair of heavy mallets, and punished those fuckers along with the "Elmo's World" beat. I still don't know anything about inner tones or audiation, but those last two minutes felt good the way a Metallica concert does. I can still see it now: my fellow cult member and I with our offspring, pounding drums like Robert Bly's wet dream, screaming "Music class" over and over until our lungs ached. And Judith, our soon-to-be-ex-leader, pleased as punch with the whole scene.

Supply Me

I'm standing in the back-to-school section of a major discount store, holding my robin's-egg-blue Elementary School General Supply List. Dwarfed by a logjam of number-two pencils and erasable-ink pens, I notice the queasy look of the other parents clutching sheets of yellow, red, or green. Even though we pack lunches in different districts and zones, we're all searching for something meaningful here in this arroyo of supplies formerly reserved for people with paying jobs who worked in offices. My quest at hand? According to my daughter's list, I need to find a four-pack of pink bar erasers. I guess she'll be making a shitload of mistakes this year.

Due to poor state and federal funding, public schools feel justified in asking parents to load their kids like pack mules from Office Depot. These "general supply" rosters have become longer and far less general. Gone are the days of sending off your little Einstein with a few pencils and a composition notebook. As both a high school teacher in a private school and an involved public school parent, I feel conflicted. Part of me wonders how much dough parents should have to cough up for a supposedly free education. My more sympathetic half has seen educators forgo luxuries like toothpaste and deodorant so their classes don't have to write with stubby pencils stolen from public golf courses. I imagine the underpaid teachers and administrators in the now sadly smoke-free teachers' lounge, tired of their requests being denied by the school board, sneaking products onto the list. Will a weary parent really question paper towels and toilet tissue buried in a table ten columns down and thirty rows across?

My daughter is entering third grade, the transition year where kids can conduct probability experiments at school yet still come home to play with stuffed animals named Bunnykins and Wee Wee. Poppy's supply list exploits the range of her development and includes everything from crayons, colored pencils, and baby wipes to a calculator and a full set of Allen wrenches. As my basket fills and my wallet whimpers, I spy a fallen soldier in this war-like supply depot, a confused dad who has obviously never been in this type of offensive. He's dressed too nicely in leather loafers and a pressed polo shirt and made the cardinal mistake of bringing his daughter on his rookie mission.

"Eight folders?" he cries out, rubbing his graying temple. "What the heck do you need eight folders for?"

"Oh, we do a lot of work, Daddy," his daughter says, playing Pollyanna as she reaches for the fur-covered binder with embedded calculator, mirror, and pockets for a cell phone, lip gloss, and Palm Pilot. These designer objects are five times the cost of the ones I bought that were made in the former Soviet Union from leftover propaganda newspaper. Little Paris convinces Dumbstruck Dad she needs a set of 120 Prismacolor pencils and the box of 64 Crayolas that include the new colors Inchworm, Jazzberry Jam, Mango Tango, and Wild Blue Yonder now that Blizzard Blue, Magic Mint, and Mulberry have been retired. Her calculator is from Texas Instruments, her school box is fashioned from 100-year-old Hawaiian koa wood, and her ruler measures digitally using state-of-the-art lasers. I want to yell to my brother in arms that the best deals are hidden on the very top or bottom rows, but in his confused state, he's not catching his kid tossing in Listerine breath sheets, gum, and a pager you can clip to your backpack so your prepubescent posse can locate you after PE.

As I make my way to the hardware section to locate a gross of 100-watt bulbs and a toner cartridge for a Canon iR1600 copier, I imagine the shock and subsequent hangover my comrade will experience when he gets his credit card bill, not unlike the diplomat's husband who spent $120,000 in a strip club in New York City. My goal is to get out of this Hades of a warehouse with a little money to spare. After all, the wrapping-paper fundraiser at Poppy's school starts in a few weeks.

What Are You Trying to Say?

Because of our hurried suburban life of practices, lessons, and never-ending meetings, my family doesn't go out and celebrate often. However, since I had just sold my first book, something I'd been working toward for over fourteen years, Lala decided we should dine outside our messy home. I was tired, having spent the whole day trying to show teachers how to use a computer, which is not unlike trying to teach the alphabet to an assembly of cheese graters. I therefore chose, as our location, an informal diner in downtown Santa Fe. This way, I wouldn't feel compelled to dust off my manners or even sit up straight.

My daughter, Poppy, loves to go out for any meal, and when we do venture into eating establishments, she becomes quite animated and chatty. This change in demeanor from thoughtful bookworm to ditzy Valley Girl sparked by the sight of a tablecloth worries me a tad in terms of her future relations with credit-card-wielding men. My son, London, is a different creature altogether, so in order to keep him seated during the meal, we cram trains and mini-backhoes into a small polka-dotted suitcase that he lugs around as though he were a short and fruity insurance salesman. After we had placed our orders, I excused myself to use the restroom, and London asked to join me. Even though he is still in diapers, he loves to explore the world of public bodily functions. Once inside the bathroom, his greatest thrill is to splash in the puddles of man piss by the urinal and pull the dirty lever down a few times as if he's driving a steam locomotive. After I washed his hands, the bottoms of his feet, and my trouser cuffs, we headed back to our booth. On the way, we passed a dwarf who was being seated at a table outside. London didn't seem to notice the man as he raced back to his mother, who was deeply engrossed in a conversation with Poppy about her costume for Halloween. Their discussion perfectly echoed the crossroads of Poppy's development. They couldn't decide which was cooler—the sullen maturity of a zombie cheerleader or the lingering innocence of Hello Kitty.

Our salads arrived and London, not interested in greenery you cannot roll around in, mimicked the city of Santa Fe Public Works Department, happily crashing his engines into his bulldozers. I listened as Lala offered to dye her own junior high cheerleading outfit Goth black if Poppy wanted to go that way. As if struck by an elfin epiphany, London picked his head up from the table, cocked one eyebrow, and asked me, "Dad, who was that little guy?"

Lala had seen the man come in, so she understood what he was referring to. She tried very hard not to laugh, but it wasn't easy for her. We had been through this before with London and her own mother, who was forever in love with all things taboo and scatological in nature. In fact, my mother-in-law, Beverly, often told us politically incorrect tales of seeing famous freaks like the Pinhead and the Bearded Lady at carnivals across Utah, Nebraska, and Wyoming. Obviously, Lala and I wanted to be open and enlightened parents of the new millennium, but sometimes your kids just won't let you keep up with the Joneses.

"He looked like he had a bump," London said, referring to the man's slight hunched back.

"He's a midget," Poppy said, attempting to educate her brother. "I've seen him before. At the mall."

"He's really a dwarf," I countered, "but I think the correct term today is *little person*."

"What's a dwarp?" London asked. His eyebrows jammed together toward his nose in concentration. Whatever I said now would never leave that pint-sized brain.

"A dwarf is a person who is little, that's all," I said, knowing that wasn't the half-pint of it.

Luckily, our meals came, and Lala and I quickly oohed and aahed over the kids' spaghetti and our own gravy-covered entrees, trying to move the conversation away from the correct terminology for an adult male under five feet tall. Since it was a celebration, I let London and Poppy pick their own desserts. Poppy chose a hot fudge sundae, which she daintily ate with a demitasse spoon like a little debutante, while London ordered chocolate cake, which he shoved down his pants.

I paid the bill and we walked toward the exit. At the hostess stand, London stopped and waited until the woman who had seated us returned. I felt proud that he had the etiquette and patience to thank her. All our hard work at home on manners was paying off.

"Where's that dwarp?" London asked the hostess, looking around. "I want to say bye."

The young woman in face-the-public makeup eyed me strangely, and I was at a complete loss. I didn't want to explain that we had been talking about midgets and dwarves during dinner, so I did what I do best, which is stand slack-jawed and gape like a zoo animal on tranquilizers.

"You know," London said, tugging on the hem of her velvet dress, "that little guy with the bump?"

Many writers I know say that having a child only helps their work, since kids reexamine everything we take for granted. Our little ones question what may seem obvious or not worth mentioning to us otherwise dull and jaded adults. I don't know what we were eating when we conceived London, but this kid somehow finds the politically incorrect nerve almost weekly. We have a friend named Denise who came over for dinner last spring. Denise happens to be African-American. London likes to tell everyone about his favorite color, which happens to be yellow. He'll greet complete strangers in Target just with that information only. Most people ignore the non sequitur from the nut job in the cart, but once in a while he'll get a "Good for you!" from a sympathetic parent who has her own self-narrating kid at home. After London informed Denise of his favorite tint, he decided, like some pigment psychic, to guess all of ours.

"Yours is blue, Dad," he said, giving me his famous wink and thumbs-up.

"Pink for Poppy." This was an easy guess given her age, gender, and the fact she had slung a salmon-hued boa around her neck only moments before our guest arrived.

"Mama, you love purple."

Then he turned to our guest, who sat demurely on a dining

room chair. "Think, think, think," London said, poking his temple Winnie-the-Pooh style with his bent index finger. "Yours is black," he said, "like your skin." Then he turned to me and asked, "Dada, why is her skin black?"

I'm running out of delicate and diplomatic ways to excuse my three-year-old George Carlin. When London discovered we all have nipples, he mispronounced the word, replacing the *n* with an *h*. Don't ask me why. Maybe it was because it sounded like *hippos*, an animal that looks like a waddling scrotum with teeth. After his mammillary discovery, London would be riding shotgun in a shopping cart, point at any woman with a B cup or larger, and say, "Look at those hipples, Dad!" or "You like those hipples, Dad? I like them!" or "Those hipples are sooo big." I would be lying if I said that a few women didn't look at my ring finger after London's bad pickup line. I guess there's something to be learned from such honesty and directness. The majority, however, did not enjoy such scrutiny in the produce section at Albertsons.

When you lead the rushed lifestyle that most families do, our many different worlds collide at times, causing much stress and tension. Lala has been undergoing physical therapy for over two years now after a bad spill in a water park. Some days she needs to drop London off at my school for a few hours so a stocky woman with a German accent can beat the crap out of Lala's arm in the name of the healing arts. One afternoon, London stepped out of our minivan dressed in T-shirt and corduroys, a Teenage Mutant Ninja Turtles mask strapped to the top of his head. I waved goodbye to Lala and led my boy by the hand into the foyer of our school. There had been a break-in the night before and a police officer was talking to the receptionist who had phoned in the report.

"Look, Dad, there's a killer," London said, and pointed to the lawman. I almost shit in my pants. I don't have an easygoing relationship with police in general, and the he-man who was staring us down literally bulged out of his polyester uniform. I knew from past encounters that most cops feel they have better things to do than to follow up on a broken window at a private school. And here was my little Alan Dershowitz pointing the finger.

"Hey, killer," London said, winking and giving the guy a thumbs-up. I closed my hand around my son's fist and yanked him down the hall. I found out later at a toy store that somehow, probably via the evil (and favorite scapegoat) of TV, he had associated all guns with life liquidation. Not an illogical idea, I admit, yet now he calls pirates, soldiers, cowboys, and our neighbor the hunter all killers.

At the end of the hall, we ran into an administrator named Alice who happens to be Native American. London knows her from his previous visits and was very chatty, telling her all about his trains and having spotted a killer only minutes before.

"What's that on your head?" she asked, referring to the Halloween mask that looked like a green beret capping his skull.

London slipped the plastic over his face and growled through the mouth slit. "It's my Injun Turtle face," he said, and snarled again for good measure.

"Your what?" She placed her hands on her hips and stared at him and me in disbelief. I hate to think what she thought we were saying at home.

"My Injun Turtle mask." Then he paused and scanned her from head to toe. Alice has long black hair, wears glasses, and measures less than five feet. "Hey, you're not so big," London said, wagging his finger at her hipples. "Are you a dwarp?"

Telephony

Telephone etiquette is a custom most of us are never taught growing up. I'm more surprised than not when a friend or colleague answers the phone at home with the level of warmth and formality usually reserved for fragrance-free centers of holistic healing. I once worked with a wackjob of a middle-school science teacher who, while on campus, wore a leprechaun costume and erected a mini-Stonehenge in his homeroom from river rocks. He was one of those teachers you see portrayed in pot-glorifying teen films or after-school specials about loser kids no one but the faculty will talk to. These types of instructors are often both immensely popular and mentally ill. At home, however, this silly little freak of a man picked up Bell's invention with great respect and ceremony and, like Madonna, a whiff of a British accent.

"Ronald Crag speaking, how may I help you today?" he answered when I rang to ask about how one of my troubled advisees was faring with his miniature golf course project. I was startled by his manners, given that I had imagined him dressed in lederhosen doing a punk rock version of *Riverdance*. I inquired about where he had learned such an impeccable greeting.

"Oh, that," he scoffed. "My father taught us that a telephone was a tool, not a toy, and should be treated as such." Then he invited me to come over on Friday night to play with his collection of board games based on TV shows from the 1970s.

"Oh, and wear something special," he said before placing the receiver gently in its cradle.

There is a custom in my house to hand any telemarketing call to the youngest child available. At eight, Poppy is too old and savvy now to fall for the trick, but we often have a clowder of toddlers handy in our playroom knee-deep in some drama based on their distorted view of a Disney film. My favorite is the one where Hercules the firefighter marries his brother Cinderella. When the phone rings and I hear that fuzzy pause, followed by the request to speak with a male carrying my wife's maiden name, I tell the caller to hold, then hand off the receiver to the mouth below the nose with the greenest viscous liquid. It's such fun to watch the kid just stare at the piece of wire-filled plastic for three minutes or babble on about how Hercules is nice but Cinderella is mean even though he is Hercules' brother. I've listened in on the bedroom line and many telemarketers don't know what to do. After they repeat, "Can you put your daddy back on?" a dozen times and nothing changes, they just sigh because of the obvious guilt that comes with hanging up on the wee little ones.

This gag stemmed from my observations about how parents

with younger kids deal with the child's inescapable desire to talk on the phone. Parents will innocently say, "I don't know why, but Cletus junior always wants to talk." Meanwhile Mom or Dad won't even go swimming without their mobile pressed to her ear or strapped to his belt in an absurd leather colostomy baggie. It's not brain surgery to realize that our offspring are fascinated with our fascinations, obsessed with our obsessions. That's why my kids love profanity from northern Germany, *Fear Factor*, and margaritas with no salt (the crusty rim just slows you down). The real question, it seems, is how you handle your kid's phone lust while acknowledging that the person on the other line may not be as interested or charmed by your child's story of seeing a "pider in the bafftub." I limit my son London's phone participation to exactly two minutes by the kitchen timer, even if he's about to freestyle some dope rhymes or recite Martin Luther King, Jr.'s "I Have a Dream" speech in Latin. I bid London to say "goodbye" and "I love you" nicely, then I wrench the electronic communication device from his steamy grip.

Some of my friends with kids obviously haven't given much thought to how to handle the phone properly. My colleague Marla and her son, Calvin, have this disturbing dueling-banjos kind of interplay when it comes to telecommunications. When I call Marla to find out about a looming admissions committee meeting or to arrange a playdate where her son can spit on mine, Calvin will undoubtedly want to speak to London. I usually avoid this painful monosyllabic toddler connection and tell Marla that London is napping after a taxing game of Dump Mom's Handbag in the Toilet. I know lying is wrong, but I might shoot myself if I again have to watch my son holding the microphone to his ear, the speaker at his mouth, yelling, "Calvin? Calvin? I can't hear you!" The first time it was call-the-wife-over cute, the second time mildly entertaining, but after that the scene became too much to bear, like the last three seasons of *Friends*. Calvin will happily accept me as a stand-in, and Marla, trying to avoid his breaking all the mirrors in the house with his Home Depot—for-kids hammer, will cave and put him on.

"Calvin?" I call nicely.

Silence.

"Calvin?"

"Londy?" he asks, with a voice not unlike the mayor of Munchkinland's.

"No, this is his dad. How are you?"

Silence.

"Calvin?"

"Londy?"

"No, I just sold him. Put your mom back on the phone, please."

Silence.

As thrilling as this might seem, our Mister Rogers-meets-Sartre conversation only gets worse. When Marla comes back on, she continues to parent even though I'm still stuck on the line.

"Calvin," she says, "the Play-Doh stays on the worktable, not on the dog."

"Do you need to get off?" I ask, praying.

"No, it's fine," she assures me. "Take your soy nuts out of your nose, food is for eating."

I sigh loudly like the telemarketers I love to torture.

"Sweetie," she calls to her boy, "we don't stand on chairs. Want me to pull up your stoolie?"

I wait politely while she strings together commands, bargains, pleas, and first-aid tips in baby talk. Calvin will soon notice the banana-shaped device still stuck to his mom's head and will beg to be let back on. She's too exhausted to resist.

"Calvin?" I groan.

"Londy?"

"No, Londy is my spawn. Where's your mom?"

Silence.

A sane individual will wonder why I don't just hang the hell up. My painful patience comes from the few bits of etiquette I have picked up in my life, mostly from girlfriends who took a helluva long time dumping me. Hanging up on someone is just not nice. Lala has this great line when she wants to get off the phone: "I'll have to let you go now." The sentence is brilliant because the person she's speaking with has never actually asked to be let go but submits nonetheless. When Lala utters it in her soft western drawl, the offer seems gracious and hospitable and goddamn it, people buy the crap she's selling. I tried letting people go too, but either my delivery or my friends suck because each one said, "That's OK, I've got plenty of time," and then they put their Siamese cat on the phone.

My niece Marcy has developed a telephonic tic due to a phone custom her family may have overstressed. Crazy Eddie and his wife, Sandy, are an overly friendly couple, the kind who spend every weekend or holiday flying and driving to watch other people get married. They attend every function they are invited to, even if it includes an offer on a time-share, dinner at Chick-fil-A, or a room full of pale-faced Mormons. Part of their friendly family credo is to allow every person in their trio to speak to relatives or friends who are kind enough to call. Unlike other clans, who pick up all the receivers in the house and shout simultaneously (you know who you are), Eddie's *familia loca* passes the cordless around. When I call to see if Eddie has passed his Professional Education Test, I speak first with Sandy, who answers, then with Marcy, and finally with the guy I was trying to reach. Seems simple, linear. However, after four years of this hot-potato routine at home and with cells, Marcy has become hardwired with fiber-optic cable. If she receives the phone from one person, she has to hand it off to a different human. No exceptions. The other day I called to ask if Hurricane Charlie had canceled their plans to attend a Wal-Mart opening followed by a Christian scrapbooking party. After my brother assured me they were fine except for a few uprooted trees, he put my niece on. Marcy is a happy kid who speaks in a bright and constant "gee willikers" type of intonation. Sandy was out on errands, but Eddie's actor friend Tony had dropped by. I've met Tony once when he smuggled us into Disney World for free under his costume, but other than that, we've got nada to say to each other. Marcy had different ideas. Because of her routine when it comes to the phone, we all had to participate equally in a merry-go-round of salutations.

"Hi, Uncle Rob!" Marcy chirped.

"Hi, Marcy."

"Hi from Uncle Tony," my brother's friend slurred speedily, trying not to annoy either one of us. Then I'd talk to Eddie for three minutes about his new idea of handing out clown noses to all the clinically depressed and ADHD students in his school before the communication carousel started up again.

"Hi, Uncle Rob!"

"Hi, Marcy."

"Hi from Uncle Tony."

Then back to Eddie. There was no way around this spinning nightmare. Eddie had tried to substitute toy phones, stuffed animals, Halloween masks, and videos of Jerry Lewis telethons, but like angry senior citizens calling large corporations to complain, Marcy needed to have a real human come to the phone. Eddie explained that if a third person leaves the equation during the call, "oh, baby, Marcy loses her shit." One Saturday, Sandy had answered the phone and passed it on to Marcy, who, after squeaking, delivered it to my brother in his bedroom. While he was chatting to some upcoming bride or groom, Sandy ducked out to the drugstore. Eddie made the fatal mistake of returning the caller to Marcy's blithesome grasp so she could offer another salaam. After she had finished, she searched their house for her mother. Not finding her, Marcy started screaming as if her legs were being sawed off, the phone's receiver still centimeters from her mouth. Eddie alternated between trying to console his irate daughter and shouting assurance to the person on the line, who formerly wanted children, that everything was in fact just fine.

Nothing worked with Marcy. Not bribes of bathtubs of ice cream, armies of dolls and stuffed animals, not even a promise of three hours of uninterrupted *Wiggles* episodes thanks to the always reliable, never knocked-up babysitter TiVo. Eddie, like most parents would, surrendered and strapped them both into his car, cell on his ear, cordless on Marcy's. He knew hers would give out soon due to the range of coverage or the amount of tears and snot invading every orifice in the plastic mold. I imagine how another driver might have seen this father and daughter racing down Lord Barclay Avenue in Orlando that Saturday morning. "They sure must love the telephone. What a great invention!" he'd say as he turned up the volume on his radio and hummed along.

Creature Comfort

When my brother Rich's daughter Maddie was born, an old friend of his sent him a baby gift by mail. It was an eleven-inch doll called So Soft Baby, a pudgy pink thing with a bonnet framing a sleeping face, a sprig of yellow hair peeking from the cap, and a satiny stomach underneath a soft cotton nightshirt. Like many such gifts, Rich and his wife, Mimi, thought it was cuter than the Olsen twins eating solid food. One night when Maddie was restless, he threw So Soft Baby in the crib as casually as he threw me down a flight of stairs when we were growing up. Little did he know that such a small gesture around an innocent infant could change the course of his life for the next seven years.

Because of its folds of baby fat and rounded features, Rich and Mimi referred to the doll, which after that fateful night never left Maddie's tenacious grip, as Mrs. Marshmallow. When

Maddie started to utter her first words, *marshmallow* was a mouthful, especially for the offspring of a Wilder, so the doll became known as Ish or the even more sickeningly cutesy Ishy. The doll went everywhere—to the store, on car trips, even to the bathroom when my niece started potty training. Life without Ishy was just not possible for Maddie. One weekend when my brother was away on business, Mimi decided to take Maddie on a weekend trip to see her parents. She left early in the morning so she could cover some ground before the trip took on its annoying stop-and-start pace that comes from having a kid on a long car ride without the hypnotic combination of cough medicine and a portable DVD player.

"Ishy?" Maddie called upon waking. She didn't care about her mother, father, or that she was strapped in a moving vehicle far away from her home. "Ishy?" she cried, panic-stricken at not seeing or feeling her raggedy sidekick.

Mimi realized while traveling at 58 miles per hour that they had left the doll at home on Maddie's bed. Without hesitation or comment, she took the next exit and doubled back to get it, her daughter screaming in the backseat the whole hour.

"Weren't you pissed?" I asked Mimi on the phone, imagining a full hour of crying based upon the attachment of her daughter to an item worth less than $15 on the open market.

"Are you kidding?" she asked. "I was going away for the whole weekend. I thought you were a teacher. Do your math."

The reason for my newfound interest in the history of my niece and her doll is simple: my son, London, and his nuzz. Before he was a year old, London started sucking his middle fingers. Due to years of sleep deprivation, Lala and I can't pinpoint the exact moment when he started sucking so hard, yet we have a photo of London sitting on the carpet in our living room, his fingers happily down his throat like a supermodel at an all-you-can-eat buffet. He hasn't stopped spit-polishing those two appendages since. Shortly after the addiction started, his fingers weren't giving him enough of a buzz, and he found that by pulling the fuzz from one of my wife's sweaters and rubbing it under his nose he could console himself. It seems that for some kids one comfort addiction leads to another the way the guidance counselor told us in high school that pot was the gateway drug to heroin and angel dust, a narcotic that sounded far too Peter Pan—ish to me to be that dangerous.

Like Maddie, London dragged his sweater around everywhere. The initial nuzz was blue in color and made from lambswool. At first, like with anything your kid does that doesn't require stitches, we thought the whole nuzz thing was awfully sweet. When London was nuzzing during the day, he was happy and hit his sister a lot less. At night, its calming influence made getting him back to sleep easier, especially after Lala or I rolled on top of him. But soon, what began as an infantile accessory evolved into our family's ball and chain.

Lala's sister Emily has an amazing house on Maui, and we are lucky to freeload every June for a few weeks. Traveling such a long distance isn't easy with two kids, and the nuzz was just one more item not to forget as we lugged two car seats, a stroller, and four suitcases to the airport. The nuzz had to travel loosely outside all the other gear, so Lala and I sounded like Clara Peller in those old Wendy's commercials, but instead of "Where's the beef?" we called "Where's the nuzz?" every few minutes or so. People started staring at these two adults jerking their heads around like frenzied seagulls asking the location of something that sounded like a character out of a book by Dr. Seuss. The looks from our fellow travelers grew even more intense as we boarded the plane from L.A. to Maui. Everyone around us was dressed in shorts and floral shirts in anticipation of the warm June weather and here I was forced to carry a bulky wool sweater around my neck since my hands were busy dragging suitcases and children.

On Maui, the only way London would nap during the day was if I strolled him up and down the street, the nuzzy covering half his body like a shroud. The weather on the island is idyllic if you are by the ocean, but if you are pushing a stroller repeatedly up and down the blacktop, it gets pretty damn hot. Emily and Thom's house was in the final stages of construction and the workers, when they weren't tinkering with the garage doors, moved quickly and smartly into the nearest patch of shade. Like a Greek chorus covered in paint and dust, they collectively shook their heads at me in disbelief as I endlessly pushed my son, who was dressed for Colorado in January. "Stupid mainlander," one guy muttered under his breath, and I answered, "You got that right," as my flip-flops started to melt to the soles of my feet.

Rich and Mimi are smart people. He's a successful executive who could sell sea monkeys to Jacques Cousteau and she is a former engineer for GE who now owns a string of fitness centers targeted to women who only have twelve minutes each week to exercise. After Maddie left Ishy on the tram at Disney World and they spent all day trying to locate the lost-and-found at the world's biggest theme park, they stocked up. They bought another Ishy as a backup, attaching it like an oversized novelty chain to their key ring the way gas stations do so that their seedy customers won't claim the restroom as their permanent residence. When my niece started preschool, they bought another for the new caregiver who, upon seeing Maddie's withdrawal symptoms when the woman stupidly decided to wash the filthy doll, bought her own stunt double out of the school's discretionary fund. Finally, because Maddie's constant girlhandling of Ishy turned the pink Rubenesque doll into a gaunt, grayish homeless shell of a comfort item, they bought Ishy number five, which leaves its plastic bag only for show-and-tell, class photos, and the grand opening of another exercise franchise.

London traded the blue nuzz for a brief flirtation with an orange crewneck number, but most of his affection has been showered upon a fancy red mohair sweater that my wife believes originally cost over $300. We have never lost the nuzz or forgotten it at crucial times, and besides the future orthodontist bills that will inevitably come from two fingers pushing his teeth in hillbilly directions, I no longer care if other people think we are a strange family. I know that much is true. What concerns me is the freakish ways London interacts with ladies' apparel. I was rushing home late one day after a parent-teacher conference I hosted had unfortunately turned into weepy family therapy. When I walked in the front door, I couldn't believe my eyes. London had put bits of red mohair inside every one of his forty or so train cars, and even in the houses and buildings on his train table. I shuddered in an *Exorcist* kind of way, and then he turned and smiled at me. He had shoved little morsels of sweater into his two ears, into both nostrils, and in between the middle fingers he was adamantly sucking upon.

"Hey, Dad," he said, as if it were any other day. I was afraid to move. If I took the wrong step, I knew I'd be smothered to death by these little woolly tribbles.

"What are you doing, Londy?" I asked, trying to remain calm.

"Playing."

"Why are there nuzzies in your ears?"

He shrugged.

"In your trains?"

" 'Cause it's a busy day on the island of Sodor, silly," he told me as if the scenario weren't apparent to any stranger happening by. He reached into his right ear, retrieved the crimson ball, examined it, then jammed it right back in again. I hear many parents complain that they don't understand their kids, but on that day, I thought Lala had been impregnated by an alien neighbor and had hatched a creature from a planet that used cardigans as a form of legal currency.

London's addiction to nuzzing has spread outside the confines of the red sweater and our home in general. If we are playing tag, he will stop in mid-stride if he spots an errant nuzz on the floor. He'll scoop it up, run the puff under his nose a few times like an addict needing a fix, then hand it to me for safekeeping until his buzz wears off. At night, when I'm getting undressed, flecks of red fur will be embedded in the jumble of my keys and loose change. *I have become my son's dealer,* I think as I use an old album cover to separate the stash from the shit.

Even though she is his loving mother, Lala does not escape the icy grip of our son's addiction. The other day she was leaving the house in a pair of Uggs, those Australian boots made from sheep that baa like Paul Hogan with a bad hangover.

"Is that a nuzz?" London said to her, leaving his train table, which he had covered in baby powder because, as he so aptly put it, "it's snowy this time of year on the island of Sodor." He squatted down and pecked at the fleece on a boot's exterior even though Lala hadn't stopped walking. Our boy is unafraid to pick up dropped cotton balls at the doctor's, errant packing foam in the post office, or loose strands of pink fiberglass on the cement floors of Home Depot. When I yell that the item he's about to rub all over his face is dirty or toxic, he gives me that "you don't know where I been" look so common on hoboes searching for cigarette butts in the gutters outside convenience stores.

London's fleecy obsession continues to grow in strange and unnerving ways. Being the sentimental historian, Lala has kept a few specimens of London's different sweaters in a small apothecary jar on top of a cabinet in our dining room. Even though London still clings to the mother lode, he frequently asks to view the contents of the jar as if they were organic traces of his origins as a human. Lala retrieves the nuzzy collection and allows London to look at the blue, orange, white, and red samples, reminding him of his past through a furry version of history.

"Can I have them, Mom?" he says, shaking at the sight of all that precious smack.

"No, you have your own," Lala tells him, screwing the top back on and placing it well out of his junkie-thin arms.

"Please," London pleads, trembling from his ever-growing jones. Even though he has the big red nuzz at hand, an addict constantly wants more, and the other guy's drugs always seem more potent.

So every week, instead of a cookie jar, Lala retrieves the container of fuzz and they privately view the exhibition. Poppy thought it was funny for a while and would stay and watch, but now she realizes what kind of family she was born into, so she goes off into her room to practice inappropriate dance moves. She figures that if she works hard enough, one day she will get free from this odd tribe that idolizes what other families scrape from their lint tray and toss into the trash.

Since London is denied access to Lala's premier compilation, he's created a museum of his own. Our week is crammed with meetings, practices, lessons, and therapies, both physical and alcoholic in nature, so we clean our home only on weekends, if at all. One Saturday I was trying to impose some semblance of order and hygiene in our bedroom, when I came across about a dozen flocculent bits on an old trunk that once belonged to Lala's mother. London was reclining happily on the bed, watching an early morning cartoon about a killer robot with a deep concern for the environment. I cupped my hand at the edge of the trunk and was about to sweep away the tiny heads, when London wailed, "Don't touch those!"

"Huh?" I said, confused by my automatic compliance with the commands of a creature still in diapers. I don't even pause when one of my teenage students screams for help.

"That's my c'lection," he said, the new word sticking to the roof of his mouth.

"Col-lect-ion?" I said, failing to stop myself from the teacherly habit of correcting my kids' pronunciation.

"Dad, please leave that alone."

I did, we did, and now the dozen blossoms have grown into a full garden, extending across the top of the chest like red tide. Everything inside that trunk is no longer accessible to us. In fact, Lala and I have forgotten what we stored in there in the first place. Parents are quick to give up inessentials like winter clothing, alcohol, oral sex, and food with spices if it means placating an otherwise ornery child. At night, we all watch London sort and re-sort, catalogue and classify these little pieces of loose nap as if they were the remains of King Tut's textile fetish.

Last year, Maddie had stopped sucking her thumb cold turkey and given up Ishy, who suffocates in the top of her closet, still unsoiled in a plastic bag. London is far from being nuzz-free, however. A few days ago he had a bout of the stomach flu and hurled all over the red sweater. It wasn't the first time Lala had to wash the fraying garment in Woolite and air it out on the rack across from our washer and dryer. Even though the arms still have some tread left on them, the body of the sweater looks like fishnet, thin with huge gaps between the weave.

"That makes me so sad," Lala said, spreading the wool across the top bars of the drying apparatus.

"He pukes on it all the time, not to mention other crap," I said, trying in my own pathetic male way to comfort her. I recalled the time he dragged it through a puddle of gasoline outside a service station, and once where I found him holding it on the couch and what I believed to be raisins were really dead flies caught in the web of Italian knitting.

"Not that," she said, welling up. "It means he's getting older."

"I guess you're right," I said, not exactly sympathetic. I don't know about other fathers, but I selfishly look forward to the next stage of development as a way to convenience my harried life. When my kids were infants, I longed for speech so I wouldn't have to order for them at restaurants. Fine motor skills meant Poppy could brush her own teeth, get herself dressed in the morning, and with a little training be my designated driver. No longer worrying about where this fabric was all the time seemed like the removal of a painful boil.

I left Lala weeping into the open Maytag and wandered back into the living room, which now was covered in fluffy white snow. London had removed the filling from inside the couch cushions and created his own nuzz igloo. Middle fingers in his mouth, he nuzzed madly, moving from one fresh snowball to the next like Al Pacino nose-deep in coke in the movie *Scarface*. I expected London to yell "Meet my little friend" in a Cuban accent at any moment. Without their stuffing, the cushions wilted on the floor like deflated balloons.

"London, where did you get all that?"

He shrugged, cotton beard on his face like Santa Claus. "Mexico?"

"Lala," I called, "you may want to wait on that crying for a while." London smiled at me while jamming huge clumps of cotton down the front of his pajama pants. His groin grew to Fatty Arbuckle proportions. "And get the phone book. We need to buy a new couch." I looked again at London pulling the guts from our sad sagging sofa. "Preferably one made from cement. Do they make a Flintstones line of furniture?"

Everything and Its Place

After dinner the other day, I was straightening up the kitchen and dining room, my nightly routine of trying to keep at least one part of the house from caving in on me. Like many families', our dining room table is the depository for everything that does not have an obvious home—car keys, hardened Play-Doh balls, overdue legal papers, and items to be returned to friends like forgotten hats, gloves, or the occasional baby tooth lost during horseplay. Even though we have sacrificed valuable square footage for his creation of play and art, London had been working at the table in our tiny dining room, drawing on paper and using old office supplies to stamp his naked body. I viewed his pencil scratches, drawn on the backs of guest checks we had purchased so our children could get a leg up on their future careers in the service industry. London's scribbles appeared fairly primitive to my eye, not as elaborate as the railroad track map he had drawn earlier in the week on the back of the kids' menu at the Santa Fe Bar and Grill. I scooped up the pile and strolled over to our trash can, which is really a laundry hamper with a Hefty bag secured inside. We had a fancy stainless-steel job with a domed top and swinging door, but we found out the hard way that the wings of a scorched turkey get stuck in a small opening even if its cover swings effortlessly. After I dumped the art, I crawled under the table and scraped Cheerios from the kilim rug with my fingernail.

"Daaaaaaaaaaad!" London squawked from behind me. He had somehow slipped into the kitchen without me noticing his naked body stamped in red and blue postal commands like Cancel, Paid, and File. He's about as tall as the garbage can and his eyes barely reached over the rim. He squinted at me like Clint Eastwood just before he shoots someone full of lead.

"Dad," London said, grabbing his work from the mess of granola bar wrappers and congealed macaroni and cheese, "don't throw these away. I want you to save them."

Those last two words sent shivers up my sore spinal column. I had to brace myself on the butcher block so I wouldn't faint. "Lala," I called, barely able to choke out the words, "it's started." I looked to the overflowing wire inbox under our pie safe and the banker's boxes on the top shelf in the art room. I thought of the storage bins in the hall closets, and the crates in the metal shed cowering in the southwest corner of our backyard. All of these archives had sprung from the eight short years of Poppy's life so far. I had to stop myself from running out into our street and intentionally getting struck by a drunk and uninsured motorist. I had a pretty good chance given the recent stats on our enchanted state of New Mexico.

When Poppy was London's age, we saved everything that even grazed her hand—colored scrawl on napkins, finger paints, and pieces of dirt she collected from the riverbed behind our house.

"Isn't this sweet?" Lala would say as she added the syringe or bullet casing Poppy found to the collection of other memorabilia placed on the windowsill over the kitchen sink, next to the refrigerator that was plastered with all of Poppy's personal handbills. And things only got worse when she started preschool. We enrolled her in a little house of instruction that's based on an Italian philosophy whose name reminds one of fancy hard cheeses. The school offered pages and pages of elaborate teaching methods and pedagogy, which in practice boiled down to ignoring the kiddies until they bled or dropped their pants in unison. It was fine for Poppy. But every day we picked her up, she'd hand us rolls of butcher paper with thick streaks of paint, balls of clay glued to a wedge of cardboard, and peanut husks she'd found in some vegan kid's cubby. Pretty soon our house was becoming a shrine to our daughter and all that she surveyed. One closet held over a dozen shoeboxes filled with photos and videotapes documenting Poppy's birth and every sneeze, shit, and smile thereafter. In another, we had crammed reams of her artwork, everything that didn't fit onto the fridge, microwave, doors, and any remaining blank wall space.

At the end of Poppy's initial year of preschool, Lala and I started a routine that I know many parents practice annually: the culling. Soon after we had cleaned out Poppy's cubby and said goodbye to the skittish class rabbit, Lala and I gathered all the crap accumulated from that year and piled it in the center of the living room. Then, like snobby art historians employed by

Sotheby's, we tried to decide the value of each and every piece—which to keep and which to toss.

"This one is a bit reminiscent of her bird series," Lala said as she held up a scrap of cloth that looked as if it had been stained by a downpour of chewing tobacco. I nodded and placed it on the catalogue couch.

"Not her best work," I said, picking up a piece of construction paper by the corner. "Look at the uneven strokes and noticeable lack of intent. Does not contain the iconic images of, say, her blue period or sun study."

While I saw this process of clearing out the clutter as vital to our survival, Lala became haughtily proprietary in her selection process, moving past evaluating our young Picasso's work toward guessing at what kind of adult she'd be in the future.

"She's really going to want this." Between her fingers, Lala held a walnut lathered in red paint. It looked to me like a bloody testicle.

"What for?"

"She'll drill a hole, attach a hook, and hang it on her very first Christmas tree." Lala smiled, imagining the scene in far more detail than a mother of a preschooler should be allowed.

"Oh, come on," I said, unrolling a piece of burlap that had rotten seeds still planted in the weave.

"You just wait. If you throw this away, she'll hate you—her own father—on Christmas Day." She turned away in what seemed like disgust.

"No way." I wasn't buying it.

"Probably will disinvite you from the holiday buffet and open house," she continued.

I laughed. "Like you know what she's planning before she does."

"I do," she said, and her eyes told me that she would be happy to pass a polygraph just to prove me wrong.

"And what her husband will be like," I said in a well-polished mocking tone.

"And the names of her children, but I'm not telling you any more, since you'll just gab and they'll steal the ones Poppy and I are saving," she said, nestling the rusty-colored nutlet on the catalogue couch.

My frustration with the never-ending parade of motley mishmash manifested itself in all areas of my waking and sleeping life. I stuffed piles of projects and papers deep into the laundry can, but Lala and Poppy got smart and checked nightly—*CSI* style, penlights in their mouths, poking the trash with long forks stolen from my gas barbecue grill. The probing pair even found a plastic bag hidden in my messenger bag, and from then on I succumbed to daily searches and pat-downs before work.

Once Poppy started elementary school, the take-home trash grew in number and variety. She still lugged home art projects, but now her backpack also carried class photos, announcements for class photos, reminders for class photo retakes, handwriting worksheets, newsletters, report cards, school policy contracts, brochures, fund-raising sign-ups, permission slips, prepayment forms, and postpayment forms. And that was just on the opening day of school.

"Look, her first cafeteria menu!" Lala said, holding the two-sided color page that would visit us monthly for the rest of our living days. "Sloppy Joes. I loved sloppy Joes when I was in school," Lala told no one in particular, slipping the memento into one of the many boxes marked for future use when they break ground on the Poppy Wilder Memorial Library. I wonder if Bill Clinton's lunch menu is encased in glass in *his* presidential center, whether visitors walk by and say, "Look, he had catfish and greens in his Hot Springs cafeteria. I'm so glad someone had the foresight to save this valuable piece of Americana."

Even Lala has her limits, I found out a few weeks ago. I had picked Poppy up from school and we arrived home to Lala sitting on the couch watching London land Jay Jay the Jet Plane and Herky the Helicopter and their accompanying speech impediments at the imaginary Tarrytown airport. Poppy excitedly opened her backpack and retrieved a large zip-top bag. The contents were small and dark and fibrous.

"What is that?" Lala said, a note of alarm in her voice.

"Owl pellets," Poppy said, proudly puffing out her chest feathers.

"Owl poop!" London screamed, throwing Jay Jay against the wall and running toward the specimen bag.

"Don't worry, Mom. It's not poop," Poppy said. "It's really their vomit."

"You have got to be kidding me." Lala stood up, raking her fingers through her hair. "Your teacher sent that home with you?"

"We all get to keep our own!" Poppy shouted, the edges of her smile touching her ears. She then went on to tell us that as part of their science block, they dissected owl vomit to find the remains of smaller animals, much lower on the cuteness scale—ugly enough to eat and then spit back up. Each third grader attempted to piece the owl food skeletons back together with Elmer's on construction paper. Not only would she be allowed to keep the vomit, but puke-covered skulls, vertebrae, and undigested rat hair would be arriving home at the end of the month clipped to the new cafeteria menu.

"I love owl poop, Dad," London said, hugging me.

"I told you it's vomit, not poop. Jeesh." Poppy was embarrassed at her brother's obvious lack of education in raptor retchology.

"Put that outside this instant," Lala demanded, pointing to the front porch.

"But I want to save it, Mom. Forever!" Poppy pleaded, her smile wilting. Her own mother—clutter comrade in arms—was turning on her.

"You'd hate to have her not invite you to her first Christmas when she can't string the pellets like popcorn and cranberries," I said.

"Shut up and figure out what we're going to do with whatever the hell that is."

Even though I enjoyed having Lala see the world through my eyes, if only for a moment, the owl puke episode was the last straw. My life was closing in on me. I had nightmares of being buried alive in an avalanche of math worksheets and clay dioramas based on Anasazi Indian cave dwellings, all dripping with the bodily excretions of rodents and raptors. I dragged myself to work after a sleepless and most suffocating night. My friend Marla was making copies in the mailroom while I tried to pour a pot of coffee down my throat before first-period American lit class.

"You look like ass," she said.

"Nice of you to say," I replied between gulps of French roast.

"What's going on?"

I told her I was like the Pigpen character in *Peanuts*, only none of the shitcloud was of my own making.

"My friend Kathy scrapbooks all her kids' stuff," she said, and shrugged.

"Huh?" As an English teacher, I'm always amazed how we

effortlessly turn nouns into verbs. *Vaporized. Microchipped. Dogged.* Where will it end?

"Scrapbooking. It's a way of organizing photos, papers. I think there's a store just off the plaza that sells the supplies."

During lunch, I sped downtown and climbed the stairs over Starbucks to find a small shop filled with rubber stamps. Thousands of small squares lined the walls, each showcasing images that you'd see on paper if you owned an inkpad and a working wrist. In the far corner was a kiosk and area devoted to scrapbooking supplies—organizers, punchers, edgers, fixatives, ribbons, and even a utility belt in case you want to create lasting memories on the fly. A big woman with orange hair and matching drawn-on eyebrows oohed and aahed at the selection while a clerk stared dumbly from behind the counter.

"Are you a scrapbooker?" I asked the woman, whose nails hosted the same hue as the hair on her head.

"I'm more of a stamper myself," she said, "but I have scrapbooked, yes."

"What's the difference?"

"Oh, well, that is a question," she said, fluttering her fingers like the Artful Dodger after he's nicked a rather thick wallet. "A stamper deals mostly with rubber stamps, making cards and such. In fact, I just got back from a stamping cruise."

"A what?" I thought she'd said *stomping bruise.* I had noticed a man wearing the same University of New Mexico Lobos coat waiting in a chair outside the store. It was her husband, no doubt. People who scrapbook were obviously cut from the same cloth as those couples who choose to dress alike at theme parks.

"About fifty of us took a cruise out of L.A. and went down the coast. Whew," she sighed, wiping her damp widow's peak with a tissue. "We must have sat twelve hours a day, making cards, taking advanced stamping classes. Oh and we ate," she added, nodding with a sense of accomplishment. "You can't go on a cruise without eating."

"I guess not," I said, realizing we both had never missed a meal. We had that much in common. "Was it fun?"

"More fun than clubbing rats at the dump," she said, "and let me tell you, I've done my fair share of clubbing rats."

I had no idea what to make of her odd quip, so I peppered her with questions about scrapbooking—could I include report cards, photos, fingerpaintings? She guided me through the store, handing me how-to books, supplies, and samples, all the while explaining how scrapbooking has eased her pain of living.

"See," she told me, "I have these two titanium rods inserted in my back and I'm in constant pain, but stamping and scrapbooking help take my mind off it."

I thought of my pain, more of the emotional sort—the panic attacks, the suffocation—and I started seeing scrapbooking as a possible form of salvation. I piled the expensive supplies on the counter and followed the heavy rod-bearing woman around like she was my own personal Jesus, if the savior had been bathed in orange juice. I even considered waxing my eyebrows and drawing them back on in a show of faith.

"Here's a way to cut up your photos and insert them into maps, menus, or what have you," she said, pointing to a busy page that looked a bit too much like Poppy's last collage for school.

"Amen," I said, picturing a day of cutting up all the items in the storage shed, gluing them to a page, and then adorning my creation with lace, ribbons, and life-affirming phrases razored from *Cosmo* or *Good Housekeeping*. With this woman's help, I could make my life both highly organized and ornately beautiful.

In a fit of excitement, I yanked the zip-top bag from my jacket pocket and shook it in the air like the Golden Fleece.

"Is that a bag of shit?" the salesgirl behind the counter asked.

"It's owl vomit," I said, correcting her, then turned back to my new master. "What can we do with this? Where can we go? Tell me all your ideas!"

"You can get that excrement out of my face," the woman said, turning her back on me. The growling wolf head stamped on her jacket warned me to take a step back. "Come on, honey," she called to her husband. "I've had enough. Let's go put on the feedbag."

I eyed all the stuff we had selected, and it looked familiar, all neatly piled up on the counter. Even though I had come to reduce the number of objects in my home, I would return carrying another set, albeit in a variety far more frilly and craft-oriented. I spun around in a state of vertigo, hundreds of wooden blocks each stamping out the same message: CLUTTER CLUTTER CLUTTER.

The Rising

Kids London's age go through stages of discovery and development that are not so easy for adults to talk about. Even though we pretend to walk around in a "it's perfectly natural, not that there's anything wrong with that" world, many parts and functions pertaining to the human body still embarrass us. Take the penis. London has recently discovered that he indeed owns such an organ, and it's kind of freaking him out. Since Lala and I are trying to potty-train him the low-pressure way by letting him run around the house bottomless, his johnson has figured more prominently in his life. Previously, it had been neatly tucked away in his Pampers as he ran from the working-class train table in the living room to the bourgeois kitchen set in the playroom. But after the diaper came off and he started bumping into things, he realized this little flesh pipe was worth some exploration and experimentation, especially when he went to use his Safety First Potty 'N' Step Stool in the hall bathroom. Even though I suffered through four years of Catholic school and Lala's cousin is a sacred-undergarment-wearing Mormon, London's phallic fiddling around was fine by us. Sometimes, though, just when you think you're doing the right thing by your child, your kid will react in ways you vowed you never would.

Lala creates her little matchbox shrines in her studio right off our kitchen. A former garage, her workspace is long and white and brightly lit so she can see the detail of a stroke of paint the size of a toothpick. Three mornings a week, Lala and London are at home together. London plays solo, darting in and out of the studio with updates on his various adventures. He's pretty content to play with his trains on his own, creating plot lines cobbled together from *Thomas the Tank Engine* videos, Poppy's Barbie, or Polly Pocket dramas, and even bits and pieces from *Survivor* episodes I guiltily enjoy on Thursday evenings. If you can spy on London without him seeing you, his imaginary playscapes are pretty hysterical. Picture a boy dressed in a *T. rex* pajama top, hair messy as a mental patient's, nothing below his waist but a cute white bum and his little antenna sticking out searching for the nearest FM station. As he pushes a string of ten trains around a wooden track, London self-narrates in a dramatic voiceover: "Here comes Peter Sam around the bend, but oh, no, he runs into Mr. Topham Hat, who says he has to take his trains to tribal council. Will Barbie vote off a Bratz when they have trouble on the tracks?" We're thinking of selling his scripts to the WB network.

"Mama! Mama!" London screamed one day, and tore into the studio. Since she could detect a note of true panic, a literal far cry from his regular doses of melodrama, Lala rose from her chair, frightened that London had finally poked his eyes on the metal flower sculptures on the fireplace or sliced his hand open on the iron candleholders near the entrance to the hallway. (Needless to say, our house is not childproofed.) On the surface, nothing on London appeared to be bleeding or broken.

"What's the matter?" Lala asked him, stretching out her arms, but he did not jump into them as usual. Something was holding him back.

"It's too big, Mama. It's too big. It scares me," he said, crying.

"What's too big?" The monster Lala imagined had at least one more eye than the one disturbing London did.

"Look." He pointed downward at his penis, which was in the middle of a major erection. London shook from fear, his member quivering like the needle on a Geiger counter in downtown Los Alamos. "Make it smaller, Mama. Make it small," he pleaded, his hands clasped in front of him like a shrunken and horny Al Jolson.

Lala is from a family of women, and I'm sure no visiting male ever made that request, even when the four Carroll sisters lived on their own and held the wildest parties Cheyenne, Wyoming, had ever seen.

"Well," Lala said matter-of-factly, "stop touching it and it's bound to get smaller."

"But, Mama," London countered, "I can't stop touching it."

Lala placed her hands firmly on her hips and told him, "Then welcome to the puzzling world of men."

About a quarter mile from our house, my friend Marla and her son, Calvin, were wrestling with their own genital difficulties. Calvin, however, has always approached childhood issues differently than my boy. While London uses a red mohair sweater for comfort, Calvin carries around an industrial cord-less drill. When a fellow toddler on the playground confronts London, he runs away. When Calvin is approached, he hisses first, then strikes back with vengeance. I'm secretly hoping they attend school together because London will definitely need a bodyguard. Calvin has always viewed his penis as a point of pride. His family spends a great deal of time outdoors, taking long hikes in the woods behind Marla's grandfather's house or in the front yard, where Calvin has a small tree fort. When he was being potty-trained, Marla and her husband let their son uri-nate outside. After studying some macho river guides on a trip they took down the Colorado, Calvin started arching his back, thrusting his pelvis outward, and shouting, "Big penis sticking out!" as if he were warning some passerby not to trip on his thrill drill. Now that he's enrolled in a preschool based on an old Italian woman's philosophy on helping "unhappy little ones," Calvin is forced to use the toilet like the rest of us city slickers. However, just because he's pissing into sanitary ware and not a murky river, his tune hasn't changed one bit. While all the other kids quietly create groupings by human tendencies, Calvin yells, "Big penis sticking out!" like some hillbilly mating call.

Calvin is extremely bright and can name twenty-five types of heavy machinery. London will spot a backhoe and say, "Look, Dad, there's a scooper!" Calvin will see the same machine and say, "Look, a Volvo BL 70 backhoe loader with axle oscillation, hydraulic oil cooler, and flip-over pallet forks." Instead of a *Bob the Builder* book, for his birthday we gave Calvin the reference edition of *How Things Work*, which Marla says they read from nightly as if Calvin is studying for the NCCER heavy equipment operation licensing exam. So it's natural that as Calvin plays with his penis, his vocabulary usage moves beyond London's monkey-like screaming and pointing. Marla told me that one Saturday she, her husband, and Calvin were hanging out in bed, slowly recovering from a hectic workweek.

"Marla," Calvin said, having discovered the joyful accuracy of using his parents' first names, "the tippy-top of my penis is hot." Marla and her husband have learned that when dealing with such a bright child, it's better not to play your hand until the kid shows where he's headed. So they waited.

"Marla," Calvin called again, "the tippy-top of my big penis is hot because I'm touching it!" He seemed proud of his ability to make fire with neither flint nor match. Meanwhile, back at our house, London had an ice pack on his package, trying to extinguish the same type of flame his pal Calvin was so fervently fanning.

I'm a high school teacher and writer, and penis bravado doesn't come up that often at faculty meetings or literary round-table discussions. Even when I was in a fraternity in college, we were all too overeducated and politically correct (the film *PCU* was based on our school) to brag about our purple-helmeted yogurt throwers. It strikes me as ironic that my fraternity brother Drew and I finally broached the subject fifteen years later around the endowment of his son, otherwise known as Allergy Boy or A.B. for short. Allergy Boy is Drew and his wife, Sue's, second child. Like Lala and I, Sue and Drew have an older girl and younger boy. Unlike London, however, Allergy Boy is hypersensitive to at least twenty food items they know of, including all dairy, nuts, legumes, most fruits, and any fish with eyes. A.B. is a sweet kid with the face of a sixty-year-old shoe salesman, a slight case of eczema, and, as I learned last summer, the penis of Ron Jeremy.

Drew had rented a house in Southampton, and we were

hanging out in the slate pool. I was swimming with my two kids and Drew's older daughter, Dayna, while a dot-commer Drew knew professionally was with his wife and their son at the other end. Allergy Boy had just come off a serious bout of diaper rash, so Drew was walking him on the flagstone patio sans diaper. Dot-commer's kid saw A.B.'s nudity and decided that he too wanted to go naked. His dad asked us if we cared, we said no, and so we had two naked boys instead of one. No big deal.

"Come on, my little ladykiller," Drew said to A.B. as he held him by his hands orangutan-style around the pool's edge.

"Ladykiller?" I asked.

"I didn't tell you?"

He said that when A.B. was born, Sue and Drew were a wreck, so they had a hospital nurse watch the boy while the weary parents tried to get some sleep. The nurse was a big black woman from the South. "A.B. loved her," Drew told me, "but we kept hearing her say strange things to him."

"Like what?"

"Oh, 'You're gonna make some girl very happy someday,' 'You are gonna be the ladykiller.' " Sue and Drew thought the nurse was just being kind, so they forgot about it until they hired a part-time nanny at home. Sue was coming out of the shower one morning and heard her say, "You may be a little boy now, but someday, you'll be a *big* man."

"What did you think?" I asked him, treading water.

"What could we think? Come on, they're babies. They all look the same."

I looked at A.B.'s organic frank and beans, and besides it being nicely shaped, I didn't notice any record-setting potential. It wasn't as easy as spotting breast implants or a bad toupee. I had another model to use as comparison, so I turned to see the dot-commer's kid, who was banging his own junk against the pool's jagged stone edge.

"Drew, look," I said, and flicked my nose toward the rocky form of self-exploration.

"Oh, man," he said. "That's gotta hurt."

If it did, Dot-com Junior wasn't wincing one bit.

After the "*big* man" comment, curiosity was killing Drew and Sue. It was only after A.B.'s bris that they finally got the expert testimony they needed. They hired a *mohelet,* a female circumciser, to perform the ceremony. She was chatty and slightly funny and even had her own cheeky Web site. After the ceremony, they pulled her aside to ask her if all the accolades were true. "I've seen hundreds of new penises," she declared, "and your boy has one of the biggest I've ever circumcised."

I was feeling halfway excited about A.B.'s future. So what if he couldn't eat much? For him there would be plenty of other kinds of nourishment. We both looked over to Dot-com Junior, who was still slamming his little search engine against the lip of the pool. His parents swam lazily in the warm water, unconcerned with his mashing.

"You still have that *mohelet*'s number?" I asked Drew.

"I'm sure it's somewhere. Why? I thought London was already snipped."

"He is," I said, "but your little buddy over there might need some reconstructive surgery."

I wonder if males ever feel truly comfortable with the tube of flesh that hangs between our legs. It seems as if we are still wrestling with the issue well into our thirties and forties. The same week or so that London was trembling in awe of his penile power and Calvin was heating up his hood, I went out for a late dinner and drinks with my friend Joe Ray. Around these parts,

Joe Ray is the goateed king of hip-hop culture. He dresses the role with slick Armani eyewear, a Yankees cap, black pressed jeans, motorcycle boots, and a leather wallet attached to a thick silver chain. In a small city like ours, he's the closest thing we have to a rock star.

We had just given a reading together at a small bookstore in downtown Santa Fe. He read dark, musical poems about heroin addicts, DJs spinning vinyl records, and sippin' on gin 'n' juice. I followed with an essay about different ways to deal with toddler tantrums. It was Cool Chicano meets Dull Diaper-Changing Dad. For a guy like me, just standing next to a guy like him makes me even whiter than a bar of Ivory soap. Afterward, a bunch of us went out to a local steakhouse where Joe Ray has a dish named after him, but he's so hip it's not even on the menu. We were the only two men with a group of five women, including Lala. I've hung around artists and entertainers since I joined the student events committee my sophomore year in college, and I know that after a performance, one person often feels "on" more than the others and should be given his time to shine. There's nothing more frustrating than a group of comics trying to out-joke each other or a gaggle of academics trying to sound smarter than the last doctor's comment on Milton's use of ivy imagery in *Paradise Lost*. From his energy, material, and the fact he wore bling-bling, I knew it was Joe Ray's night, so I shut my trap. He sat in the corner with his back to the wall, snapped the brim of his cap, and laughed heartily. Every six minutes, his cell phone, which lay on the table like a pack of cigarettes, would glow and emit a set of beats downloaded from his personal DJ, who goes by the name of Rockwell.

"That's a stripper from Vegas," he'd say, reading the little blue window. "Should I get it?"

Since Joe Ray is single, the topic of sex and his latest girl-friend invariably comes up. One of the women at the table asked if Joe Ray ever worried about dry spells, gaps in his famously active sex life.

"Hell, no," he said. "There hasn't been a day since I was seventeen that I haven't taken care of myself."

"What?" one of the women asked, leaning in to hear better.

"You know, masturbated."

We all gasped. "Come on," I said. "Seriously?"

"I'm not shitting you. I can't think of leaving the house without helping my own damn self if no one else is there to do it for me," he said proudly.

"But you're always running late." Besides running a hip-hop night each week at a local nightclub, Joe Ray also teaches poetry to kids in public school. It's not unusual for him to be tackled by a gaggle of eight-year-olds after breaking up a gang fight only a few hours before. I call that lifestyle bipolar; he calls it getting paid.

"Man, there are some days I really have to concentrate to get out of the house on time. People will be calling me up and shit, and I have to really focus 'cause if I don't put my time in"—he moved his curved hand up and down in the air—"I can be one cranky son of a bitch."

As he was speaking, I noticed that the women around the table were mesmerized. He was both a manly man and the poster boy for Dr. Ruth's guide to healthy sexuality. He not only had dozens of beautiful young women throwing themselves at him at the club, but he'd also built a handy relationship with his own damned self, as they say on the street. I thought of Calvin's aplomb and London's fright, and I figured why can't a white professional guy like me freely express his sexuality? This was, after all, the new millennium.

"Well, for me," I began, almost starting to feel my proverbial big penis sticking out.

"That's it. Let's go," Lala said, pulling me up by my collar. Just like London and his thang, Lala was worried that the tool she'd married was indeed growing too big for his Dockers. She dragged me out, and as I turned back to say goodbye, I slammed—junk and all—into the nearest wall.

"That's gotta hurt," Joe Ray said to his peeps, and flipped open the cover of his cell phone.

Little Creatures

When it starts getting colder, I take the kids to our local children's museum on Sundays. The jaunt gets us out of the house and allows Lala to catch up on her rest or her work without London jumping on her head or Poppy asking if you can wear leather pants with Doc Martens after Labor Day. Unlike most films rated G these days, the children's museum is an activity that appeals to adults and their offspring as well. This house of hands-on entertains Poppy and London and makes me feel as if I'm doing something to broaden their educational horizons, more so than my previous Sunday lessons of explaining the nutritional content of beer, how a couch is constructed, or the evolution of the football helmet in the NFL.

This past week, Poppy invited her friend Emma, a wispy blonde with green eyes and metal on her teeth, to tag along.

When we arrived, the two girls scurried quickly to three chairs facing a metal pole, each seat hooked up to a series of pulleys and lengths of knotted rope. The goal of this interactive exhibit is to show how the use of a block and tackle can make work easier. London is not as fast as his older counterparts and landed in the seat with only one pulley. The older girls were smart enough to secure chairs that required one-half and one-third of the force needed to lift roughly the same weight.

"Hey, Dad," London called after yanking unsuccessfully on the rope. "Pull me." I tugged hard on the cord, handing the excess to London as I went. I beat the girls the first time up, but then it became abundantly clear to the parents, kids, and volunteers around us that this was the only exercise I'd had in weeks. London and I lost the next rounds by more than a few yards. I could see in his disappointed face that he was embarrassed that his father lifted slim volumes of nature poetry during the week and not barbells or loads of roofing material.

Try as he might, London could not keep up with the two older girls, and they lost him (and me) between the rabbit village and the greenhouse. In a fit of despair, London threw himself to the ground, which was paved with fund-raising bricks etched with the names of individuals or families who had donated at least twenty-five bucks. He cried loud enough for a set of twins, who were standing in the observation deck above us, to call down and ask if he still had all his teeth.

We went back inside the museum to the manipulative play area, located conveniently near the restrooms, which for kids is a form of manipulative play in its own right. From tables of blocks, magnets, and other lethal throwing objects, London chose dominoes. A basket of white dominoes sat next to another basket filled with an equal number of black ones, surrounded by what seemed like flea circus stairs and slides to set the wooden squares upon. On the floor next to London, a girl just under a year old sat gumming a domino of the same race as London's choice. I couldn't help but stare as this small creature shoved a whole block into her mouth, keeping it there like it was a communion wafer from the church of Milton Bradley. I took infant rescue breathing and CPR almost seven years ago and tried to recall the stages of saving that this oral fixator would no doubt require. Was there something about "shout and tap"? Open the airway? Tap the airway? Tap the shouter? This kid's licking was almost methodical; she'd carefully choose a domino from London's basket, jam it in her mouth, roll it around, withdraw it, then lick all the sides like it was a three-dimensional postage stamp. Having successfully completed the necessary lickage, she'd slap it down on the table like some mah-jongg mama in Central Park. Then she'd grab another. Pretty soon my concern about choking was eclipsed by deep unease for sanitary conditions.

The children's museum runs on a volunteer workforce, which means the place is manned by pimply teenagers fulfilling a court-mandated sentence of service to the community. The disinterested kid assigned to our play pod wandered over in his baggy jeans and hoodie and plopped the spittle-dripping pile back into the general population. Before I could spray the area with bleach or grab London and run, the mother of Saliva Sally came out of the restroom. She had a newborn on her back, a second grader at her feet, and hickeys peppering her neck. I wanted to put a condom on just looking at her.

"I'm so sorry," she said, retrieving the tainted dominoes from the basket.

"Thanks, I appreciate it." I watched as she wiped the pieces off on her jeans, which were stained with what appeared to be pureed peaches and motor oil. I looked around in a can-I-get-a-witness moment, but all I had to choose from was London, Vapid Volunteer, and Baby McLickme, who was trying to re-create the famous Bergen move in her mouth.

"Let's go," I said to London, and moved him across the main room to the Houser Art Start, a four-by-six-foot area encased in etched glass. Inside the prison-like structure, bins of recycled materials—yarn, corks, film canisters, and absentee ballots—were available to be transformed by tiny hands into art. Lala and I have decided (or surrendered) that only two rules apply when dealing with this type of messy activity: wear a smock if you can find one, and spot the stains when you get home. Given the fact that my wife's business involves paint, glue, and glitter, I buy Shout stain remover in ten-gallon drums at Sam's Club. After those two rules, everything is fair game. London immediately grabbed a cube of Styrofoam that had once braced a large television set, and poured glue into the various cavities. Two teen moms strolled by on cell phones, the Y straps of their thongs visible above low-cut jeans. A first-time dad tore by, jumping and playing harder and sweatier than his toddler. Later, I would see him arguing with the climbing wall instructor, whining that he was not too big to scale the faux rock face. Emma and Poppy would drop by now and then to let me know they were having fun but they wanted to be little Gloria Steinems—on their own, no boys allowed.

By now London had lacquered his side of the table in Elmer's and was hacking his Styrofoam soup tureen to bits with the almost pointy end of a pair of safety scissors. I wasn't worried about injury, though. London has watched the movie *Psycho* enough times to know to hold the scissors by the handle and to strike away from his body.

A smartly dressed mother-and-son combo walked up the carpeted stairs to the Art Start cell, and the curly-haired boy positioned himself at the near end of the table. He had obviously been clothed by upscale kid outfitters like Hanna Andersson and Oilily. He wore corduroy overalls, brown leather driving shoes, and a brightly patterned shirt. His mother looked as though she had just left church or was scheduled for high tea after slumming in this unkempt playland. The boy reached for a container of glue, but his mom intercepted it. "Sterling, we cannot get glue on our hands or our clothes," she said, and waved the brush over the butcher paper in front of him, never fully touching down. His face melted into a half-pout as he glanced at London, who was now holding his leaking container over a pile of mucilage-drizzled photo canisters. His mess resembled a Barbie toxic waste dump.

Sterling then reached for a set of Fiskars to his right, but his mom snagged those too. "No sharp scissors," she said, sliding the deadly weapon onto a storage shelf behind her. London, not getting ultimate leakage, stabbed new holes into the thermoplastic bottom. Meticulous Mom deposited a dry clump of yarn in front of her boy, who lifted and dropped it limply like a bunch of leftover spaghetti. He repeated the action, hoping for some spontaneous combustion or perhaps a dormant bug to emerge from the twine and bite his mother in the eye. Across the table, London had his face crammed inside his creation and was trying to blow the glue out of the puncture holes. Realizing his clean and dull fate, Sterling dropped the yarn and walked out, his relieved mother behind him.

Down the stairs, just past the bubble play area, there's an alcove that hosts various reptiles, insects, and other creatures that might end up on a spear or in the grass-clipping bag attached to your lawn mower. Two of the interns huddled around a snake cage, and after I scraped the glue from London's face, I carried him over. My son's not so enamored with anything lower on the food chain than a Labrador, so it took some convincing to assure London that we were indeed safe from attack. The younger of the two interns, a ten-year-old boy with a fetching blond ponytail, was instructing the older, a sixteen-year-old Hispanic girl, on how to properly hold the corn snake.

"You need to cradle it here," he said, pointing to a loop at what would be the neck if a snake had one, "and what you do is tell people about the snake as you hold it. No, not like that." He slid the older girl's hand upward, away from the tongue-shooting serpentine head. "Gently now," he cautioned her.

"London, do you want to pet this nice snake?" I asked, rubbing his back to reassure him.

"Has he washed his hands?" the intern asked me, flipping his ponytail off his shoulder. I could tell his parents were hippies from his unicolor clothes, made from refined hemp, and his shoes, which were the same kind as David Carradine used to kick ass in the television show *Kung Fu*.

"Why, yes, he has," I said like Mister Rogers, hoping to signal the boy that he needn't be so bossy. I've taught these types of "genius" kids before, and while they can cite *Othello* and play chess blindfolded, they are severely lacking in the social cues department.

"Good," he said without any trace of irony, and turned his attention to his partner. "They need to wash their hands before and after touching."

"That's what she said," I joked under my breath, but I think Ponytail Boy heard me because he stared at me a bit longer than most men find comfortable. "We saw a rattlesnake, didn't we, Londy?" I said, trying to change the subject. I was referring to a hike we'd taken with London's friend Calvin where we almost tripped over a diamondback.

"What did you do?" Willie Wunderkind asked me.

"Huh?" I didn't understand.

"How did you react?"

"We froze and backed away."

"Good for you." He turned to his assistant. "A snake can only strike half its length, you know." Then we were lucky to get his full attention again, only this time he stepped in. Besides being a prodigy, he was a close talker. Luckily, he only came up to my neck. "Know what to do if you encounter a mountain lion?" he asked.

"Run like hell?"

"Nice way to die," he said, and rolled his eyes at his partner.

"Excuse me?"

"The proper way to ward off a mountain lion attack is to make yourself appear larger by holding up your coat like this." Since he wasn't wearing a jacket, when he held out his arms it looked as though he was being crucified.

"Didn't work for Jesus."

"What?" It was obvious he didn't get the joke.

"Never mind."

"Fine." His partner sided with him, impressed by his knowledge at such a young age. That, or she marveled at how he avoided split ends while her hair was a total rat's nest.

"I was only joking about the running, by the way," I said, trying to explain my humor, which is always a bad idea.

"I have no idea what you are saying." He stared at me flatly.

"Before, you know, when you asked about the mountain lion. I was just kidding."

"That kind of kidding will get you mauled," he warned.

"Daddy, let's go," London said, starting to squirm.

"Hold on, Londy. How do you survive a bear attack?" I asked him.

"Simple." He shrugged the question off. "Back away slowly, avoid eye contact, throw something to distract him. A sandwich, say, or a camera." He turned to his ally, the snake still enjoying the crook of her bare neck. "Bears are more inquisitive than people think."

"Airplane crash?" I asked.

"Remove sharp objects like pencils, wet a handkerchief to breathe through, use a pillow to protect your head." He smiled smugly and crossed his arms.

"Come on, Dad. I don't like that snake; he's not a useful engine. He's a rude diesel." London's judgment of character came from the Thomas the Tank Engine school of morality: you were either a useful engine or a rude diesel, nothing in between. I put him down.

"You think you're pretty smart, huh?" I asked the young intern.

"Smart enough to realize that your son doesn't like reptiles," he said, and we all watched as London scurried away.

We caught up with Poppy and Emma inside the steamy greenhouse, where they were elbow deep in the earthworm exhibit. By digging through a coffin-shaped trough filled with ripe compost, the duo had collected about fifteen or so earthworms and gathered them in a plastic pot they had placed precariously on the box's edge. The greenhouse doubled as an aviary.

Finches, sparrows, and other warblers flew overhead back and forth from a row of birdhouses and tree branches mounted on the far wall. Exhausted from our various glue- and geek-filled adventures, London and I silently gawked at the girls, who giggled and squealed with each new vermicular discovery. The pot overflowed and a poor little dirt crawler fell to the ground, where he slithered like a miniature version of the snake we had just run away from. London pointed but said nothing. He was too tired. A yellow finch spotted the escapee and swooped down, scooped it into his beak, and devoured it whole.

"Isn't learning fun?" Emma asked Poppy, who concurred by nodding. The rest of us—London, a dozen tiny birds, and me— waited for the next casualty to fall.

Things Are Heating Up

When I was growing up, my father was invariably cheap. If you ask him today, he'll say that he was a product of the Depression, when people couldn't afford air to breathe, and that this upbringing, coupled with having to raise four boys virtually on his own, gave him every right to deny us such luxuries as brand-name soap, water pressure, and home heating oil. Every winter, my brothers and I would crawl from under the military surplus blankets my dad had stolen during his stint in the navy and run through the icy air to dress by the fireplace downstairs. According to my dad, not only were we resisting the evil clutches of OPEC by freezing to death, we were building up our resistance to successfully battle future colds as well. Since I was raised in a house of men, I'm not sure if my inner temperature gauge runs hot because of genetics or because of the influence of arctic temperatures in my ancestral home. Either way, it makes for some conflict now that I'm a husband and father living in a house full of wussies.

A few days ago, I came home from coaching my daughter's soccer team, and Lala looked like a wrestler trying to shed a few pounds before her pre-match weigh-in. She had on four or five layers of clothing, a down vest, a ski cap, and mittens covering her frigid hands. Running in place, she worked diligently on our children's Halloween costumes. I was dressed in shorts and a T-shirt, tracking mud from the bottom of my turf shoes onto our tile floor. My daughter, Poppy, is smart enough to recognize two cultures when they are about to clash, so she quickly grabbed herself a post-practice snack and positioned herself neatly on the couch.

"Jesus, it's like a furnace in here," I said, walking toward the thermostat. Lately I've been sounding a lot like my dad, which up until recently gave me the creeps, but now I realize I can channel him when I need to cast off my sensitive superdad persona to act more like Robert Duvall, daddy doctrinaire in *The Great Santini*.

"Don't you touch that," Lala said, her voice a bit muffled by the scarf wrapped tightly around her mouth. She shook a mitten in what she believed to be a threatening gesture but which to me looked more like a coatrack asking to be let outside. Since I was unencumbered by my sporty outfit, I easily evaded her lumbering attack. Feeling quite spry, I danced around her like a campy leprechaun, threatening to lower the thermostat and shut off the heater.

"It's not funny," she said. "I'm freaking freezing in here." She clapped her arms around her biceps, the international sign for impending hypothermia.

"You're forty," I reminded her. "What will you be like in ten years? Twenty? We're going to have to move to Florida. I don't want to learn to golf." I imagined myself in a lime green polo shirt, matching white slacks and shoes, and one of those hats with a ball of yarn glued to the top.

"Couldn't do Florida, hate the humidity," she said. I then realized that the only place Lala would ever be comfortable would be some sort of temperature-controlled bubble or a fully staffed nursing home, whichever came first.

It's amazing to me the lengths women will go to get warm. Each November, I have to prepare myself for our annual weatherproofing dance. Just after Halloween, I'll come home to see Lala in her studio, wrapped in blankets and quilts, a circle of electric space heaters creating a ring of fire around her gelid body. Like every other healthy American male who still has his hair, I'll ignore her issues and retreat to the television to see what type of live vermin *Fear Factor* is having supermodels eat this week. Lala will limp after me and, like our current political leaders frightening us with threats of terrorists stealing our pets, invoke the children.

"We need to do something about this house," she'll say. "I don't want our kids getting sick."

"That's not how kids catch colds," I'll respond, using my matter-of-fact gassy-windbag-of-a-teacher voice.

Nothing will deter an unwarmed woman, however. "Freezing all the time will weaken their immune systems," she'll tell me, and cite some odd piece of news about the condition of Russian orphanages or hillbilly babies left in drafty trailers during a twister. If she's really desperate, she'll send my son London to me, having rehearsed and bribed him thoroughly in the back bedroom beforehand.

"Daddy, I'm c-c-c-cold," he'll say, and shiver like a wet cat.

"Can I get you a sweater?"

"No," he'll answer stiffly, like a pint-sized Keanu Reeves. Bad actors are so easy to spot. "You can get me a warm house. Even Thomas the Tank Engine has a warm house, Dad. And he's a train."

So each year, I surrender. Lala and I haul the kids to Wal-Mart or Home Depot and spend a month's salary on various types of plastic to cover, fill, wedge, or ooze over the many evil drafty cracks in our igloo. I feel like the artist Christo, wrapping my entire home in cellophane and then using a hair dryer to make this high-tech heating solution even that much more efficient. Honestly, I don't think these artsy-craftsy home improvement kits change things dramatically, yet Lala likes to curse the cold air as it presses up against a sheet of Saran Wrap blanketing our kitchen window.

My friend Nell also belongs to the order of forever-frosty females. She rents a lovely home on the east side of Santa Fe, and when she travels, I look after her dusty plants and make sure that no one gets inside her house to steal her Zen pillow or old Bob Dylan cassette tapes. I think of her house as cozy, but she doesn't.

"I can't take a winter here. I'm freezing," she said to me on the phone a while ago.

"But Nell, it's September." Outside my office window, I saw wildflowers blooming under piñon and juniper. The sky was so blue and the sun so bright, I was getting a nature headache.

"See what I mean?" she said. "Imagine what it will be like in January."

Nell is a tough cookie when it comes to any type of negotiation, but I had to question her wisdom when she decided to split the cost of installing radiant heat with her landlord. Her cut was about $5,000 on a house she would never own and continue to pay rent on. Away when the plumbers came, she asked me to drop by to water her ferns and to make sure the overweight plumbers weren't meditating on her personal cushion. Upon her return, I came over for tea, and she was as happy as George Hamilton sealed inside a tanning bed.

"See? See?" she screamed, twirling around like a Jewish Julie Andrews. "Can you feel how warm it is now?"

I could feel the fervidity, but it was more of a $250 comfort adjustment to me. For a $5,000 investment in a rental home, I expected palm trees growing in her living room and a naked servant willing to provide extended hugs on command. But Nell was ecstatic and shared her toasty life with Lala on the phone. Unless I find ten grand on the way home today, my wife and good friend are about to become roommates.

Best Buy

Lala had been bugging me for three years to buy a new refrigerator. According to her, the one we owned was too small for our growing family and in an embarrassing state of ill repair. She pointed to the bungee cords strapping the condiments inside the door, a solution I saw as crafty and quite ingenious actually, and the layer of frost covering the eggs on the top shelf like a light dusting of snow. I had purchased the small Tappan brand in 1994 in the dusty hamlet of Las Cruces, New Mexico. Having just enrolled in graduate school, I needed something to hold my beer, discount cold cuts, and milk for my morning coffee. The Tappan was the cheapest machine I could buy that could pass as an appliance for someone close to thirty years of age. It was like the slightly older brother of the midget fridge my dad had rented me in college.

To me, our icebox still worked fine, and except for the occasional jar of pickles slung across the kitchen if I opened the door too forcefully, I had no problem digging through the narrow confines to find the leftovers necessary to a make a scary yet tasty scrambled egg frittata. I'm not saying that Lala didn't have a point from where she was pacing; I just have a hard time throwing things away if, as London would say, they are still useful engines. I suppose that's why I drive such a crappy car and still wear tube socks from my high school gym class.

Lala and I scouted out all the different showrooms, superstores, and home centers in Santa Fe, and I did a bit of research on the Internet between teaching classes. Our needs weren't extravagant; I required a major brand that could be serviced in our area and included two separate cooling zones—the most energy-efficient method, according to some former Maytag repairman's blog. Lala wanted a stainless-steel front and a freezer at the bottom so the kids could retrieve their own post-injury ice packs if she was in the middle of filling a big order. Maybe because my wife grew up on a farm, the idea of automatic ice cube makers and water dispensers just pissed her off, so I warned myself to stay away from such frigid luxuries. Besides, I was happy to save myself the embarrassment of feeling like a helpless little child as some hairy plumber hooked up a water line with tools I could not name.

While we were still shopping around, we went into Best Buy, a flashy consumer electronics store with bright colors and a sales force that reminded me of the Stepford children if those creepy wives did breed. After we were greeted sixteen different times by nine different employees, London and Poppy raced toward a double-door refrigerator with a flat-screen TV embedded in the right-hand panel. This refridgervision was showing clips of *SpongeBob SquarePants*, a show we have to rent since we still live like it's the 1980s, without Nickelodeon or the Cartoon Network.

"Can we get this, Dad?" London asked, patting the belly of the beast.

"We don't have cable, guys." I sounded like poor Tiny Tim's dad before Scrooge has acid flashbacks and drops a pile of money in his employees' laps.

"We could buy it, Dad," Poppy said in a sweet yet conniving tone. "You could watch football while you cook. We'd let you." She patted me on the back to try to seal the deal.

"We should get you a job application form, Pops," I told her. "You'd fit in quite well here."

The kitchen in our home is about four feet wide and ten feet long. The only way you could watch the refridgervision would be from inside the old Mexican *tristero* we use as a pantry. With the proper lubrication, we could squeeze London between the Goldfish crackers and granola bars, but it would be too tight for anyone else, even petite Poppy. While Lala opened doors and measured storage space, I waited around for the George Jetson that would seriously consider this Hummer of the appliance world: the guy who didn't want to miss a single second of the next NBA brawl or steamy moment of *Desperate Housewives* as he left his couch to grab a brew. Sadly, most of the customers I saw just pointed to the oddity like it was an exhibit at the World's Fair of Conspicuous Consumption, continuing on in search of some newly released computer war game.

The four of us ended up at an appliance warehouse. It wasn't as sexy as Best Buy, but its cavernous hall offered more of a selection, and the salespeople weren't required to dress exactly alike. The store was cut in two, kitchen appliances on one side

"Not this time, Julia the child," I said, watching a different salesman repair the knobs that London had removed earlier during his culinary casualty spree. "Let's go see the TVs."

"In fridges?" Poppy asked.

"No, just TVs." Best Buy had embedded the wrong idea in my daughter, and it would take a while to undo.

"Are we getting cable?" Poppy asked, slightly hopeful that she could someday speak the same language as her hooked-up friends.

"No, we are just looking," I said, employing the parental vernacular of a person I swore I'd never be.

At the warehouse, just like its kitchen counterpart, a portion of home entertainment was divided into little den-like areas with plasma screens, high-fidelity sounds, and huge La-Z-Boys with racks, drawers, and holders for porno mags, adult beverages, and up to a six-pack of remotes. I plopped Poppy and London down in a recliner that was wider than the aisle they were spazzing out in. Unlike the plush chairs in the other home theater soundstages, this recliner was covered in thick faux leather. I could tell by the industrial carpet, cheap end tables, and plastic artwork that this setup was for the guy who gets loaded and throws up all over himself and his furniture. Everything in this three-sided room could be washed off easily with a garden hose. The 50-inch screen was playing a film that combined Jackie Chan, hot air balloons, and costumes that looked as though they came from those photo places at the mall where you can dress like Wyatt Earp. In the chairs next to Poppy and London, a gangbanger dad and his son reclined in ways that made me think they might actually live there.

I walked back toward Lala and Farmer Joe, passing through the freeway of gas grills. I drive-by-marveled at the size, scope, finish, and features of all these shiny cookers, each more elaborate and impressive than the next. When I reached the Amana subdivision, Lala had decided on a model that, according to our guy, they did not have in the warehouse.

"I thought this was the warehouse," I said, confused.

"There's the warehouse and then there's the *warehouse*," he said, rocking on his heels.

"Right," I said, not knowing what in tarnation he was talking about.

The fridge Lala had her head inside was remarkably similar to one Farmer Joe was leaning against. "I like the feel of this one," she said, her voice a bit muffled from the efficient insulation.

"Feel?" Like one of the Three Stooges, I glanced back and forth far too rapidly. I tried to see what Lala saw, but with me as a witness, the lineup of fridge felons would prove inconclusive.

"Come on, you cannot tell me that you don't feel a difference. That one is so much more claustrophobic." Lala crossed her arms over her chest.

"This one actually has more cubic feet, ma'am," Joe said, looking around for a place to spit.

"I don't care what that sticker says," Lala shot back.

I had to move this along. "Can we get this one?" I asked nicely, referring to the good-feeling model. "And will you knock off 10 percent, seeing as it's a demo?"

"Well, let's just see here," he said, pulling a calculator from a pants pocket as big as London's sleeping bag. "If I cook these figures right, we might be able to work out somepin'."

Smelling victory, Lala started peeling off the cluster of yellow stickers posting features and prices for the white, almond, and ebony versions of our possible new purchase.

"What are you doing?" I asked her. Joe and I still hadn't spat in our palms and shook on it yet.

"Getting these off," she said, viciously ripping the plastic from the metal.

"They'll do that."

"We're not spending this much money," she said, waving a sticker in my face, "to have scratches."

After Joe and I settled on a number that was three times the cost of the bungee-cord model still running at home, I went back to check on the kids but ended up in front of a glorious machine. I started thinking that since I was going to blow so much money on a fridge that was really for Lala, why not treat myself to a better grill? All our friends, before they stopped coming over, loved my marinated flank steak and chicken, and hell, I'd been wanting to work on improving my ribs so they were as tasty as my brother's. When the drool hit the lid of the deep-fat-fryer attachment, I woke up and ran to the kids. Poppy and London, or the gangbanger dad, who was now awake and guffawing as Jackie Chan did backflips, had fully extended the La-Z-Boy so it looked more like a large sponge than a chair. Both of my kids had their hands behind their heads in full repose. They looked happier than they had on Christmas morning.

"Hey, Dad," London said, his lap littered with remote controls, "I changed my mind."

"About what?" Given his new friends, I worried that he had decided to leave us for his new, more high-tech family.

"I don't want that kitchen anymore. I want this," he said, freeing his hands and waving them around the real man's slice of heaven. I know he didn't have the language to say *rec room, bachelor pad, love den,* or *fortress of solitude,* but I knew what he meant. In my home full of trains, Barbies, and folk art, my macho side has been a bit squelched. I too have often longed to be bunkered in my own man sanctuary, snoozing in the overstuffed recliner, all the gender-specific items at my disposal: La-Z-Boy, Bud tall boy, *The Man Show* flickering on the big-screen television. I had been slain by my own treachery, however. I married an artist and studied so much feminist theory in college and grad school that it made my penis shrink.

Knowing the kids were adjusting well to their new crib, I went back to sexually harass an outdoor grill. I touched my new love lightly with the tips of my fingers, inhaling the freshness of metal that had yet to sear meat. What was a few grand considering the enormousness of our mortgage and credit card debt? So what if I die owing another 3K? Life insurance would easily cover it.

Farmer Joe was perspiring like a pregnant nun on the Pope's visit day. Marbles of sweat rolled around his bald head. Lala and Joe had three types of cleaners in spray bottles clustered next to a pile of rags. My wife picked at a piece of tape with her fingernail while bossing around my stand-in. "Can you get this spot?" she asked him, pointing to the smudge where a yellow tag once adhered. He shot me a desperate look, then went over to address the mark.

"Why don't you use magnets instead of tape with those signs?" I asked, but just like at home, Lala answered for her male compadre.

"It's stainless steel," she said like I was an idiot. "Magnets won't stick. I can't wait to get all that crap off your shitbox at home."

"We're going to start posting them on the inside only," Farmer Joe said weakly.

"Go check on the kids," Lala said to me, then turned her

attention to her new butt boy. "We still have a lot of work to do, you know."

As I paused in front of my dream grill on the way back, a salesman trolling the aisles approached me. He wasn't like Farmer Joe. This guy was good-looking, dressed a little nicer than I was, and quite well groomed for a hoofer in a warehouse. He even smelled charming.

"Nice one, huh?" he said, patting the domed top.

"Indeed."

He walked me patiently through each feature, explaining how the fire was divided into hundreds of tiny flames, each no larger than a pinprick.

"Such temperature control!" I said, imagining the grilling possibilities—wild game, Asian fish, even the most delicate of fruits and vegetables. "Can I do a turkey?" I asked him. After all, Thanksgiving was only weeks away.

"No problem. Best damn bird you've ever tasted." He rubbed the long silver rotisserie shaft. "Slow-roasted to perfection."

I've always hated such hackneyed food porn descriptions, but out of his mouth it sounded so right.

"Step away from that grill," Lala called, marching up the aisle, her personal bitch behind her clutching a mess of rags and yellow stickers. "Where are the kids?"

"Over there in the, um, um . . ." I stumbled on my words just like London had. Can we not give a mortal name to heaven? "Over there," I said, pointing in the general direction. I went off with Joe to settle up while Lala tried to extract our TV twins from their pleather womb.

In the car, the kids' eyes seemed glassy as I strapped them into seats far less luxurious and more confining than their Naugahyde nest. They stared blankly at the seat backs in front of them, having endured close to an hour of the limited humor of a guy who tells kids, "Don't try to be like Jackie. Study computers instead."

Smelling of lemony Pledge, Lala happily settled in for the ride home. She had gotten what she wanted and made a new friend along the way. "You know, Tom works on 100 percent commission," she said, leaning back and slipping her hands beneath her head.

"Tom? Who's Tom?" I asked.

"Our salesman, silly. Two percent across the board. No salary."

"Two percent?" I'm no math genius, but I realized that the poor man had just earned $25 for playing cleaning lady to a woman he wasn't married to. "That's not a lot of money," I said, recalling his balls of sweat and the scared way he looked as our kids scampered around his pant legs. "I wonder how he feels about our sale."

"I'm sure it was fine," Lala said. Turning around to face the backseat, she asked, "So, did you kids have a good time?"

"It was bootiful," London answered, his eyes still as cloudy as milk.

"Did we get cable?" Poppy asked, a bit confused, as we drove home to wait for delivery.

Acknowledgments

I am deeply grateful to Christopher Schelling for laughing first and last, and all the fine folks at Ralph Vicinanza, Ltd. At Bantam Dell, I'd like to thank my tireless editor Danielle Perez as well as Barb Burg and Nita Taublib for believing. In addition, I'd like to thank Julia Goldberg and the *Santa Fe Reporter* for allowing me to ramble on.

Deep thanks and love to the following people and their families: my father Ben, the Wilder brothers, the Carroll sisters, Natalie, Boz and Toni, Kath and Tony, Andy and Sue, Marta and Charles, Tom and Katie G-Funk, Mc, Jim and Mary, Lauren and Adam, Joe Ray, Henry and Clare, Tom and Mary, and Honey Harris.

I'd like to thank the following communities for their lessons, support, friendship, and allowing me to be a member: Santa Fe Prep (Go Griffins!), New Mexico State University (Go Aggies!), Warren Wilson MFA Program for Writers (Go Owls!), and the Mabel Dodge Luhan House (no mascot yet).

About the Author

ROBERT WILDER is a writer and teacher living with his wife and two children in Santa Fe, New Mexico. He has published fiction and nonfiction widely, has been a commentator for NPR's *Morning Edition*, and writes a monthly column for the *Santa Fe Reporter* called "Daddy Needs a Drink." His website is www.robertwilder.com.